DATE DUE

D1249399

The Story of Emoji

The Story of Emoji

Gavin Lucas

Prestel

Munich · London · New York

CONTENTS

SPEAKING IN PICTURES

Mankind's earliest and most ancient writing systems were based on pictures. Now, it seems we've come full circle and are again embracing imagery and symbols in our written (now typed) messages.

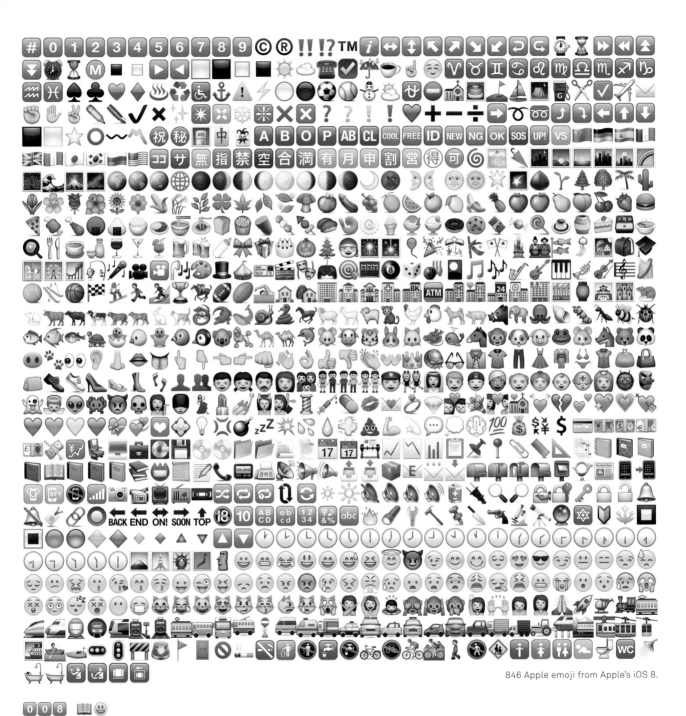

846 Apple emoji from Apple's iOS 8.

THE EVOLUTION OF THE DINGBAT

Long before written language was developed, humans drew pictures and created symbols to communicate and record narratives. From crude paintings in caves to carved and painted hieroglyphics and rebuses (picture puzzles) on ancient monuments and artefacts, drawn imagery – both figurative and symbolic – has long played a vital role in the development of human civilization. The very first writing systems were built around characters and glyphs designed to visually reference what they represented. It was the ancient Greeks who first successfully abandoned visual cues altogether as they developed an abstract form of writing that favoured phonetics, focusing on the sounds of the spoken word rather than referencing physical objects to communicate ideas.

Now, some 40,000 years since the earliest known cave paintings, we exchange information using different languages and alphabets, aided by home computers and mobile phones. We can talk to or send text messages to anyone anywhere on the planet. However, despite the sophistication of our written language systems, millions of us are still harnessing the potency of symbols, pictograms (images or icons, such as the heart symbol ♥, that convey meaning through pictorial resemblance to the physical objects they represent) and ideograms (written characters that symbolize ideas without indicating particular words or speech sounds, such as the universal symbol for recycling ♻) in our everyday communications – thanks largely to a set of internationally recognized symbols called emoji.

If you use Twitter or send text messages, it's highly likely that you've used, or been sent, emoji. You might even have received and sent messages composed entirely of emoji – they're the characters such as heart symbols 🤍 🤍 or smiley faces 😀 that denote a whole range of emotions (from happy 😄, confused 🙂, sad 😞, fearful 😨 and anxious 😬 through to angry 😠 and *really* angry 😡). They also come in the form of icons depicting foodstuffs 🍔, animals 🐿, office equipment 🖨, rain clouds ☁, flowers 🌼 and hundreds more.

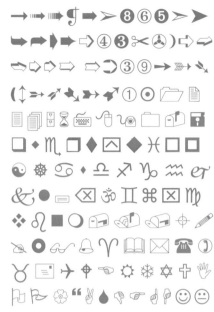

You can access emoji characters through the keyboard on your smartphone and intersperse your typed communications with tiny images.

The word 'emoji' comes from the Japanese words for 'picture' (*e*) and 'character' (*moji*). The core set of emoji characters that has found its way into the digital communication devices of millions of people around the world in recent years was first conceived of specifically for a mobile-phone provider in Japan in the late 1990s. However, when 722 emoji characters were included in version 6.0 of Unicode (the computer industry standard for encoding and displaying most of the world's writing systems) in 2010, and Apple subsequently incorporated an easily accessed emoji keyboard in its iOS5 iPhone operating

system the following year, emoji became a global phenomenon.

That said, the idea of special, non-letter characters that can be interspersed with type was nothing new when emoji emerged. Anyone who has used a home computer in the last 20 years will probably have come across typefaces Zapf Dingbats or Wingdings and realized that they can integrate symbols and pictograms into bodies of text by accessing these specialist 'dingbat' fonts using their keyboard. Emoji are themselves a kind of dingbat – non-alphabetical characters or glyphs that can be typed. However, emoji aren't restricted to single-colour icons in the same way that dingbat characters are. It's as if emoji fuse the concept of clip art

(crude rights-free illustrations that used to come packaged with word-processing programmes such as Microsoft Word) with that of the dingbat. Emoji were the first collection of symbols and icons to be widely usable using the keyboards of mobile communication devices.

Just as there are thousands of digital typefaces in use around the world today, so there are a huge variety of non-letter (often called 'symbol' or 'pi') fonts, which roughly fall into two distinct categories: those which allow the user to create patterns and ornament, and those which provide handy symbols, illustrations and graphic tools for use in specific circumstances. Long before emoji arrived on our smartphones, if you needed a picture of a party balloon

Various characters from Zapf Dingbats and Wingdings.

Fleurons, or 'printers' flowers'.

or the symbol for Mastercard , well, you could find a dedicated symbol font for that. There's even a dingbat font that features dozens of record-label logos. Handy.

While the notion of gathering such marks and devices into typefaces has gained popularity in the digital age, the use of typeset ornaments (also known as 'fleurons' or 'printers' flowers') is as old as printing itself. As retired professor of Old and Middle English and author Peter J. Lucas explains: 'At the beginning of the era of printed books in Europe at the end of the 15th and beginning of the 16th century, books followed manuscript tradition and had a colophon at the end which stated the name of the printer and usually the date and place of publication. This was not very

commercially useful, so printers and publishers (usually the same person) started to use title pages at the front of the book to display this information. These needed to look attractive to customers visiting their shop, so a decorative woodcut with a frame in which to print the title, author's name and printer/publisher was introduced. It was attractive to look at as well, giving the essential information about the book. Some printers used a bar with a geometric design so that several pieces could be set together to create a frame.'

For as long as typesetting was done by hand, ornamentation in typesetting was hugely popular and served to help identify publications as being by particular publishers. But with the advent of machine typesetting in the

20th century, says Paul Barnes of type foundry Commercial Type, the production of ornamental type characters went into decline. 'For foundries selling type for hand composition, [ornament] was of huge importance for the jobbing printers they sold to,' he explains, 'whereas with machine composition primarily for books, magazines, et cetera, it wasn't so important. Ornament was increasingly out of fashion in the 20th century and the skills of using ornament were dying out. It wasn't just a design skill but a composition skill and, with less and less hand-setting, there was less and less time for ornament.'

This didn't mean the end of non-alphabetical or numerical characters. Instead, the emphasis

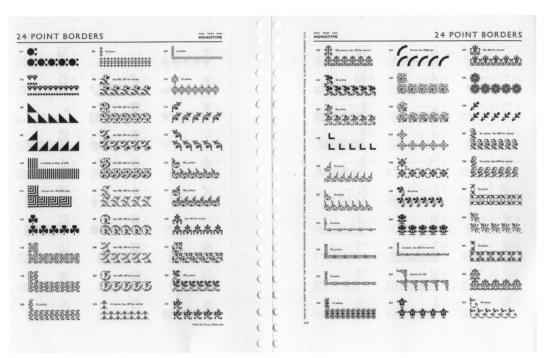

Spread from an old Monotype catalogue showing a selection of the company's range of border ornaments (at 24-point size) and the way in which their repeated use can make patterns.

switched from the ornamental to the practical as printers used graphic elements for, as self-confessed type obsessive Erik Spiekermann explains, a variety of tasks that, 'can today be done using other graphic tools, like the criss-cross pattern under a signature field or the black marks invalidating a carbon copy (remember those?). These had to be composed from bits of metal and the typographic duodecimal system with its 1, 2, 3, 4 and 6 dividers was the perfect way to work out multiples and endless combinations of these elements into whole pages, strips or frames. Even complete typefaces could be made up from graphic elements, like Super Veloz, created by Joan Trochut in the

early 1940s and since digitized by Andreu Balius [this was a dedicated system of lines and other shapes created specifically for combining to form type or illustration, inspired by the efforts of Catalan printers during the Spanish Civil War to create modernist illustrations using whatever pieces of metal they had to hand]. Futura, created in 1927, had its own "typosignals", with arrows, squares, triangles, circles and other bits that could be combined into typographic illustrations.'

When technology shifted again and digital type came into being, printers and designers were able to draw on a huge variety of specially designed

symbols created as fonts. A recent catalogue from Monotype, one of the world's oldest, largest and most highly regarded type libraries and providers of typography and related technologies, devotes some 34 pages to pi and symbol typefaces encompassing everything from species of fish, signs of the zodiac and foodstuffs to road signs, dinosaurs, facial expressions and decorative borders.

While many dingbats have a practical use (the foundry Linotype's Warning Pi, for example, is a collection of hazard warnings for signage use), others appear to have been created just for kicks: the dingbat is where type designers let their hair down.

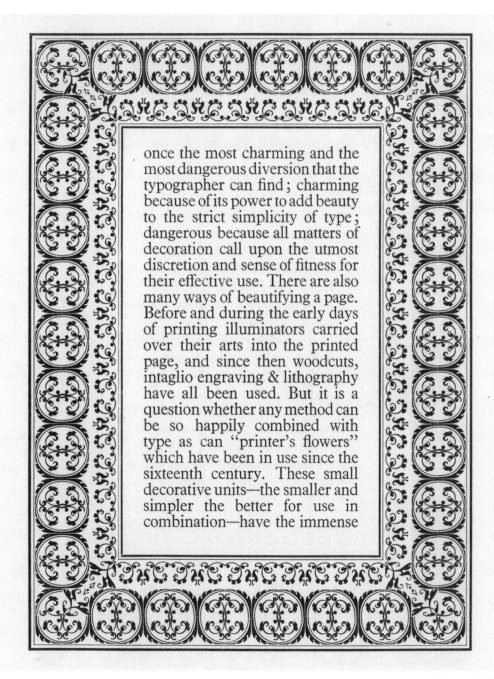

once the most charming and the most dangerous diversion that the typographer can find; charming because of its power to add beauty to the strict simplicity of type; dangerous because all matters of decoration call upon the utmost discretion and sense of fitness for their effective use. There are also many ways of beautifying a page. Before and during the early days of printing illuminators carried over their arts into the printed page, and since then woodcuts, intaglio engraving & lithography have all been used. But it is a question whether any method can be so happily combined with type as can "printer's flowers" which have been in use since the sixteenth century. These small decorative units—the smaller and simpler the better for use in combination—have the immense

A page from Frederic Warde's book *Printers' Ornaments Applied to the Composition of Decorative Borders, Panels, and Patterns*, published in 1928 by the Lanston Monotype Corporation, Ltd.

Examples of Linotype's Warning Pi.

Characters from Rian Hughes' Box Office dingbat font.

They can even be a forum to do good, as the Font Aid series of collaborative typefaces sold for charity demonstrates.

Dingbats have also benefited from the demand for bespoke typefaces. Just as companies want to commission and own unique corporate typefaces, some require their own sets of unique symbols and icons. Prolific type designer Rian Hughes was originally commissioned by *Radio Times* magazine to create his Box Office dingbat font for its TV and film listings. For the commercial release available from his site, it has been augmented with an extended international set of icons covering a broader range of uses. 'Dingbat fonts are especially useful in situations like *Radio Times*' listings because they flow with the text box and are easily editable,' says Hughes. 'It's much simpler to choose a glyph from a font than find and insert an EPS vector file.'

Making things simpler is, of course, a much wider trend in digital communication. As we type messages using our mobile phones and tablets, we've been creating linguistic shorthand for commonly used expressions such as LOL (laugh out loud) and OMG (oh my God). Emoji have emerged as a fun visual shorthand for a huge range of human emotions thanks to the many different versions of the yellow 'smiley' face as well as a wide variety of day-to-day objects, actions and activities. Visual shorthand transcends written language in a way that textual shorthand simply can't.

The power of emoji, and the key to their growing number of users, lies in how they allow textual messages to be combined with visual symbols that allude to the sender's frame of mind at the time of sending, very simply denoting whether they're happy, sad, angry, annoyed or tired. Emoji can, to some extent, make up for the lack of visual conversational cues such

as facial expressions, gesturing and intonation that are present in face-to-face communication but missing from textual exchanges. A text message that reads 'you're an idiot' is blunt and could be taken as an insult. Add a 😄, and the tone is completely different.

Another key to the popularity of emoji lies in their simplicity. However, version 7.0 of the Unicode Standard became available in the summer of 2014 and it included the addition of approximately 250 new emoji (though most of them were lifted from well-known dingbat fonts Wingdings and Webdings). And in early 2015, Apple introduced the ability to choose from a range of 'ethnically diverse' skin tones when using the hand symbols and some of the face character emoji. This complicates using these particular emoji somewhat – not least because it makes you really think about skin tone (there are five to choose from) unless you simply choose the yellow default. But realistically drawn yellow hands look very weird. And surely the tiny image of two hands raised as if to receive a double high-five sent by text means 'well done', not 'here is an accurate representation of my hands'. There is a danger that the larger the set of emoji becomes, or the more complicated the ideas represented, the less intuitive they will be to use. There are, however, new ways of accessing and utilizing emoji that look to address issues around ease of use as character sets expand. The global

The LINE app has an auto-suggest function that suggests stickers and emoji as you type.

mobile messaging platform LINE (which has become known for its emoji and 'stickers') has developed a nifty 'auto suggest' feature into its messaging application that sees suggested emoji pop up in response to certain words being typed – a kind of emoji equivalent of predictive text. This means that users don't have to trawl through vast character sets to find the right emoji, but simply choose from a selection of word-relevant emoji at any one time.

The idea of sending images embedded in our text communications has clearly taken hold, but is it just a passing fad? It seems unlikely. Combining word and image in digital text messaging is too powerful a communicative tool for us to abandon it anytime soon. On the contrary, emoji and other illustrated or graphic devices are fast becoming as important to the millions of people that use them in their typed communications as the letters and words they use – not simply because they're fun, cool or on-trend, but because they allow us to inflect added layers of humour, emotion and meaning into concise textual messages.

Vyvyan Evans, a linguistics professor at Bangor University in Wales, suggests that emoji are the fastest-growing form of language of all time. His research suggests that 72 per cent of people between the ages of 18 and 25 find it easier to express their emotions if they use emoji. Furthermore, 50 per cent of the people in this age group believe that emoji enable them to be better communicators.

According to a rather different study by dating website match.com published in early 2015, the emotional expression facilitated by the use of emoji means that people who use them in text messages have more active sex lives than those that don't. Dr Helen Fisher, a biological anthropologist at Rutgers University in New Jersey who led the study, told *TIME* magazine, 'It turns out that 54% of emoji users had sex in 2014 compared to 31% of singles who did not.' Her study even found that people who have more sex tend to use emoji more. Fisher's study (which polled 5,675 singles whose demographics were representative of the national population, according to the U.S. Census) maintains that this held true across both men and women in their twenties, thirties and forties.

'Emoji users don't just have more sex, they go on more dates and they are two times more likely to want to get married,' Fisher says. '62% of emoji users want to get married compared to 30% of people who never used an emoji.' It seems that emoji make our short-form digital communications more powerful and, apparently, improve our love lives. Thanks, emoji!

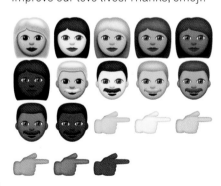

Apple's range of 'ethnically diverse' skin tone emoji choices was released in 2015.

The characters shown here were designed by different contributors for Font Aid, a series of collaborative typefaces that were sold to raise money for charitable causes.

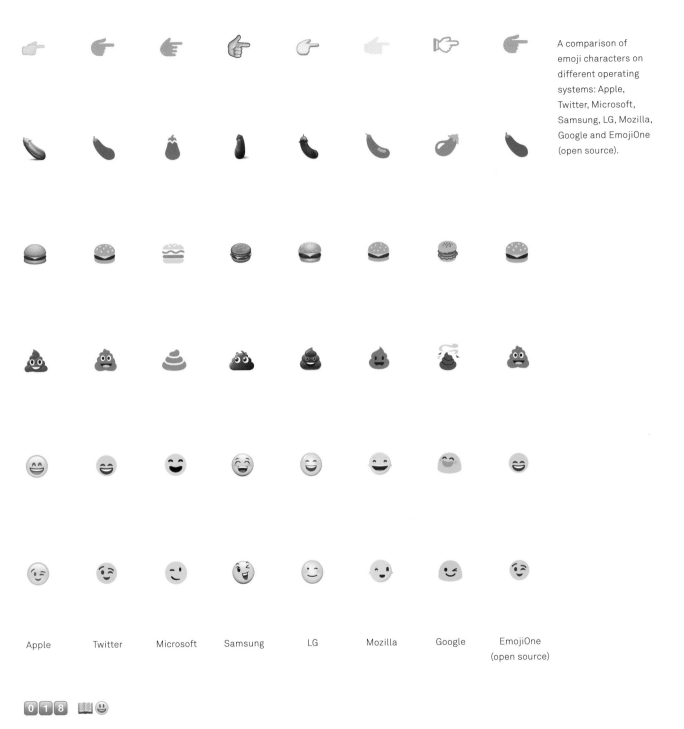

A comparison of emoji characters on different operating systems: Apple, Twitter, Microsoft, Samsung, LG, Mozilla, Google and EmojiOne (open source).

Apple	Twitter	Microsoft	Samsung	LG	Mozilla	Google	EmojiOne (open source)

LOST IN TRANSLATION

Emoji were developed in Japan and so, perhaps inevitably, the standard set includes various cultural references that don't quite translate into Western ideology. Add to this the fact that there are no hard and fast rules regarding emoji interpretation – and that different brands are creating their own proprietary emoji character sets, which all look slightly different – and it becomes clear that there's plenty of room for emoji-caused miscommunication.

The intended meaning of a particular emoji can become confused across different operating systems because emoji look different depending on the OS or application used. The many people who associate the use of emoji with their Apple phones think of emoji as looking a certain way. However, Microsoft, Google and Twitter are among many companies that have commissioned their own emoji sets to give them a particular proprietary look and feel. Apple, for example, put a smiley face on its pile of poo emoji. Google waived this jolly touch in favour of pushing the stinky aspect by including a couple of buzzing flies.

Another potentially easily mis-construed emoji across platforms is the aubergine (or eggplant) emoji. The Apple version has been used widely to indicate sexual attraction, for fairly obvious reasons, and because of that it is the only emoji that can't be hashtagged on the social media app Instagram. However, if a text is being sent to someone reading it on a Windows device, the meaning might well be lost because a Microsoft aubergine emoji is considerably less suggestive.

Additionally, there are some commonly used Apple emoji symbols that have different meanings or can be more or less potent depending on different cultural points of view. For example, not many Westerners are likely to use the emoji, or realize that in Japan it means 'well done' or 'you did very well'.

Outside of Japan, it's unlikely that people would use the tengu mask emoji to denote big-headedness or conceit, though that's invariably what it is used to represent. In Western culture, we're more likely to assume that the big-nosed, red-faced guy with the impressive eyebrows represents anger and so are more likely to use it in that context.

Another emoji regularly misconstrued by Westerners is the sleepy face emoji. It has a sad expression and what looks like a teardrop under the right eye, so Westerners tend to use it as a crying emoji. But the droplet actually emanates from the nose area of the face, because in Japanese anime the device of a snot bubble emerging from one nostril shows that a character is asleep – in a similar way to how Western cartoons might have the letters 'zzz' emanating from a sleeping character to suggest snoring.

Then there are simple cases of mistaken identity. Apple users tend to think of the grinning face with smiling eyes emoji as a grimace, and so tend to use it in that context. This is possibly because the dedicated grimacing emoji is so similar.

There's also some confusion as to whether symbolizes someone praying or a high five. Staying with hand gestures, is the symbol to choose if you're suggesting that high praise is in order or is it to be used when you want to receive a textual two-handed high five?

The great thing about emoji is that there is no wrong or right way to use them. This is why they're so much fun, but also why there's plenty of room for misinterpretation. Despite the cross-platform issues, it's possible to communicate almost any short message just using emoji without recourse to alphabet-based language at all – something no other dingbat or symbol font has really attempted to achieve, apart from a number of symbol fonts devoted to sign language. There are even emoji-only social networks where you message in emoji characters. Whether these become as popular as, say, Twitter remains to be seen.

PAVING THE WAY

Emoji weren't designed out of the blue. They were preceded by numerous cultural and literary phenomena and reference points, from the 'original smiley', to various attempts to introduce expressive punctuation and beyond, to kaomoji and ASCII art.

The interrobang combines a question mark and an exclamation mark, but hasn't gained widespread usage.

 The percontation point, a reversed question mark, was devised (and used) by English printer Henry Denham in the late 16th century.

The irony mark, an inverted exclamation mark, as proposed by John Wilkins in his 1668 work *An Essay towards a Real Character and a Philosophical Language.*

 The *ironieteken*, designed by Bas Jacobs of type foundry Underware.

 American typographer Choz Cunningham's snark mark – comprised of a full stop followed by a tilde.

 This is the love point, one of several punctuation marks proposed by French author Hervé Bazin in his 1966 book *Plumons l'Oiseau.*

EXPRESSIVE PUNCTUATION

Now that the use of emoji and emoticons to succinctly express mood in typed messages is widespread, it seems astonishing that the English language only really has two commonly used punctuation characters that denote expression or intonation. The question mark and exclamation mark, of course, are indispensable, but other similar functional glyphs that have been proposed simply haven't caught on in popular use. There's the brilliantly named interrobang – ‽ – a combination of question mark and exclamation mark that can be used to punctuate rhetorical statements such as 'Say what!?' or 'You're telling me you've never had a cheeseburger!?' It was devised by advertising man Martin K. Speckter in 1962 in an article written for *TYPEtalks Magazine*. The interrobang featured in the American Type Founders' 1966 metal type Americana, and also as a key on Remington Rand's 1968 typewriters. Although it's not widely used, there are no fewer than four variations of the interrobang in Microsoft's Wingdings 2 typeface and it also appears in Lucida Grande, the default font for many user interface elements of Apple's operating systems from 2001 to 2014.

Speckter was by no means the first to propose a new typographic symbol that could suggest tone of voice. Back in 1580, English printer Henry Denham proposed (and used for several years) a percontation point, or reversed question mark, to clearly mark rhetorical or ironic questions that require no answer.

In his 1668 work *An Essay towards a Real Character and a Philosophical Language*, another Englishman, the clergyman and natural philosopher John Wilkins (brother-in-law of Oliver Cromwell, no less), proposed that irony should be punctuated with an inverted exclamation mark. In 2007 Dutch typographer Bas Jacobs of type foundry Underware designed a new irony mark called the *ironieteken*. It also took the exclamation mark as a starting point, but kept it the usual way up and gave it a zigzag shape. Unfortunately, if two *ironieteken* are placed side by side, they look a little like the Nazi SS logo – which might, on a psychological level, go some way towards explaining why they haven't caught on.

French author Hervé Bazin proposed not one but a number of punctuation marks in his book *Plumons l'Oiseau* (1966), including the love point, a backwards and a forwards question

mark that share the same point and form a heart shape – a device that could be used in messages of affection, not unlike the hearts available in the original emoji character set.

According to the exhaustive research of Keith Houston, author of *Shady Characters: The Secret Life of Punctuation, Symbols and Other Typographical Marks* (2013), American typographer Choz Cunningham is the man responsible for the snark mark, a full stop followed by a tilde that Cunningham proposed should be used to denote sarcasm. While this mark, like all the others listed above, has failed to gain traction, it is formed by using two typographical glyphs readily available in standard alphabetical fonts; you simply combine them to create a new meaning. In other words, no new character needs to be designed and introduced. It is this concept that forms the basis for emoticons.

```
:)      <:-)    :-7     :-)~~   =|:-)=  (:>-<   '-)     (-_-)   :-{}    :-X     :<      :-D

:-)     |-(     (@ @)   |-)     7:)     &;-P    (-:     D :-)   }:-(    <|-)    :{      G-)

:>      :^)     :-"     :~)     :~I     *;-~I   (-)     Q:-)    :-[     <|-(    :O      :-J

;)      :*)     :-V     :-?     :~J     >:-)    (:I     O_O     :-E     *<:-)   :C      :-K

;-)     :-{#}   :-V     :-8     :/I     >;-)    {:-)    >:-|    :-F     (8-O    :Q      :-L

;>      &:-)    :-O     O=      :-I     :-)##   +:-)    :-/     :-)~    *:O)    :,(     :-Z

(*_*)   @:-)    :-W     -=      :-B     &:-]    =:-)    :-{)}   :-~)    O!O     :*      :-B

B-)     #:-)    :-W     .-)     O.O     &8-]    %-^     <>:{(}  :'-)    3:]     :-`     .-]

8-)     O:-)    :-R     :-:     ):-)    ;|8-)   @:I     **:-)   :-@     3:[     :-%     ,-}

8-(     C=:-)   :-F     :<)     :-)     7:^]    :-!     ])      :V      D8=     :-6     0-)

:D      :-) )-: :-P     :^{     (:-)    *<|:-)  #-)     [:-|    -:-(    E-:-)   ):-)    ~~:-(

:-D     (.)(.)  :-1     8*)     (^.^)   )-:|<*  :-(*)   {(:-)   :=)     :-9     ):-(    O |-)

:-O     :/)     :-,     B*)     #:-O    [:-)    %-\     }(:-(   +-:-)   %-6     )8-)    8 :-I

:-P     :-)))   <:-O    :<)=    (:-$    D:-)    :-)8    8(:-)   `:-)    <:-I    =:-(    E-:-I

:-J     :->     :-T     :-=)    (:-&    :-\     :-)-{8  *:-)    ,:-)    K:P     :-Q     >:-I

:-#     :-C     :-Y     :-#|    (:-(    ;-\     :X(     >:->    |-I     :-0     :-E     3:O[

:-$     :-C     :-|     ::-)    (:^(    :-S     8:]     >;->    |-O     :}      (_O_)   |-P

:-&     :-<     :'-(    8:-)    (:<)    -:-)    (:)-)   [:]     :-Q     :@      :-T     <:I

:-*     ;-C     :~-(    B-|     ?-(     O^O     (-:|:-) B:-)    O-)     :I      :-]     :-8(

:-X     :-}     :~(~    P-)     <{:-)}  :N)     {:V     :-)-8   O :-)   :(      }:-)    >:-<

:-(=)   :-I     :-)....  :-{    <:-)<<| :U)     %+{     :-{)    :-S     :[      :-A     8-|
```

First published in 1648, Robert Herrick's poem 'To Fortune' features one of the earliest examples of a printed emoticon (albeit an unintentional one).

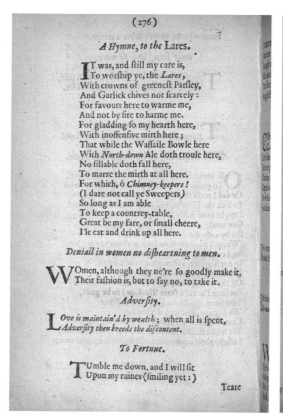

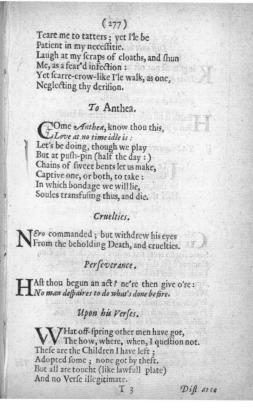

EMOTICONS

An emoticon (a composite of the words 'emotion' and 'icon') is a combination of typographic characters hat look like a face when viewed sideways. All emoticons are comprised of combinations of readily available and familiar typographic marks and symbols, and are used to imply tone in a text or typed message where body language, facial expressions or vocal intonation aren't able to denote the tenor of the communication. The most common and recognizable emoticon is the smiley face represented by a colon, dash and closed bracket **:-)** known simply as the smiley emoticon. There can be no doubt that the smiling yellow-face emoji characters took inspiration from the way emoticons were previously being used in typed messages.

When or where the smiley emoticon was first used is something of a mystery. Poetry fan Levi Stahl blogged in 2014 about his discovery of a possible emoticon used by 17th-century poet Robert Herrick in his poem 'To Fortune', published in 1648:

Tumble me down, and I will sit
Upon my ruins, (smiling yet :)

'Lest it be an aberration in the edition I own,' wrote Stahl in a blog post on 13 April 2014, 'I checked it against the new, authoritative two-volume edition of Herrick's work edited by Tom Cain and Ruth Connolly (Oxford University Press, 2013). The emoticon is there. Herrick's poetry is rich in wit,' he continues, 'so it is not entirely out of

(applause and laughter ;)

the bounds of possibility that this is something more than a punctuational oddity.'

Although the context of the word 'smiling' in this particular verse does perhaps suggest that Herrick (or the typesetter of his book) had used an emoticon, Stahl failed to mention the various other incidences of similar punctuation constructs littered throughout Herrick's collection *Hesperides* (published in 1648), including the one that appears in the very next poem, 'To Anthea', shown in the right-hand image on the previous page. Look at more 17th-century texts and it becomes clear that Herrick's emoticon was nothing more than coincidental.

A *New York Times* transcript of an Abraham Lincoln speech published in 1862 contains a similar punctuation construct used next to the word 'laughter', which has led to speculation that it should be read like an emoticon. The transcript features the phrase '(applause and laughter ;)' as one of 14 instances of the crowd's reactions to the speech that are included in brackets in the transcript.

There does seem to be an inconsistency in these transcribed crowd reactions: of the 14 included, two appear in round parentheses, while the other 12 appear in square brackets. A further two also contain the word 'laughter', but neither includes an emoticon. Furthermore, the final audience reaction note in the speech contains what looks to be a punctuation typo, as a quote ends not with a quotation mark and a full stop, but with two commas followed by a single quotation mark: '[cries of "No, no–go on,,']'. Typesetting inconsistency and punctuative error appear to be the most likely explanation for the supposed emoticon here.

Less than 20 years after Lincoln's speech transcript, in 1881 four vertical emoticons that covered the emotions joy, melancholy, indifference and astonishment were published by *Puck* magazine in its 30 March edition under the headline 'typographical art'. Here, we see combinations of punctuation marks, full stops, parentheses and dashes combined to create simple faces showing different emotions. They were accompanied by the presumably tongue-in-cheek message, 'We wish it to be distinctly understood that the letterpress department of this paper is not going to be trampled on by any tyranical [sic] crowd of artists ...'

However, perhaps the best-documented early and deliberate use of emoticons in digital communications is by Scott Fahlman, a computer able you to bring suit. They always give a man such facilities gladly."

"But say she refuses to marry?"

"There is no precedent for a woman refusing to marry, in the law."

At this point Mr. Ryan left to get his dinner, and Mr. Burke indicated to the jailer his desire to take a lease of his cell (with privilege of renewal) and to fit it up on the installment plan.

The next day Mr. Ryan made application at one of the higher courts for a mandamus compelling the jailer to show cause why he should not release Fortunatus.

"I am going," said Ryan, "to make this a TEST CASE."

Burke said he was sorry to hear it.

The jailer got five days to file answer, then an extension of twenty, two postponements of ten days each, and three privileges to "amend" his reply, with three days along with each one. Meanwhile Mr. Burke languished in jail. Ryan came to see him, spoke hopefully, and said:

"We must move slowly but surely. I will make the jailer pay the costs. This is some satisfaction."

At the end of seven weeks the jailer filed his answer, which was:

"Demurrer to the complaint, as it is defective. Redress in equity is a suit against committing magistrate. I am only his agent."

Mr. Burke was cast for $413.75 costs.

Mr. Ryan, however, continued to make it a "test case." He carried it from one court to another; he took it from the general term to the special term; he wrote and filed 320 pages of manuscript; he furnished bonds to the amount of $20,000, the arts of a Choate in law, a Fox in eloquence, and a Macchiavelli in strategy, he employed unstintingly. At the end of a year and a half he got the case to the Court of Appeals, in Albany, and it was put "peremptorily" on the calendar for June 16th, 1886. With this cheering information he returned to poor Burke, who still languished in jail.

"Well," said B., "what has all this thing cost?"

"Nothing! I brought it *in forma pauperis.* Constructively, you are a tramp. That will appear on the record if you are discharged."

"If?" said Burke. "Is it not all settled?"

"A decision," said Ryan, will be handed down from the Bench in Albany within five years."

Mr. Burke said nothing. He arose from his bench, took off his coat, and inquired of Quirites what was the way he came in. Mr. Ryan told him.

"It is the shortest way for you out," said Fortunatus fiercely. "Jailer," he said, "take me before the judge."

Ryan retired discreetly, and Mr. Burke was led into court and placed before the bar.

His Honor.—"What do you want?"

Burke.—"I wish to plead guilty."

His Honor.—"Of what offense?"

Burke.—"Murder."

His Honor.—"Murder!"

Burke.—"Murder in the first degree."

His Honor.—"What is your defence?"

Burke.—"Insanity."

His Honor said:

"Burke, the point is well taken. A man charged with murder who pleads insanity is always acquitted. There is no use holding you. I discharge you. You are free."

Burke.—"Don't you want bail?"

His Honor.—"It is useless. There is no the faintest possibility of a murderer with such a defence being condemned. Why didn't you enter this plea before?"

Mr. Burke did not answer.

But he took from his pocket two crisp five dollar bills, and handed one to the judge and one to his clerk.

"Ryan," he said, "has my bank-book and jewelry. The jailer has my life insurance policy. I leave the court a poor but a free man."

* * *

The feminine character is everything that is true, loyal, loving, noble and sincere. The woman waited. They were married. Children blessed their union, and now play sometimes with the gun which is waiting for Ryan in the hall. But the lawyer's clerk has moved to Ohio, and has the people of the United States for a client just now. Mr. Burke says that the day that case is called up for trial in the Court of Appeals, he will send Clerk Perrin a card of which this is a copy:

Mr. and Mrs. Fortunatus Burke,

(*And don't you forget it.*)

ERNEST HARVIER.

TYPOGRAPHICAL ART.

We wish it to be distinctly understood that the letter-press department of this paper is not going to be trampled on by any tyranical crowd of artists in existence. We mean to let the public see that we can lay out, in our own typographical line, all the cartoonists that ever walked. For fear of startling the public we will give only a small specimen of the artistic achievements within our grasp, by way of a first instalment. The following are from Studies in Passions and Emotions. No copyright.

Joy. Melancholy. Indifference. Astonishment.

A NUISANCE AND ITS REMEDY.

THE HOLY KISS.

THE MANLY KICK.

END OF THE WORLD.

"Say, what is there in this talk about Old Mother what-you-call-her, the conjugation of the planets, and the world comin' to an end this year?" asked a grizzled old '49er, stopping Prof. Legate as he was turning the corner of G and Union streets with a big telescope under his left arm. "Do you think the old world is going to pass in her checks?"

"Well," said the Professor, "we certainly have had, during the last year, some remarkable movements in the principal planets."

"Anything liable to bust loose very soon?"

"Before long. Let me see—at 9 o'clock on the night of April 21, Saturn will be in conjunction with the sun."

"Good for a starter. What next?"

"At 7 o'clock next morning Saturn and Jupiter will be in conjunction."

"Bully! That's business."

"At 9 o'clock that morning Jupiter will come into conjunction with the sun."

"Hurrah! All getting in their work on the sun. I can see old Sol beginning to get shaky on his pins. What next?"

"On the second of May Venus comes into conjunction with the sun."

"Glory! The old gal gets in her lick on the sun, too. It's gettin' hot now. Hit him again, old gal!"

"On the 11th of May Neptune will be in conjunction with the sun."

"Tiptop; old Nep and all of 'em goin' square at the sun, like so many butting billy goats. I'll live to see it yet. Who goes at him next?"

"On the 14th of May Mercury comes into conjunction with the sun, and Uranus will be at right angles."

"My what will be at right angles?"

"Uranus."

"The h—l! Then I'll be in the grand bust up, sure. Is that all?"

"Those will be the principal occurrences."—*Virginia (Nev.) Enterprise.*

"Is the Oilymargarine all out?" asked farmer Traddles of his wife at the breakfast table the other morning. "Yes," replied the good woman; "John, the hired man, took the last lump yesterday to grease the axles of the cart." "Well, John is getting altogether too economical," petulantly exclaimed Mr. Traddles. "He thinks common tar is too good for axle grease."—*Norristown Herald.*

NEW HAVEN people will remember the big whale that passed through this city on a couple of flat cars a few weeks ago. Well, it is on exhibition in Cincinnati, and one of the wicked papers of that city suggests that some one take the character of Jonah and give a Sunday-school entertainment.—*New Haven Register.*

PRESIDENT CHASE, of Haverford College, says the Bible has 120,000 errors which the new revision will make straight. Considering how our forefathers were handicapped, it is a wonder how any of them figured out their eternal peace.—*Somerville Journal.*

THE Parisian Jardin Mabille is to be closed. We were going over to Paris in company with three deacons to study the art works in the Louvre, but we have given up the idea.—*Boston Post.*

SHREWDNEES AND ABILITY.

Early examples of emoticons in an 1881 issue of *Puck* magazine.

```
19-Sep-82 11:44     Scott E  Fahlman                    :-)
From: Scott E  Fahlman <Fahlman at Cmu-20c>

I propose that the following character sequence for
joke markers:

:-)

Read it sideways.  Actually, it is probably more
economical to mark things that are NOT jokes, given
current trends.  For this, use

:-(
```

Computer scientist Scott Fahlman believes he invented the emoticon in this 1982 online bulletin board post.

scientist at Carnegie Mellon University in Pittsburgh, Pennsylvania. On an online bulletin board on 19 September 1982, Fahlman proposed that the character sequence **:-)** should be used to denote joke messages. 'Read it sideways,' he wrote. 'Actually, it is probably more economical to mark things that are NOT jokes, given current trends. For this, use **:-(**.'

'This convention caught on quickly around Carnegie Mellon,' Fahlman recalls on his website, 'and soon spread to other universities and research labs via the primitive computer networks of the day. Some CMU alumni who had moved on to other places continued to read our boards as a way of keeping in touch with their old community.'

While Fahlman believes that he invented this glyph and the 'turn your head to one side' principle independently, he doesn't doubt that others have used such typographical devices in a similar way. 'Some people have told me that the **:-)** or **:)** convention was used by teletype operators in the old days,' he says. 'Maybe so. Others have written to tell me that their father or uncle or they themselves used to type these symbols, or something close to them, in private letters (or, in one case, on punch cards) long before 1982. I haven't (yet) seen any hard evidence of this, but I have no reason to doubt their accounts. It's a simple and obvious idea after all, and the independent invention of this idea by multiple people would not be implausible.' Meanwhile, the term 'emoticon' appeared in print publi-

cations for the first time in the *New York Times* on 28 January 1990 and was added to the *Oxford English Dictionary* in its print edition of June 2001.

Of course, the use of emoticons in written communication has had its critics over the years. Journalist Neal Stephenson's piece in *The New Republic*'s edition of 13 September 1993 described the smiley face emoticon as 'the written equivalent of the Vegas rimshot' (a typographic 'boom-tish' to signify a joke); in other words, the very nadir of linguistic sophistication.

In the same year in which Stephenson's derogatory article was published, the use of emoticons in the Western world became more and more established. Californian

The cover of David Sanderson's emoticon dictionary, published in 1997.

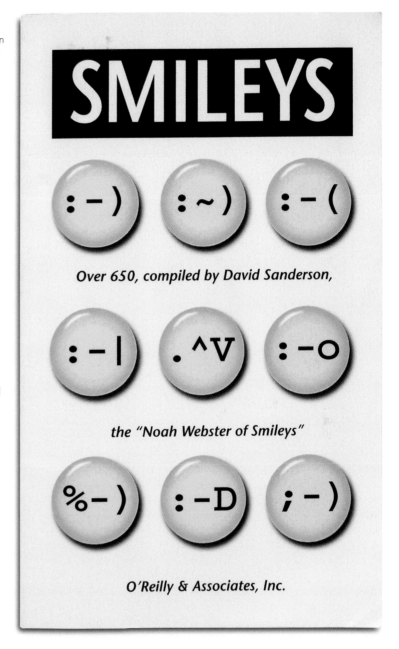

computer book publisher O'Reilly & Associates published a 93-page emoticon dictionary entitled *Smileys*, compiled by David Sanderson. The cover of this book shows a grid of nine emoticons arranged as if printed on yellow button badges. The direct line of influence of emoticons on emoji couldn't be clearer. At around the same time, James Marshall, a graduate astronomy student at the University of Maryland, began compiling an online emoticon dictionary, which is still online and now has thousands of entries.

KAOMOJI AND ASCII ART

Around the time that emoticons were coming into popular use in the West, Eastern cultures were developing their own version. In the late 1980s users of Japan's ASCIInet online bulletin board network developed emoticons that could be read without having to tilt your head.

As with Western emoticons, faces are created using combinations of typographic characters and symbols. However, Japanese kaomoji – from the words for 'face' (*kao*)

and 'character' (*moji*) – can be quite complex and can even be made up of more than one line of text to build up an ASCII-art-style image. In Japan, this is referred to as either Shift JIS art (Shift JIS is a superset of ASCII intended for Japanese usage) or AA, standing for 'ASCII art'. ASCII (American Standard Code for Information Interchange) is a character-encoding scheme based on the English alphabet that encodes 128 specified characters into 7-bit binary integers to allow communication equipment and other devices to process and represent

text. 'ASCII art' is the term given to graphic designs and illustrations created using lines of text typed using (usually) a monospaced, fixed-width font.

Japanese kaomoji can be as simple as just two characters – ^^ – or made up of many more:
＼ (ˆ∀ˆ) ╱ (ˆ∀ˆ) ╱.
Because of the increased number of available Eastern characters, there is great potential for stylistic creativity, which has led to a vast number of different kaomoji.

THE ORIGINAL 'SMILEY'

The original 'smiley' – a yellow circle with two black elliptical dots for eyes and a smiling mouth – was designed by American commercial illustrator Harvey Ball in 1963. He was commissioned to create the graphic device when the State Mutual Life Assurance Company of Worcester, Massachusetts, purchased and merged with the Guarantee Mutual Company of Ohio. After the merger, employee morale was low and Ball was tasked (for the princely sum of $45) with creating a smiling face that could appear on button badges, desk cards and posters which would be distributed and displayed internally within the company. The idea was that employees would 'Have a happy day' and smile more when using the phone and performing other tasks. The button badges became super popular: by 1971 over 50 million of them had been sold and the smiley was dubbed an international icon.

However, neither Ball nor State Mutual registered the design as a trademark and so have never made a penny from its success outside of its original purpose within the company. Philadelphian brothers Bernard and Murray Spain, on the other hand, were more enterprising, designing and selling products in the US sporting the smiley logo along with the phrase 'Have a happy day', which soon changed to 'Have a nice day.'

It was a Frenchman, Franklin Loufrani, who successfully (and cannily) registered the image of a round yellow circle with black dots for eyes and a smiling mouth as a trademark in 1971; he did this after he had started to use it in the newspaper *France Soir* to head a column of good news that aimed to make readers smile. His son Nicolas now runs the company,

The original 'smiley' designed by Harvey Ball.

which licenses the use of the smiley to other companies. Sales of products with a SmileyWorld licence purport to be in the region of millions of dollars every year. The company even has its own Smiley London store, from which it sells various smiley-adorned products.

In 1999 Harvey Ball set up the World Smile Corporation to pursue smiley licensing opportunities (primarily in the US), determining that all after-tax profits generated would be given to charities. Now called the Harvey Ball World Smile Foundation, the non-profit organization's remit is to raise

'I Want You to Smile' poster designed by Harvey Ball, 1997.

money for and awareness of small, grassroots charitable efforts. It receives funding from donations and from licensing the smiley image. The foundation is also the major sponsor of World Smile Day on the first Friday of October each year.

In the UK, the happy yellow face has been associated with psychedelic culture and in particular with the anarchist and free festival campaigner and organizer Bill 'Ubi' Dwyer. Dwyer helped organize the Windsor Free Festival (1972–4) and utilized the smiley as a kind of personal logo, which he sported on his hat and clothes and even his letterhead.

The smiley face is also strongly associated with electronic dance music culture, particularly with acid house, rave culture and the 'second summer of love' in the late 1980s. A yellow smiley face appeared on the cover of Bomb the Bass's 1987 single 'Beat Dis'. The design, complete with a red splat, referenced the bloodstained smiley badge that features on the cover and in the opening pages of Alan Moore and Dave Gibbons' *Watchmen* series of comics, first published in 1986 by DC Comics.

Fashion designer Jeremy Scott arrives at the 2014 MTV Video Music Awards wearing an outfit created in collaboration with SmileyWorld.

'World Smile Day' poster, 1999.

Bill 'Ubi' Dwyer, an early smiley face enthusiast.

Beat Dis, 12" single by Bomb the Bass,
Mister-Ron Records, 1987. The record sleeve's
design paid homage to the cover of DC Comics'
Watchmen issue 1, published in 1986,
which featured a bloodstained yellow smiley
button badge.

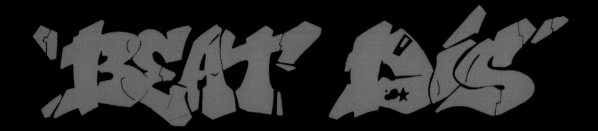

1 😴 B 4 ✈️ 2 ☀️ 🏖️ 🏄 🍹 😎

EMOJI: BORN IN JAPAN

The story of how emoji came into being, initially as a strategy by one enterprising mobile network service provider, and evolved to become a global communications phenomenon.

Japanese mobile service provider Docomo's Pocket Bell pager, a must-have gadget for teens across the country in 1995.

The inclusion of emoji on Apple's iPhone software in 2011 undoubtedly helped them on their way to becoming an international phenomenon. However, emoji were originally conceived in Japan in the late 1990s and rolled out in February 1999 by a telecommunications service provider looking to make Internet use on mobile phones and pagers more engaging and intuitive.

In 1995, pagers were hugely popular with teenagers in Japan. NTT Docomo, one of the country's largest mobile service providers, had created the Pocket Bell pager device that was seen as the must-have gadget of the time. This was not so much because of its aesthetic appeal, but because Docomo had added a heart symbol that allowed the school kids that favoured it to inject a new level of sentiment (and cuteness) into the millions of messages they were keying into telephones every day. But when new versions of the Pocket Bell abandoned the heart symbol in favour of more business-friendly features like kanji and Latin alphabet support, the teenagers that made up Docomo's core customer base had no problem leaving the network for upstart competitor Tokyo Telemessage. By the time Docomo realized it had misjudged the demand for business-focused pagers (and the power of the teenage market), it was badly in need of a new killer app that could re-engage teenage customers.

In the wider context of digital communications in the mid-1990s, Windows 95 had just launched and

Heart symbol included on NTT Docomo's Pocket Bell pager

NTT Docomo's i-mode team visit San Francisco to check out AT&T's Pocketnet mobile phone

NTT Docomo release its original set of 176 emoji

Japan's top three mobile networks map incoming signals to their own character sets

email was taking off in Japan alongside its pager boom. But people in Japan, for the most part, were having a hard time getting used to these new methods of communication. In Japanese culture, personal letters are traditionally long and verbose, full of seasonal greetings and honorific expressions that convey the sender's goodwill to the recipient. The shorter, more casual nature of email was at odds with this tradition. Furthermore, familiar, longer-form letters gave people important contextual information in the same way that face-to-face interactions and phone conversations allow for facial expressions and vocal intonation to play an important part of conveying meaning. The absence of all of these cues in emails and texts meant that the promise of digital communi-

cation – being able to stay in closer touch with people much more easily – was being offset by an accompanying increase in miscommunication.

At the time, Docomo had a research and development team working on i-mode, a project that would become the world's first widespread mobile Internet platform, combining features like weather forecasts, entertainment reservations, news and email. i-mode would eventually prove so popular that it would completely engulf the country, giving Japan's mobile Internet a 10-year lead internationally. However, back in the mid-1990s, the i-mode team needed ideas. In order to take a look at other work already being done on mobile Internet applications, the team – which included a young employee named

Shigetaka Kurita – visited San Francisco in 1998 to check out AT&T's Pocket Net.

Pocket Net was the first service in the world to provide amenities like email and weather forecasts over a mobile (cellular) network. Using AT&T's new cellular digital packet data (CDPD) service, it was capable of transfer speeds of 19.2Kbps (these days, average transfer speeds are around 10Mbps – around 500 times more impressive). Hardware specs at the time were also poor, and devices were simply not capable of displaying images. So, while Pocket Net conveyed weather-related news, forecasts like 'cloudy' and 'sunny' were just spelled out in text. The lack of visual cues made the service more difficult to use than it ought to

Emoji encoded
into Unicode

Emoji keyboard
included in
Apple's iOS 5
iPhone software

Japanese service
provider AU
redesigns its
primary group of
emoji characters
to look more like
the original
Docomo designs

have been, and Kurita and his team recognized that AT&T's mobile experience would benefit greatly from some extra characters and icons to show contextual information.

Kurita started to wonder if it could be beneficial to show simple faces that would help denote tone in textual messages. 'We had already had the experience with the heart symbol, so we knew it was possible,' he recalls. ASCII art and kaomoji were already around at the time, but they were time-consuming to enter on a mobile phone, since they were composed of multiple characters. Kurita was looking for a simpler solution. Not being a designer himself (he was an economics major), Kurita's plan was to draft some ideas to show to manu-facturers like Sharp, Panasonic and

Fujitsu, all large companies that had design resources to throw at the problem. However, he was surprised to find that they didn't immediately share his zeal for the project. 'They were like, "please, you design them." They had a lot of reasons – these were the first devices that supported i-mode, they didn't have the resources, that kind of thing,' he explains. Faced with few options, Kurita gathered his team, and got to work with no small ambition: he aimed to create a complete set of 176 12-by-12-pixel characters that could cover the entire breadth of human emotion.

For inspiration, Kurita looked to different elements of his childhood, including manga and kanji. 'In Japanese comics, there are a lot of

different symbols. People draw expressions like the person with the bead of sweat, you know, or like when someone gets an idea and they have the light bulb. So there were a lot of cases where I used those as a kind of hint.' From kanji, he took the ability to express abstract ideas like 'secret' and 'love' in a single character.

In order to display the glyphs, Docomo decided to exploit an unused region of the Shift JIS Japanese character encoding scheme. Each 2-byte code would correspond to a unique image, all of which would come loaded on Docomo mobile phones like any other typographic character. Users would then be able to add them to their messages by selecting them from a grid inside the mail app. Docomo wasn't only targeting email

 - 1580s

 - 1700s

 - 1880s

? - 1960s

 :) - 1980s

♥ - 1990s

⊟ - 2000s

😊 - 2011

💁🏿 - 2015

with emoji – the easily accessible images were also designed to let content providers dress up their i-mode websites. Companies Zagat and Pia were some of the first to provide content for Docomo's experimental new service, entitling them to a special perk: their logos were part of the original set of emoji installed on the company's phones (although they were removed after the first contract expired, a year or two later).

With only a 12-by-12 grid to play with, Kurita had to be economical with the use of space in his designs, and the resulting characters were exceedingly simple. For example, the original grinning face has a rectangular mouth and upside-down V's for eyes. In many ways, his original emoji look very different from the glossy yellow smileys that people outside Japan

📖😊

now associate with the word. They look like a hybrid of emoticons and early 8-bit computer game graphics.

While Kurita always envisioned emoji as symbols – something closer to letters that wouldn't feel out of place if you slipped them into a sentence – he had thought that the manufacturers who suggested he design emoji himself would be able to add some finishing touches, turning them into something more professional. 'But every single one just took what we had and implemented it the way it was,' he says. 'Then again, the good thing about that was that everyone's emoji were identical. If each manufacturer had added its own originality to the characters, the emoji would have been all mixed up and inconsistent depending what manufacturer's

device you were looking at, even if one Docomo user sent a message to another.'

This consistency, however, didn't last long. Docomo wasn't able to get a copyright on its emoji designs ('they're only 12 blocks by 12 blocks,' the company was told), which meant that Japanese competitors AU and J-Phone (which would later become SoftBank) could have simply piggybacked on Docomo's success when they launched their own emoji. Instead, they both decided to do their own thing, adding more (and more detailed) images, along with animation, in an effort to lock in customers. What could have been a single, uniform set of characters used by different service providers became a jumble of different proprietary approaches, and emoji

sent from one carrier wouldn't display on its competitors' phones. It wasn't until 2005 that the three main mobile networks in Japan began to map the incoming signals to their own character sets. Finally, in 2012, in an overdue step toward standardization, AU decided to redesign its primary group of characters to look more like the original Docomo designs – an effort that Kurita was involved in. But even so, there are still multiple sets of characters in the wild depending on your carrier and phone. Docomo's expanded set numbers around 250, not counting animated characters. Some devices display more than 800.

By 2010 emoji had been adopted into Unicode. Their various implementations had become fractured, with lots of companies

Tennis champion Andy Murray summed up his wedding in this emoji-only tweet in 2015.

having developed their own proprietary emoji sets. Although Japan's carriers don't have a standard single set of characters, this hasn't stopped emoji from catching on overseas. Apple's iPhone supported a variant of SoftBank's emoji set beginning with the iOS 2.2 update, at least in Japan. But with the release of iOS 5 in late 2011, emoji made their real international debut. And while the smileys found in communication software packages such as Google Talk or Skype have all been designed independently of Apple's emoji, there's no doubt that they are all part of the same cultural phenomenon.

As people found out how to enable the characters on their phones, little pictures of guardsmen and winking faces with stuck-out tongues started sprouting up all over Twitter, Instagram and Tumblr. Today you see them everywhere, from the texts you get from your mum, to advertising campaigns for global brands such as Coca-Cola and IKEA, and beyond to projects and memes. New York-based artist Fred Benenson's *Emoji Dick* project, an emojified version of Herman Melville's classic novel, was added to America's Library of Congress collection in 2013. In 2015 Australia's Foreign Minister Julie Bishop responded to an interview with Buzzfeed entirely in emoji (she even pulled an 'angry face' in response to a particular question during a TV interview); international tennis star Andy Murray summarized his wedding in an emoji-only post on Twitter (which has been retweeted over 14,000 times); Apple launched 'ethnically diverse' emoji by adding the option of different skin tones to all of its hand symbols and some of the available face emoji; and a Vulcan salute 🖖 has even been added to Apple's emoji character set for the benefit of *Star Trek* fans. Emoji are clearly more than just a passing fad; they really are conquering the world.

📝 Jeff Blagdon reported for The Verge between 2011 and 2013, after earning a Master's Degree in Applied Economics from Doshisha University in Kyoto. Having spent nearly a decade studying and working in Japan, he has relocated to New York, where he spends his time bicycling, taking photos and ineptly trying to program in Haskell.

Some of Shigetaka Kurita's original emoji characters have been recreated here, each drawn in a 12-by-12 grid of pixels.

INTERVIEW WITH SHIGETAKA KURITA, THE INVENTOR OF EMOJI

You were working on the i-mode development team in 1998 when you took a research trip to San Francisco to check out AT&T's Pocket Net. What did you learn from that trip?

When I looked at AT&T's Pocket Net, the thing I was most interested in was how to display content on a cell phone. In 1997 the screens were incredibly small, and also black-and-white, so you weren't able to show images. I went to San Francisco with the intention of learning how to show information like weather forecasts and news on these terrible displays, and about the kinds of interfaces needed to show it in a way that was easy to understand.

I felt that the way Pocket Net showed text like 'fine' for clear weather and 'rain' for rain wasn't intuitive. Instead, I thought they should use things like ☀ for clear weather and ☂ for rain, like weather forecasts do on TV. Up until then I had been thinking that emoji would be used for showing emotions, like the heart, but I was made to realize that since we couldn't show full images on these devices, emoji would be necessary for providing rich informational content to users as well.

Also, Pocket Net seemed to be written in a language that was similar to what would become HDML (Handheld Device Markup Language), and I felt that the interface was unintuitive. Text is the basis for displaying information, so I felt that the system should be like a tree. In that way I had the same idea as Pocket Net, but I recall the way they did it being very difficult to use because the functions for making a selection and advancing, and returning to the previous screen, were split between two buttons. I was a 'game kid' that grew up with Nintendo, so I believed that the easiest interface model to understand and use would be a D-pad and two buttons for select and cancel. You could say that through getting a chance to use Pocket Net's interface we were given an anti-pattern that let us come up with the i-mode interface. As for the OS itself, there wasn't anything in particular that caught my interest.

What made the deepest impression on me during the trip was being able to email Japan while I was riding the cable car in San Francisco. Up until that point, 'email' meant sitting down, at home, on the computer. So being able to stand on the cable car and send and receive messages on a mobile device felt really liberating.

The love heart was one of the first symbols to appear on a pager besides type characters. In a way, that was the first emoji.

In 1995 the only two symbols the Pocket Bell was able to display were a phone and a heart. The phone icon was used when you wanted someone to call you back, but the heart was a symbol that you used to express emotion. So I definitely agree that the heart was the first emoji.

What other visual cues inspired and informed the original emoji characters you created for Docomo?

The two things that served as my inspiration were *manpu* and pictograms. *Manpu* are special symbolic expressions used in manga – for example, the droplet-shaped 'sweat' mark used on someone's face to indicate things like anxiety or embarrassment, the wavy 'steam' lines above someone's head for indicating rage, or the light bulb for showing a flash of inspiration. I used them as a reference because they were simple expressions, as well as having the ability to express a wide range of feelings and situations, and were becoming shared knowledge for a lot of people through manga. Pictograms are a kind of information design used in things like public guide maps. They're something that anyone can understand with a single glance and served as a reference for the information-type emoji we came up with. In particular, I'm talking about the pictograms that were created for the 1964 Tokyo Olympics to allow visitors from abroad to navigate facilities like washrooms. It really makes me proud that emoji were inspired by manga, pictograms and things from Japan, and now they're being used all around the world.

Were there any emoji characters you created originally that didn't make it to your final selection?

The poo emoji. When I first designed it at Docomo it was deemed to be 'unsuitable for Docomo from the perspective of public morals and decency', and so initially went un-released, but because KDDI adopted it, it's now part of the standard set of emoji.

Can you explain the design process?

I presented my idea to develop emoji to the head of planning for i-mode (who was also my boss), Mari Matsunaga, who approved the plan. I took care of the planning, while two others handled the development and negotiation with handset makers, so the emoji development team was made up of three people in total. It was decided that the first version of i-mode would use 12-by-12-pixel characters, so that was our first constraint. Our staff considered how to actually implement emoji, deciding to use the free region in the Shift JIS character encoding space. A few of the free blocks were reserved for the kanji introduced in the third and fourth standards of Shift JIS, so without a reserved region of our own, we figured we could safely use enough of the free space in Shift JIS for about 200 characters. This became our second constraint. That left us with the actual work of coming up with 200 emoji and producing the 12-by-12-pixel icons. Our original assumption was that there would be three main uses for emoji: expressing emotions, mainly for messaging (the heart, for example); displaying content (such as the weather or the news); and general-purpose functions for the platform (such as user ID and password, an emoji meaning 'free' and the i-mode logo).

I started by listing, as comprehensively as possible, all the emoji that I could expect to be used on the service, then prioritized them according to their usefulness and how frequently they might be used. Finally, we narrowed what I had down to 200 ideas. As for who did what, it was only me coming up with these ideas and giving them priorities, but Ms Matsunaga, the other team members and I all decided what to include in the final release.

As for the emoji designs, I made a few samples myself, colouring in the squares on sheets of graph paper. Simple ones, like the shining sun, the emoji for rain and the smiley face. There were also a number of emoji where I didn't come up with the pixel arrangement, but I drew pictures and produced guide documents in order to show the designers what we wanted. When I think about those ideas now, one that I think I did a good job on is coming up with the golf flag for the 'location information' emoji. This was before Google's pin icon or anything. I also think I did a good job of coming up with the original designs for the emotion emoji. There were always multiple heart emoji right from the beginning, because I recognized the special importance of the heart early on.

The person who came up with the actual pixel designs, the architect Jun Aoki, was introduced to me by Ms Matsunaga. What led me to ask him was the fact that he had designed pictograms for buildings before. The most difficult part of designing the emoji was the lack of expressivity in the 12-by-12 grid's even number of pixels. There was no way to centre an image, since a dot would end up one square to the right or left of the box's centre.

I asked him to revise the pixel designs that he came up with a few times, brushing them up before the emoji were finally completed. Afterward, members of the development team produced a specification that we would have handset makers implement, giving birth to emoji.

While this was going on, the legal department was meeting to secure a patent for emoji, but the view at the time was that with a size of 12 by 12 pixels, no matter who drew the subject-matter, it would end up looking essentially the same, so it would be difficult to assert a claim to the designs. Because of that, until the number of pixels in emoji went up, they were free of copyright. I think emoji spread through Japan as a result, which ended up being a plus.

Incidentally, the total time that passed between initial planning and completion was about one month.

How does it make you feel to know that emoji are now used all over the world?

At the time, I wasn't considering emoji being used outside Japan at all. Part of me thinks the reason they caught on might be precisely because they came from Japan, where we're surrounded by kanji – its own kind of pictogram – along with *hiragana*, *katakana* and the Latin alphabet. Emoji have permeated throughout the world, enabled by the spread of smartphones and their adoption into Unicode, and they have become an important element of digital text communication. Digital text is different from speaking face-to-face or over the phone, or writing letters even, in that it makes it difficult to express emotional information. And because of con-fusing input methods and the very nature of texting in a mobile setting, messages tend to be short. Emoji become necessary for making that kind of communication go more smoothly. I consider them the newest form of written language in a world born of digital text communication.

Why did you recently work with Japanese mobile phone brand au by KDDI to create a set of symbols more like your original emoji?

In Japan the three major mobile carriers are Docomo, KDDI and Softbank, and each one pretty much adopted its own version of emoji. They each believed that emoji were a killer service for their users, and as a result, the number and design of characters in each of their sets came to differ quite a lot. When emoji were adopted into Unicode in 2010, the Unicode Consortium took a comprehensive approach and added all three carriers' emoji. Because of this, it was able to maintain compatibility between each company's emoji, but only for those characters that they all had in common, and because each carrier had a different number of characters it meant that there wasn't complete interoperability for everything.

Because of that, Docomo and KDDI decided to consolidate their emoji in 2012. They normalized not only the types of characters, but their designs as well, deciding to go with Docomo-style emoji across the board. For that reason, they asked me to oversee a new uniform design for the project, since I had produced the original designs for Docomo.

Are emoji here to stay?

Emoji are a communication tool, so they will likely continue to change as a result of their surrounding environment. Of course, I don't think that emoji will ever disappear.

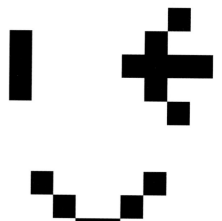

Your move. Btw, you're red!

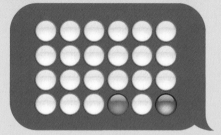

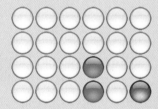

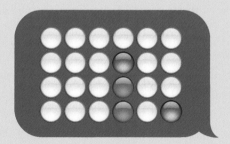

INSPIRED BY EMOJI

Here, we take a look at projects that have been inspired by emoji, from visual art and fashion design to advertising campaigns.

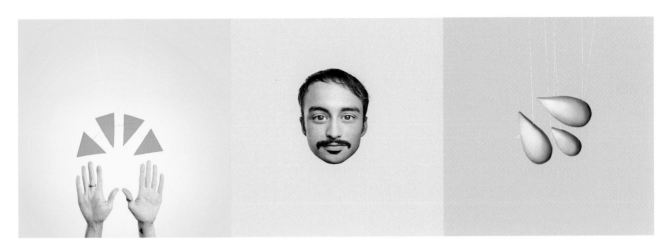

EMOJI IRL.LOL.
Art project
Liza Nelson

Emoji IRL.LOL. is a project by Los Angeles-based artist Liza Nelson, who has selected a number of classic Apple emoji and recreated them photographically or sculpturally. 'I did this project because I felt like the tiny 20-by-20-pixel images most of us are using every single day deserved to be examined more closely,' explains Nelson.

She continues, 'We seriously *think* and *speak* in emoji now, and it hit me one day that we take this new form of communication for granted. We think texting back and forth for hours with tiny pictures of poop and floppy disks and tongues is normal, like we've been doing this forever. And the crazy thing is, we truly *are* expressing incredibly real and raw emotions with these things. Over the past year or two I've had hundreds of "deep" conversations with friends and fellow creatives revolving around emoji – we're all obsessed with analysing what they mean and which ones represent us, which I think is a new favourite pastime for eight-year-olds to 30-somethings with smartphones everywhere. I decided to pay homage to the individual characters that hold the most meaning for me and, as ridiculous as that sounds (because they are essentially little cartoons), emoji have become an incredibly significant part of our culture and our language. My project is both a mockery and a tribute to the individual characters that have become so much more to our culture than tiny pictures on an iPhone screen.'

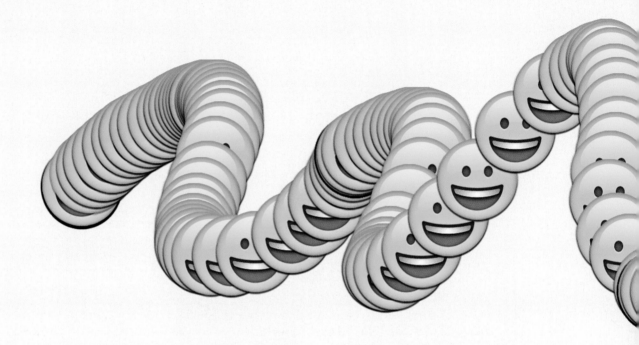

click to draw.
press any key to select an emoji.
site by vince mckelvie

save image

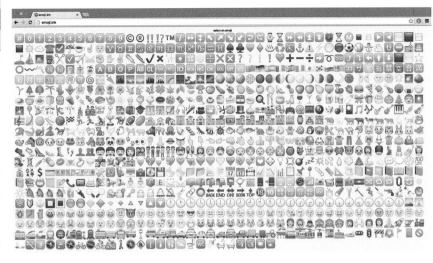

EMOJI.INK
Illustrations
Takakura Kazuki

Emoji.ink is a simple but fun online app created by Vince McKelvie that allows visitors to the site to create images using Apple's standard emoji set. When a user arrives on the site, their browser window displays all of the emoji in rows that fill the screen. Clicking on one, adjusting its size using a slider scale and clicking and dragging allows the user to 'draw' anything by leaving a trail of the selected emoji character.

Tokyo-based illustrator, pixel artist and art director Takakura Kazuki heard about emoji.ink through a friend and started to play around with it, posting his resulting illustrations on his Instagram account. 'It reminded me of Nintendo's Mario Paint video game for the SNES console and completely blew my mind,' he says. 'Emoji originated in Japan so I thought it would be interesting to draw Japanese cultural motifs and characters using them.' Typically, it takes Kazuki between two and five hours to complete one of these emoji.ink illustrations, which are shown on the following spreads.

size

pp. 64-69: Illustrations created
by Takakura Kazuki using the
emoji.ink web app, which allows
users to draw by dragging emoji
across a computer screen.

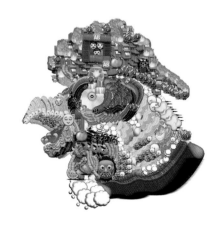

POO EMOJI LIGHT WING FRANKLIN SHOES & BUTTON-UP SHIRT

Footwear and apparel
Betabrand

Under normal circumstances, poo on your shoe is not fun. But San Francisco-based company Betabrand has changed that with these jolly poo emoji sneakers. Betabrand is an online clothing community that designs, manufactures and releases new products nonstop. Its selling point is that its fans co-design and crowdfund new ideas into existence in just a matter of weeks. These high-top sneakers were successfully funded on 7 November 2014 and are made of lightweight Tyvek – a super-strength, paper-like material that's both water-resistant and breath-able. We'd like to hope the soles are suitably poo resistant.

Betabrand also produced a cotton poo emoji button-up shirt that was funded in February 2015 – a good one to style out a hangover in.

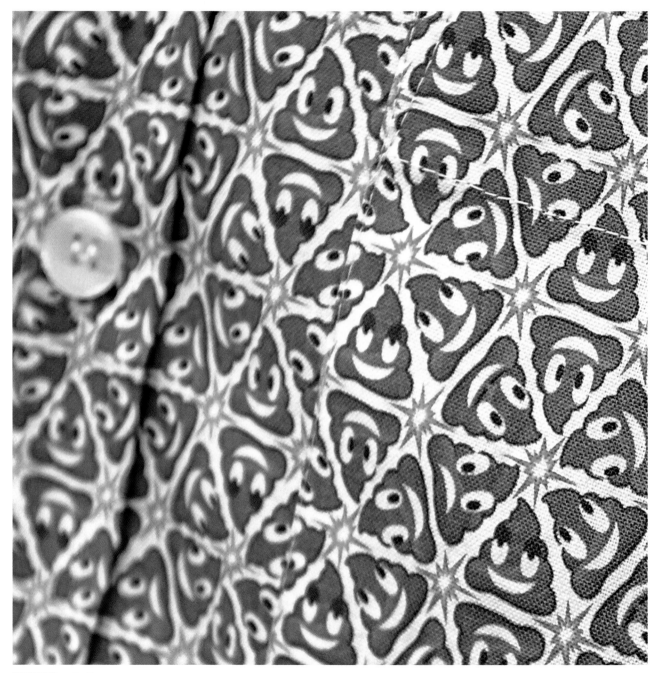

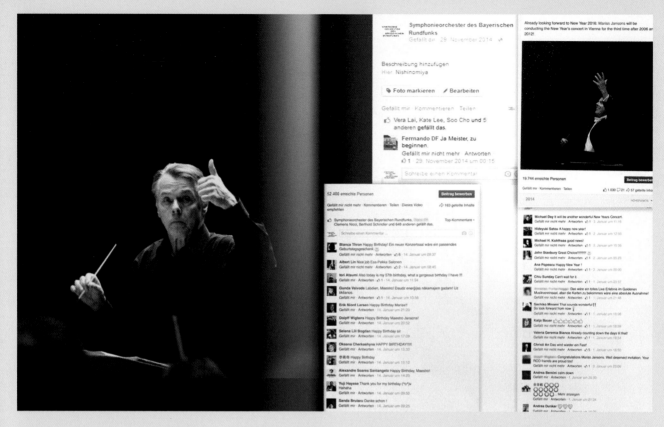

SYMPHONIEORCHESTER
Annual publication of the Bavarian
Radio Symphony Orchestra
Bureau Mirko Borsche

Munich-based design studio Bureau
Mirko Borsche has worked with the
Bavarian Radio Symphony Orchestra
(BRSO) since 2010, when it designed
the orchestra's visual identity. As
well as creating posters for the BRSO,
the studio art directs an annual
publication for them which contains
concert and event dates and other
relevant information as well as

seasonally changing editorial content.
Since BRSO tries to present a fresh
view of the orchestra with each issue
(featuring a variety of contributors),
the design differs from year to year
and is always a close collaboration.

The concept behind the 2015–16
annual's content was to give teenagers a space to air their impressions
on the work of the BRSO. With the
editorial content written by established journalists, Mirko Borsche
wanted the design of the publication
to mimic classic newspaper layouts.

'In emoji, we found a way to add a
certain playful youthfulness to the
design without having to give up or
compromise the strictness of the
newspaper design theme,' says the
studio's Lukas Rudig about the
project. 'Since this design embraces
the idea of a young generation
"taking over" an established medium,
another rather illustrative layer of
the book shows the alleged opposite:
the orchestra's communication in
social media and open discussions
by fans and critics alike.'

Symphonieorchester

DES BAYERISCHEN RUNDFUNKS

CHEFDIRIGENT MARISS JANSONS

WWW.BR-SO.DE

2015 — 2016

»Für mich ist es wichtig, dass ich mich in den Dienst der Musik stelle und dass das auch so bei der Jury ankommt. Mir geht es nicht um irgendeine Hierarchie innerhalb des Orchesters. Mir geht es um die Musik. Sie steht für mich im Vordergrund«, verrät ein Kandidat. Ein anderer betont: ›Ich möchte eine gute Balance zwischen technischer Stabilität und musikalischem Ausdruck finden. Schließlich muss es mir gelingen, die Herzen des Publikums zu erreichen und zu gewinnen. Und in diesem besonderen Fall ist das Publikum das äußerst kritische Orchester.«

HART UND WILLKÜRLICH?

Um kurz nach halb zwölf Uhr sind alle Kandidaten aufgetreten, und die erste Runde wurde beendet. Nun spielt sich – natürlich hinter verschlossenen Türen – folgendes Szenario ab: Die Stimmgruppe berät sich und gibt eine Empfehlung ab. Daraufhin diskutiert das gesamte Orchester unter der Leitung seines Vorstandes, der das Wort erteilt, und stimmt schließlich ab. Die Namen der Kandidaten, die es in die zweite Runde geschafft haben, werden verkündet. Das Prozedere der ersten Runde wiederholt sich. Als Wahlstück können die Kandidaten entweder Schumanns oder Dvořáks Cellokonzert vortragen.

In der dritten Runde gibt es nach den Vorträgen der Kandidaten, die den Ansprüchen des Orchesters standgehalten haben, eine geheime Abstimmung der Jury. Ist die absolute Mehrheit für einen der Kandidaten gegeben, geht ein Musiker als Sieger aus dem Probespiel hervor, und die Stelle kann besetzt werden. Heute jedoch hat es keiner der Kandidaten geschafft. Bereits nach der ersten Runde wird das Probespiel abgebrochen. »Heute hat das gewisse Etwas gefehlt. Das Herausstechen, der Funke, der Zauber war

nicht da«, versucht Marije Grevink etwas Unsagbares in Worte zu fassen. »Die Cellogruppe hat empfohlen, an dieser Stelle aufzuhören, und dasselbe Gefühl, dieselbe Meinung hatte auch das Orchester. Die Begeisterung war einfach nicht da. Anerkennung für die Leistung, die war da, aber die ganz große Begeisterung hat gefehlt.«

So hart und willkürlich dieses Auswahlverfahren auch scheint, ist es dennoch nicht allzu weit hergeholt. Damit das Konzert für das Publikum zum Klangerlebnis wird, hat der Musiker auch nur eine einzige Chance, abzuliefern, häufig in noch sehr viel kürzerer

Zeit als sieben Minuten. Mit all den negativen Aspekten, die ein Probespiel mit sich bringt, ist der Musiker auch als Orchestermitglied konfrontiert. »Probespiele sind gerecht, denn auch im Konzert muss ich in einem Augenblick – und sei er noch so kurz – meine Leistung auf den Punkt bringen«, urteilt ein Kandidat mit hochgezogenen Schultern und etwas Widerwillen in seinem Blick. In der Kantine ist das »Schluss« des Orchestervorstandes fast verhallt. Der Zauber des Probespiels löst sich an einem gewöhnlichen vorweihnachtlichen Montag um zwölf Uhr wieder auf.

»Im Radio höre ich entweder die aktuellen Hits oder, wenn ich mich entspannen will, Klassik. Damit stoße ich aber bei meiner Familie auf taube Ohren – die wollen dann, dass ich wieder zu den Hits umschalte.«
Sofia Ossanna

»Ich war etwas überrascht, die Musiker und den Dirigenten bei der Generalprobe in ganz normaler Freizeitkleidung auf der Bühne zu sehen.«
Leo Kapfhammer

terling«, so interpretiert Kristof Friedrich treffend. Beeindruckend ist, dass die Kinder ganz andere Dinge mit der Musik in Verbindung bringen als viele Erwachsene. Daniel Harding, der Dirigent, ist zwar einverstanden mit der Interpretation, doch hört er statt Tieren in der Wildnis Trommeln und Krieg. Bemerkenswert ist auch ein Menuett, das von den Schülern erlernt wurde und zur Veranschaulichung des dritten Satzes im beengten Raum zwischen den Musikern und Instrumenten vorgeführt wird. Genau das ist der Hauptaspekt der »Echtzeit«: Die Aufbereitung von Musik von Kindern für Kinder, wodurch sich diese angesprochener fühlen als beispielsweise von ihrer Lehrkraft.

Zum Abschluss der Moderation, nach der das eigentliche Konzert erst beginnt, wird es noch einmal besonders interessant. Von den Schülern ausgewählte Fragen stellen sie nun nacheinander dem Dirigenten des Orchesters, Daniel Harding, den sie erst bei dieser Gelegenheit kennenlernen. Trotz seiner Position als weltweit gefragter Dirigent ist er den Schülern gegenüber offen und es entwickelt sich ein interessantes Gespräch. So spricht er zum Beispiel von einem Unglück, das er wegen schlechten Befindens ein Konzert abbrechen musste. »Vermutlich haben sie damit irgendetwas ins Essen gemischt, damit sie schnell zum Fussballgucken konnten«, scherzt er und erklärt die Hauptaufgabe des Dirigenten, die viele gar nicht genau kennen; er ist praktisch ein Interpret und zeigt dem Orchester mit seiner Gestik, welche Gefühle ausgedrückt werden sollen.

Als das Konzert nach einer guten Stunde endet, ernten sowohl die Moderatoren als auch die Musiker und der Dirigent tosenden Applaus. Ein Beweis für die gute Umsetzung der Idee, dass Schüler Gleichaltrigen die Musik auf einzigartige Weise näherbringen, und sie damit begeistern können.

ffe ich auf die hüb-
aus Russland und
Criens. Sie im wun-
rkleid, perfekt ge-
nägel in Deutsch-
d er im schlichten,
rnen Anzug – sei-
agt. Sie sind zum
n Air und freuen
Nacht mit Wer-
Schostakowitsch
und dem be-
Ensemble Russ-
rtet. Nun geht
nne unter und
on der hinters-
ehen am Rand
siebenjährige
weiße Klei-
ussin hat ihr
ekauft. Ihre

ch davor shop-
pen gehen und
extra für den
Abend ein Kleid
kaufen konnte.«

IKEA EMOJI
Promotional emoji set
IKEA B.V. Nederland

Global homeware company IKEA created a proprietary set of emoji for its customers. Developed by creative agency Lemz and released by the brand's Netherlands head office in early 2015, the IKEA emoticons were made available in an app that embeds a special keyboard which iPhone users can access and use in the same way as standard emoji.

The icons, illustrated by Sue Doeksen, allow people to communicate about homeware. A press release that accompanied the launch of the app revealed the findings of a study by TNS Nipo (a Dutch survey agency) which showed that clutter at home causes tension in a third of all Dutch households. At the core of the project was the idea that emoji enable text messages to be understood more easily while also allowing for a higher level of fun and humour. Therefore, the theory goes, the IKEA emoticons might enable a cheery, rather than stressful, conversation about clutter and storage solutions at home. The set includes over 100 icons, some of which are easily recognized as IKEA objects – from the brand's blue shopping bags to its famous Swedish meatballs and even specific items of furniture such as its FROSTA plywood stools and BILLY bookshelves.

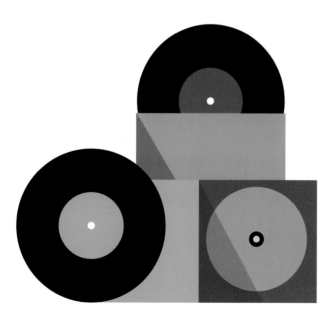

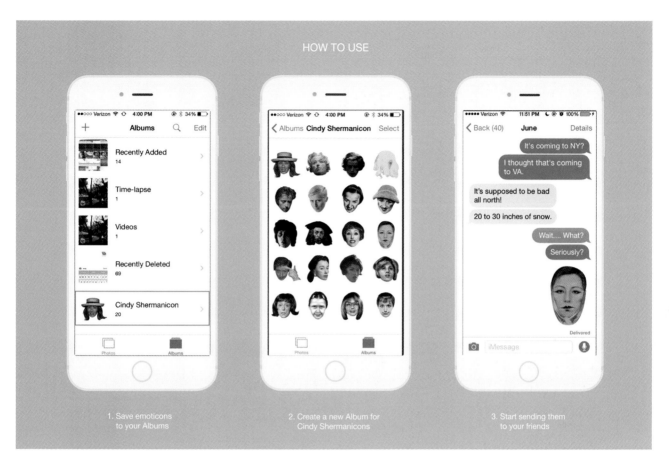

1. Save emoticons to your Albums

2. Create a new Album for Cindy Shermanicons

3. Start sending them to your friends

CINDY SHERMAN-ICON

Art project
Hyo Ju Hong

Inspired by the many faces (and facial expressions) of American artist Cindy Sherman, who often appears in various guises in her own images, Hyo Ju Hong created her own art project, entitled Cindy Sherman-icon.

'I found a connection between her self-portraits and emoticons in terms of various facial expressions from one face,' says Hong. 'We don't always want to convey that we're blindly happy, crying with laughter or horizontally-lipped and nonplussed. Sometimes, we need something a little more subtle, more human than emoticons and emoji.' Hong's solution to this problem was to create a series of images of Sherman's face, each one displaying a different facial expression. While Hong initially made 20 of the icons, she plans to extend

the project to include 'ever more complex, nuanced and disturbing emotions'. Watch this space/face.

POLITICONS
Political emoji set
+rehabstudio

Creative digital agency +rehabstudio, which has offices in London, New York and Belfast, created an emoji series called Politicons as a way of encouraging greater political discussion and, ultimately, voter turnout for the UK's 2015 General Election. The politicized characters in the set included faces of the main party leaders, a fist bump emoji with the word 'vote' appearing on the knuckles, a strong arm emoji holding the word 'tax', and a passport being held by a hand in a spectrum of skin tones.

The studio was inspired to initiate the project following an Ipsos Mori poll revealing that 34 per cent of 18–24-year-olds said that reading something on social media was likely to influence their vote – second only to the TV debates.

'Hacking emoji seemed like an obvious, fun and irreverent way to help get young people talking about the election and sharing their thoughts with mates or the wider public,' explains the studio's strategy partner, Tom Le Bree. 'Whatever their stance, they can help articulate it with a Politicon.'

Whatever your stance say it with a POLITICON

"I'm 😐 and my ✊ goes to 😢 because i want a 💰 so 🖕 😂"

Barry, 21, Hull

"The 💼 is putting 💔 on 🪑 - only 👨 can make it 🤳"

Lucy, 24, Sevenoaks

Coming soon to Messenger!

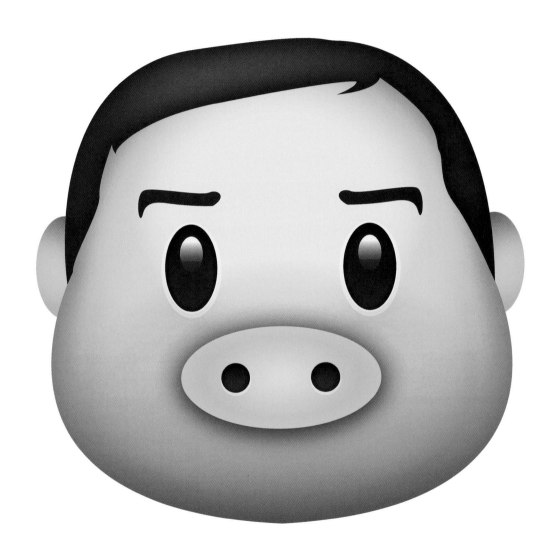

📖😃

BENEFIT STREET FS1
CITY OF THE POOR

PASSPORT

091

WHO'S REALLY CHATTING ONLINE WITH YOUR CHILD?

Ad campaign
Rosapark

Innocence en Danger is a non-profit organization that rallies against all forms of child abuse. Working with a VFX company, Parisian ad agency Rosapark transformed three emoji faces into 'real' men (to frightening effect) for an ad campaign published in early 2014 and designed to highlight the potential danger of online chatting. Each of the campaign's three executions was accompanied by the line, 'Who's really chatting online with your child?'

Who's really chatting online with your child?

innocence
en DANGER

innocenceendanger.org

Who's really chatting online with your child?

INNOCENCE en DANGER

innocenceendanger.org

#ENDANGEREDEMOJI

Fundraising campaign
WWF (World Wide Fund For Nature)

On 12 May 2015, WWF launched an emoji-based fundraising campaign to help support the organization's work to protect endangered species and their habitats. The campaign, developed with WWF's UK ad agency, Wieden + Kennedy, and technical partner Cohaesus, was based on the discovery that 17 characters in Twitter's standard emoji character set represented endangered species. The idea for the activity was to translate the popularity of these characters into donations.

The campaign kicked off with a tweet published on the official @WWF Twitter account that showed all 17 Endangered Emoji. To take part in the campaign, Twitter users were encouraged to retweet the image. For every Endangered Emoji the user tweeted, WWF added the local currency equivalent of €0.10 to a voluntary monthly donation. At the end of each month, users received a summary of their Endangered Emoji use and could then choose how much to donate.

Adrian Cockle, Digital Innovation Manager at WWF International, said, 'When it comes to fundraising, giving people a simple way to donate is key. By using one of the world's biggest social platforms to highlight endangered species, we're hoping to raise vital funds for their conservation as well as raising awareness globally.'

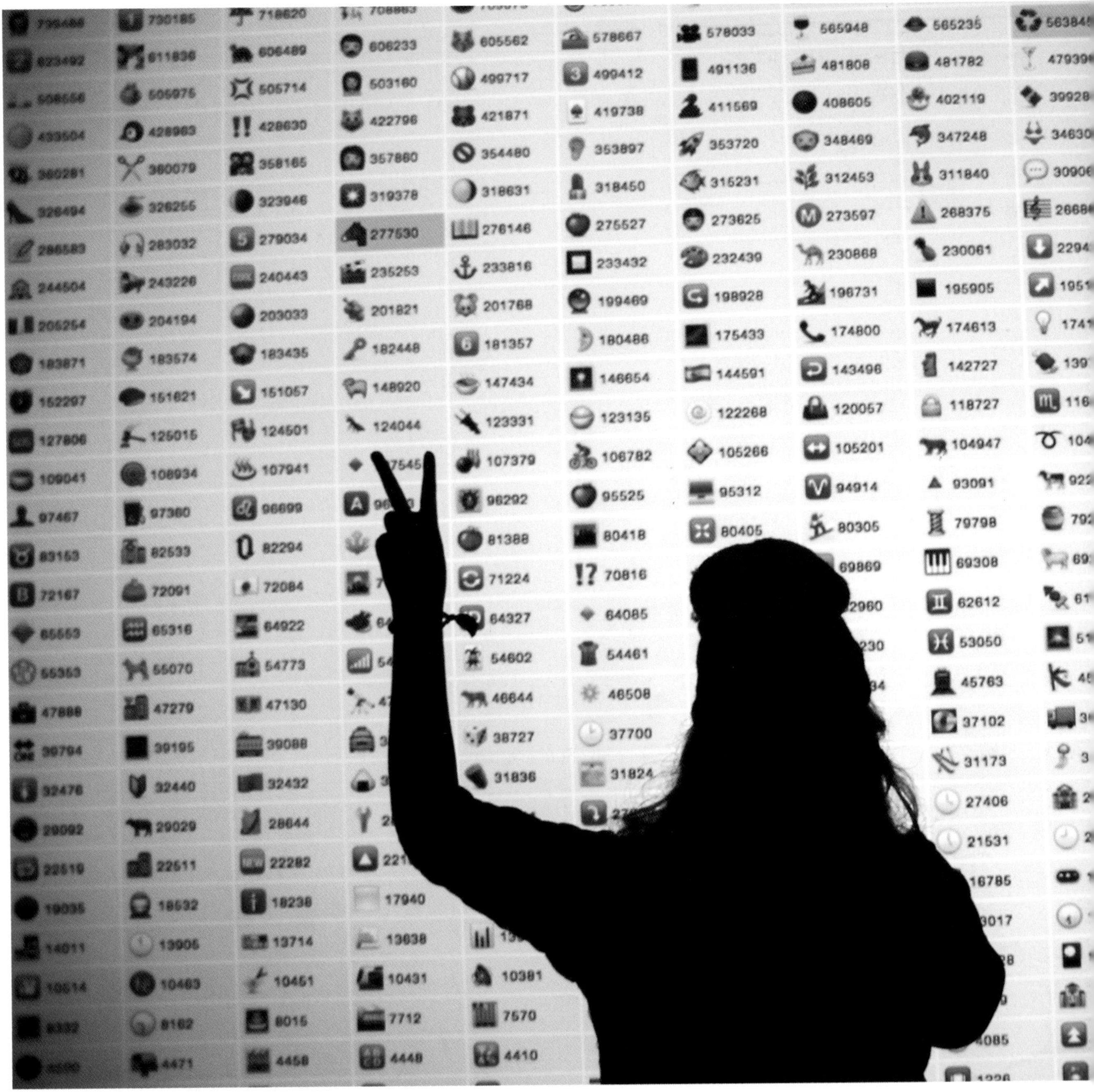

'Emojinal' T-shirt designed by KTHANKSBYE.

THE EMOJI ART & DESIGN SHOW

Exhibition
Forced Meme Productions & Eyebeam Art + Technology Center, New York City

Presented by Forced Meme Productions, Eyebeam and GroupMe, the Emoji Art & Design Show took place at Eyebeam's gallery space in New York in December 2013. The group show featured artworks created in a range of mediums, from digital prints to sculptures, video and performance art. Contributing artists included Fred Benenson, Liza Nelson, Fahad AlHunaif, Mike Burakoff, Zoë Burnett and more. The work in the show was inspired by both pop and visual culture – from appropriating and inserting emoji into the art history canon through to hypnotic moving images and emoji photo apps – as well as exploring translation difficulties and the desire for a wider range of emoji characters. A special emoji edition of *Womanzine*, edited by Mercedes Kraus, was also produced in conjunction with the exhibition, and included essays, poetry, art and other emoji-inspired musings.

EmojiTracker, created by Matthew Rothenberg, catalogues real-time emoji use on Twitter.

The nearest two framed artworks are untitled pieces by Ibon Mainar.

Emojified: R. Kelly's *Trapped in the Closet*, Chapters 1, 2, & 4

ZOE MENDELSON

The Great Lord Kells' masterpiece hip-hop opera *Trapped in the Closet* is my favorite piece of art ever created in any medium. It walks that incredibly thin line between serious and joking so well that most people really can't make the call. That's sheer genius. I love the absurdity in it, the drama in his voice as he sings, "I cloooosed my mouth and swallowed spit." Emoji are absurd, too (because their set of symbols is so random), and I figured, why not translate the absurd into the absurd? Everything about the pairing seemed well-suited—from the characters' high-running emotions to the involvement of a cop to the significance of cherries. *Trapped in the Closet begged* for emojification.

The translation should be read both as an image and as a text—at times it requires translation left to right, and at others it presents the story as an image.

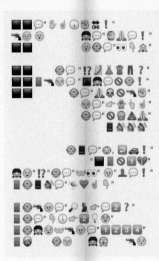
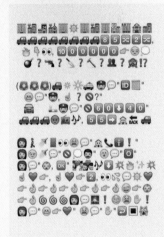

Womanzine, a publication penned only by people who identify as women, created a special emoji edition for the exhibition (the cover is shown to the left). The spread above showcases a translation of R. Kelly's 'Trapped in the Closet' by Zoe Mendelson.

Shift Key by Maya Ben-Ezer.

Emoji embroidery by Jessica Harllee.

BFF LAPEL PIN
Apparel
Valley Cruise Press

Based in Los Angeles, Valley Cruise Press is an art and design-focused label specializing in limited edition zines, art objects, accessories and apparel. Its one-inch-high enamel BFF Lapel Pin pays homage to the emoji. 'Certain emoji mean different things to different people,' says VCP's Ted Feighan, 'but the dancing twin girls emoji almost universally represents friendship. We made these pins as a sort of modern-day "friendship bracelet" to be shared between friends.'

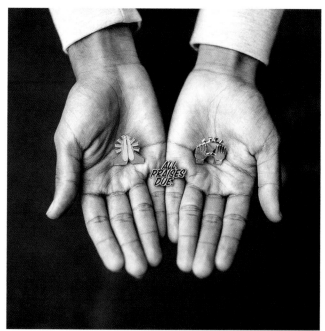

EMOJI PINS
Apparel
Pintrill

Brooklyn-based company Pintrill, co-founded in April 2014 by Jordan Roschwalb, Doni Gitlin and Andrew Yung, specializes in enamel pins and has produced not one but a whole series of high-quality emoji pins. The company has lovingly made pins of the fist bump emoji, hand clap emoji, prayer hands emoji, thumbs-up emoji and, rather brilliantly, the smiling poo emoji.

108

Emoji Passcode by Intelligent Environments is the world's first emoji security technology.

EMOJI PASSCODE
Banking app
Intelligent Environments

UK-based company Intelligent Environments has been responsible for such financial technology innovations as the first online credit-card solution, the first online wallet in the UK and, in 2013, the world's first smartwatch banking app.

In 2015 it introduced Emoji Passcode, an application that allows users to log in to their banks using a PIN made up of four emoji characters (selected from a set of 44), rather than via a traditional numerical PIN. Emoji Passcode has been integrated into the company's Android digital banking app.

Intelligent Environments says that Emoji Passcode is mathematically more secure than a four-digit code as it has 480 times more permutations (a whopping 35 million, in fact), and that hackers are less likely to identify common formulae in the way that they're able to for numerical passcodes, such as birthdays or anniversaries. Furthermore, the company suggests that humans are more likely to remember pictures than words or numbers, and that as much as 64 per cent of a youthful demographic of millennials regularly communicate only using emoji – one of the key reasons they decided to reinvent the passcode for a new generation by developing the world's first emoji security technology.

2015 NCAA TOURNAMENT EMOJI

Emoji set for the *Washington Post*
Julia Heffernan

To drum up excitement among its readers during the 'March Madness' of the 2015 National Collegiate Athletic Association (NCAA) Tournament, the *Washington Post* commissioned a set of 88 college basketball team mascot emoji characters. Illustrated by Julia Heffernan, the team mascots appeared in a mid-March edition of the newspaper and also on its website, with an invitation to readers to see who would win the tournament – based purely on which team's emoji was the favourite … All good clean fun. Fans could also download their favourite emoji and text it to friends or, in some cases, use it as their Twitter or Facebook avatar.

BYU

Alabama-Birmingham

Belmont

Villanova

Gonzaga

Albany

Boise St.

Virginia

LSU

Arizona

Buffalo

West Virginia

Northern Iowa

Arkansas

Butler

Wichita St.

San Diego St.

Baylor

VCU

Wisconsin

Northeastern

Wyoming

UCLA

North Dakota St.

Robert Morris

Xavier

Utah

Providence

Duke

Cincinnati

Coastal Carolina

Davidson

Dayton

Eastern Washington

Iowa St.

Hampton

Harvard

Indiana

Iowa

Kansas

North Carolina

Manhattan

Maryland

Michigan St.

New Mexico St.

North Carolina St.

Ole Miss

Notre Dame

Ohio St.

Oklahoma

Oklahoma St.

Oregon

Texas Southern

SMU

St. Johns

Stephen F. Austin

Texas

UC Irvine

North Florida

Georgetown

Georgia

Georgia State

Wofford

Valparaiso

Purdue

Kentucky

Lafayette

Louisville

😱

👧🏻👧🏻

EMOJI-NATION
Art project
Nastya Nudnik

Kiev-based artist and art director Nastya Nudnik has produced a number of self-initiated series of *Emoji-nation* art projects, which she has posted on her Behance feed to wide acclaim. Each of these series of images sees her select a number of famous figurative artworks and overlay them with emoji, digital speech bubbles, messages and pop-up windows familiar from various online apps and operating systems.

Nudnik's first series showed four iconic paintings next to emoji she thought looked like the characters depicted in each one. Perhaps unsurprisingly, Edvard Munch's *The Scream* was paired with the 😱 emoji.

In *Emoji-nation Part 2*, Nudnik overlaid a series of Edward Hopper paintings with speech-bubble status graphics familiar from various social media platforms, making the viewer question how we think about images and people based on the kinds of information regularly shared and pored over on social media.

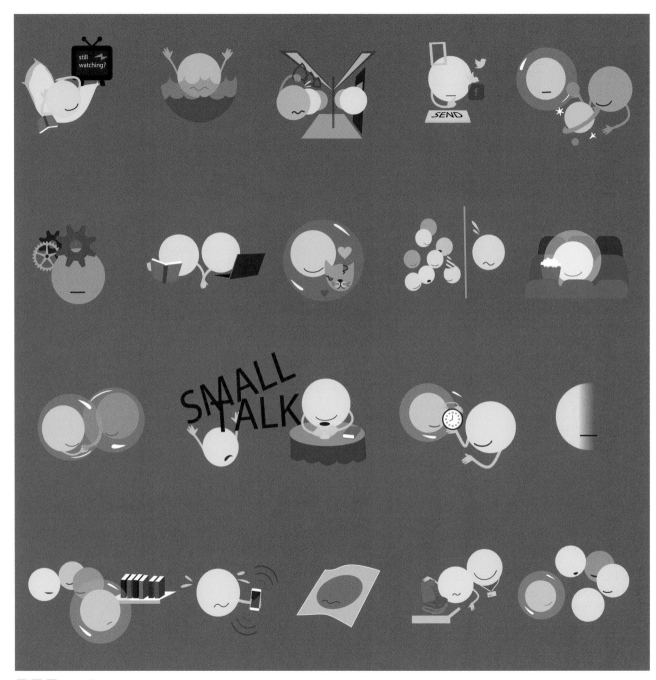

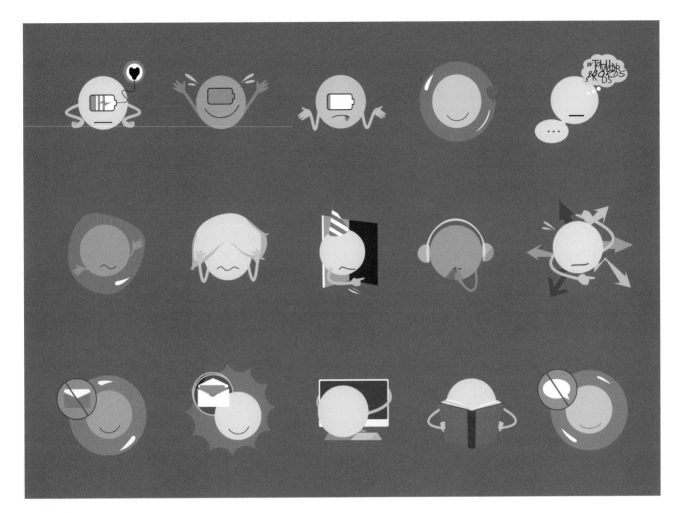

INTROJI
Art project
Rebecca Evie Lynch

As an introvert, British curator and artist Rebecca Evie Lynch wished there were emoji to convey when she needed some alone time. She set about designing a set of 'introji' characters that could express the things she found difficult to say in words. 'I love text messages but miss the reassurance of visual and physical cues like smiles and hugs,' she explains, 'so emoji give a little bit of context to messages. I hope my introji do the same, but in a way that reflects more complex aspects of human interaction.'

Some of the meanings conveyed by the initial set of 23 introji include 'happy in my bubble', 'need help getting out of my bubble', 'shhh, computer time', 'time with pets', 'TV binge' and 'crowd anxiety'.

EMOJI SPECTRUM
Interactive art installation
Callum Copley

London-based artist and designer Callum Copley created the Emoji Spectrum as an outcome of an earlier project entitled *The Short Range Future Forecasting Study*. In an essay Copley wrote to accompany the installation, he draws comparisons between emoji and the Isotype pictograms designed in the 1930s by Gerd Arntz and Otto Neurath. He explains further that the standard emoji set of yellow faces don't seem to represent a number of emotions named on psychologist Robert Plutchik's emotion wheel diagram. For example, Copley believes that there are no emoji for aggressiveness, contempt, remorse, disapproval or submission. Furthermore, Copley argues that written language is in danger of being polluted and corrupted by the use of and reliance on 'these melodramatic symbols'.

The piece explores how digitally mediated communication is changing the way we feel. 'By plotting emoji against Plutchik's Wheel of Emotion, it is possible to visualize the short-comings of the icons at expressing the full range of human emotion,' Copley explains. 'This installation invited the public to reassess the inaccuracies of such a communication method and explore the ambiguity of these pictograms that make up an ever growing proportion of our language.'

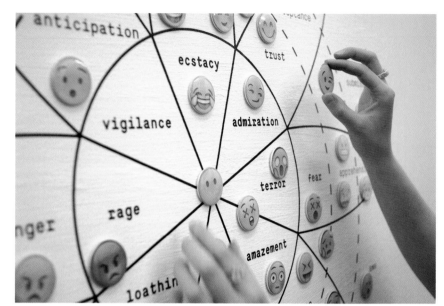

This interactive art installation aims to highlight the way emoji fail to represent the full range of human emotion.

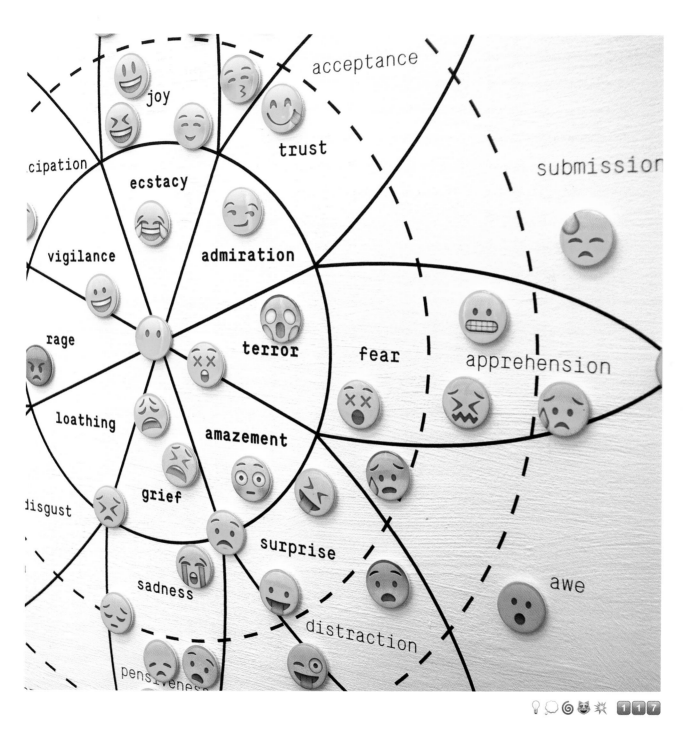

EMOJISTUFF.COM

Emoji-themed merchandise
Richard Trautmann

OK, so you love emoji. But do you love them enough to cuddle one? Emojistuff.com sells a range of 13-inch plush emoji character pillows that enable buyers to do just that! For those not quite ready to purchase a smiley cushion, you can also get emoji-adorned one-inch pin badges and simply select the most appropriate one to wear, depending on how you feel that day.

To further prove its love of Apple's proprietary emoji, emojistuff.com has created a Google Chrome extension entitled Emoji Input which allows users to view and input Apple-style emoji in a text input field on any website, including Twitter and Gmail. Emojistuff.com's Richard Trautmann explains:

'My emoji story began when I received the 💩 emoji from my sister on my iPhone. At that time, you had to either jailbreak your phone or download some special app in order to enable the option to choose the emoji

keyboard. Years went by and my friends and I used a lot of emoji. We made whole sentences and told stories with emoji. We'd create elaborate emoji art to make fun of each other. We each had a specific emoji that the rest of the group would use in place of our name.

Besides using emoji on my phone, I wanted to use them on my computer. I'm a web developer and nothing yet existed that would help me, so I built a Chrome Extension for myself. It lets you see emoji in websites and also pick emoji to use in tweets, messages,

statuses et cetera. When the popularity of emoji started to explode, I decided to publish my extension and it took off! When it reached 30,000 users, friends started asking if I was making money from it. I figured if I charged 99 cents for my extension, I'd be lucky to keep 300 users. It wasn't worth $300 to me; I'd rather have 30,000 users! What I did know is that I had a bunch of people that loved emoji. So I created emojistuff.com to start selling emoji-themed products.

I enjoy thinking about people around the world receiving my products, or

giving one to a friend and them loving it. I think emoji bring happiness and good vibes by their very nature, and that there's something extra special and happy about holding the physical emoji in your hands, or cuddling it, after you've seen it so many times on a screen.'

📖 😃

EMOTICOKE

Ad campaign
Coca-Cola/EJE Puerto Rico

For a highly unusual brand campaign, advertising agency EJE Puerto Rico registered URLs for every emoji character that conveys happiness. Entering any of the smiley-face URLs (which appeared in traditional media, including huge outdoor billboards) into a mobile web browser, along with the .ws suffix, led people directly to a landing page on Coca-Cola's Puerto Rico website addressed as emoticoke.com.

At the time the campaign was launched, emoji weren't accepted on more heavily used domains such as .com, .net and .org – but Samoa's .ws suffix was available, and EJE Puerto Rico thought that was the best fit as it could potentially stand for 'we smile'. The idea behind this activity was to offer the various smiley-face domain names as prizes to people who engaged with the campaign.

'The vast majority of our audience now visits our website via a mobile device,' explains Alejandro Gómez, president of Coca-Cola Puerto Rico. 'And since emoji have become a kind of second language for Coke's younger consumers, we felt this was a great opportunity to connect on a deeper level with our most important demographic.'

Coca-Cola Puerto Rico launched a competition that gave Coke drinkers a chance to win smiley-face emoji URLs.

LINE MESSAGING APP
Communication network
LINE

In the wake of the 2011 tsunami that struck Japan, more than 18,000 people had been confirmed dead and most of Japan's telephone systems had been destroyed. With the networks down, many people had no way of calling friends and relations to find out if they were safe. Out of this disaster, LINE was born: a global mobile messaging platform created to allow people to connect over WiFi, even if their network was down.

Now, LINE has hundreds of millions of users worldwide and has become well known for its stickers and emoji as well as for providing mobile gaming and a feature that allows users to text and call each other from their smartphones through their web data plan. Rather like WhatsApp, this means users are essentially talking over the Internet rather than on a phone line, and so can message and chat (and send emoji and stickers) for free.

LINE provides literally thousands of illustrated stickers, created by individual illustrators as well as by companies including Disney, Aardman, Sony and more. These can be inserted into text messages like emoji or sent individually at a slightly larger size. LINE has also created a nifty 'auto-suggest' feature which sees suggested emoji pop up in response to certain words being

typed. This means users don't have to trawl through every single emoji to find the one they need at any given moment.

Another innovative contribution to the culture of incorporating graphics into text messages introduced by the company is its LINE Creators Market initiative, which essentially functions like an AppStore for sticker developers. Launched in April 2014, it allows illustrators and designers to upload and sell their own stickers. LINE users can buy and use the sticker sets, which are proving almost unbelievably popular. According to figures from LINE, in the first six months of the existence of their Creator's Market, over 270,000 creators hailing from 145 different countries had registered with the service. As well as independent designers, famous entertainers, companies, local government organizations and sports teams, many other individuals and groups have also uploaded and sold their own stickers by the millions.

The number of sticker sets on sale through the platform exceeds 30,000 and, in the first six months of its life, LINE Creators Market generated total sales of 3.59 billion yen, with a staggering total of 35.95 million sticker sets purchased. The top 10 sticker sets sold each achieved an average of 36.8 million yen in sales (about £206,000), with the top 1,000 sets averaging 2.7 million yen (£15,000).

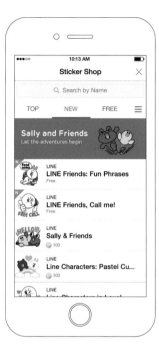

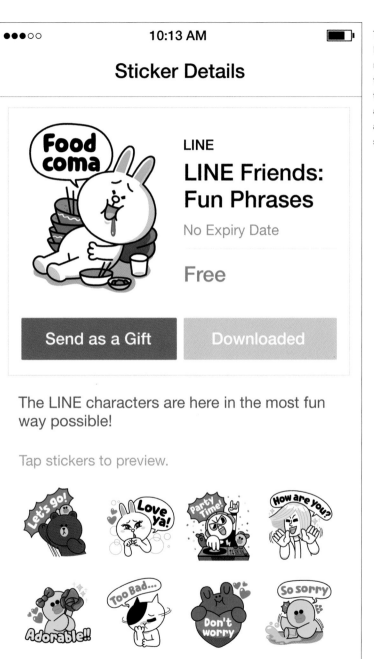

Sticker Details

LINE

LINE Friends: Fun Phrases

No Expiry Date

Free

Send as a Gift   Downloaded

The LINE characters are here in the most fun way possible!

Tap stickers to preview.

The interface for LINE, a global mobile messaging platform that allows people to connect over WiFi as well as create and send emoji-style stickers.

EMOJI SET FOR LINE

Emoji stickers
Dan Woodger

As well as encouraging entrepre-
neurial designers to create and sell
(or give away) their own stickers and
emoji, LINE proactively commissions
stickers and emoji from illustrators
whose work they love. This spread
and the next show just some of the
1,000 illustrated emoji created for
LINE by UK illustrator Dan Woodger.
He explains:

'I was approached in January 2014
by the Art Director at LINE LA to
produce a set of 1,000 emoji for
an emoji library they were building
for use with the LINE app. It was
an incredibly challenging project –
especially putting in such long hours
– but it has been hugely rewarding.
My illustrations are now being used
by millions of people every day.'

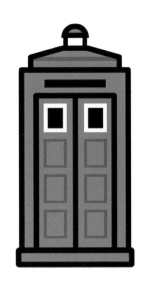

![ELECTIONS IN EMOJI]

ELECTIONS IN EMOJI
Voting initiative
Preston City Council

Preston City Council in the UK looked to the power of emoji to galvanize young voters in the run up to the general election in May 2015. Stephen Parkinson, Preston City Council's head of communication, briefed local illustrator and animator Dave Robinson to create an animated campaign film that used emoji (all drawn specially by Robinson) to highlight myriad reasons why it's important to vote.

'My real inspiration is my 19-year-old daughter,' says Parkinson of the project. 'We exchange emoticons and emoji in texts, we make stories using emoji and have fun with emoji. But we were having a conversation one night – I was telling her about what I do and she said "But Dad, my vote doesn't make a difference, does it?" – and it struck me: emoji are how we can engage with a young audience. If we create a narrative using emoji, it could explain in a really simple way why you should vote.'

Stills from
Elections in Emoji
by Dave Robinson.

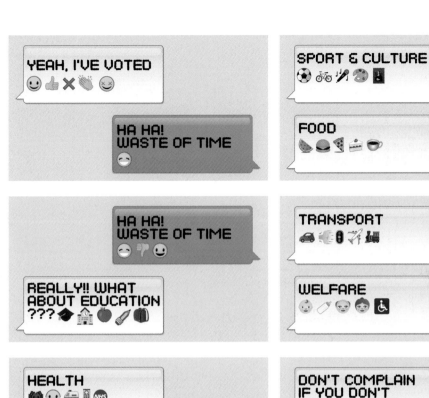

Cat Emoticons

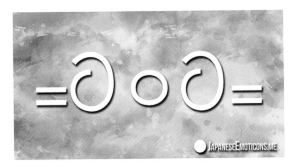

Cats are probably my favourite animal and what better way to celebrate that then with a giant page of kaomoji cat emoticons! Seriously, how cute are some of these kaomoji cats? Fun fact: the Japanese word for cat is "neko" and the sound they make in Japanese is "nya". Feel free to add a little "nya" to any of these emoticons to make them extra Japanese.

Cats are pretty much just most regular Japanese emoticons with ='s added to them as whiskers. ^'s can also be used for ears and you can use ·I· for a cat's nose. Some of these cats get pretty elaborate and I'm highly impressed with some of them!

Cats with Anime Eyes

These cat emoticons look like they'd belong in an anime. Something about Φs for eyes especially makes me think of the Azumanga Diaoh cat.

(ΦωΦ)	((ΦωΦ))	(*ΦωΦ*)
(=ΦΙΦ=)	(ΦωΦ)	(Φ3Φ)
(Φ∀Φ)	(ΦΔΦ)	(ΞΦÅΦΞ)

Table Flipping Emoticons

The original table flipping emoticon is (ノ °口°) ノ ⌒━━┻ followed by the guy who puts the table back ┳━━┳ ノ(• ∵ノ) and then followed by flipping the guy who put the table back (ノ °Д°) ノ ⌒/(.□ .)

There are however a ton of other table flipping emoticons, so many in fact that I felt they deserved their own category instead of being included in the other actions section. There are people flipping tables, bears flipping tables, flipping tables with magic and even tables flipping people in this category of Japanese emoticons. I also included in here some other things being flipped as well.

Some of these kaomoji are even throwing tables at people! What jerks! You can also take pretty much any emoticon with raised arms, put on of these flying tables in front of it and just like that you have a new flipping table emoticon.

(ノ °口°) ノ ⌒━┻	┳━━┳ ノ(° -°ノ)
(ノ °Д°) ノ ⌒/(.□ .)	(ノ♂益♂)ノ彡┻━┻
(ノ♂∩♂)ノ彡 (o˚o)	(ノ °口°)ノ ⌒ Facebook

The site catalogues over 10,000 Japanese-style kaomoji.

JAPANESEEMOTICONS.ME
Web resource and smartphone app
Peter Saydak

Canadian emoticon fan Peter Saydak has compiled an impressively vast number (over 10,000) of Japanese-style kaomoji emoticons on his website japaneseemoticons.me. He's helpfully grouped the emoticons to guide users to the one they need – whether it's to convey a particular

emotion such as happiness (ˆ 凹 ˆ) or sadness (✖ ∩ ✖) or a specific activity like dancing ┌((= ̄(ェ) ̄=))┘ or even different animals including bears ൠ? and cats (=^..^=). There's even a whole section devoted to table-flipping emoticons starting with the original (╯°□°)╯︵ ┻━┻ .

As well as the website, Saydak has developed a smartphone app (for both Apple and Android platforms) that

allows users to easily find and copy kaomoji to use in their text messages. Users can add certain emoticons to their favourites list, which can be reorganized easily to make finding specific emoticons super quick and easy. The app also includes a design-your-own-emoticon feature.

EMENTICONS
Promotional emoji set
Mentos

Working with advertising agency BBH London, mint brand Mentos created its own set of 10 'ementicons'. Each ementicon character takes the form of a round Mentos mint sporting a face created by illustrator Geneviève Gauckler. The character set incorporates crazy faces to mean 'awkward', 'romantic' and the super-enthusiastic 'double-like'. In addition, a free app was created for both Apple and Android users that would embed an ementicons keyboard in phone operating systems, enabling the use of ementicons in precisely the same way that regular emoji are used.

EMOJI DICK
Book/art project
Fred Benenson

Emoji Dick is a crowdsourced and Kickstarter-funded translation of Herman Melville's novel *Moby Dick* into emoji. In his 2009 Kickstarter proposal for the project, its creator Fred Benenson explained, 'I'm interested in the phenomenon of how our language, communications and culture are influenced by digital technology. Emoji are either a low point or a high point in that story, so I felt I could confront a lot of our shared anxieties about the future of human expression by forcing a great work of literature through such a strange new filter.'

Each of the book's 10,000 sentences were translated three times by crowd-workers via the Amazon Mechanical Turk website (an online marketplace where workers can choose to take on small tasks and get paid). The three translations were then assessed and voted on by another set of workers, with the most popular version of each sentence selected for inclusion in the book. Benenson calculated that over 800 people spent approximately 3,795,980 seconds working to create the book, with each contributor being paid five US cents per translation and two cents per vote.

The US Library of Congress added *Emoji Dick* to its collection in early 2013. 'I am very pleased that the Library was able to add this work to its collections,' said Michael Neubert, a recommending officer for the Library of Congress' collections. 'There is, in the literal sense, no other book in the Library's collections like it. What is striking for the Library's collections about this work is that it takes a known classic of literature and converts it to a construct of our modern way of communicating, making possible an investigation of the question, "Is it still a literary classic when written in a kind of smartphone-based pidgin language?"' he added. 'Simply demonstrating that it is possible is interesting in that regard.'

(- / 5 , ! + & :

0;;<=>?@

🗳😎⛵🐢👌
Call me Ishmael.

🔇🔈🥢
Some years ago--never mind how long precisely--having little or no money in my purse, and nothing particular to interest me on shore, I thought I would sail about a little and see the watery part of the world.

🔝✖🥄🖼❓👇👤
It is a way I have of driving off the spleen and regulating the circulation.

😵🕯🔱🐌👃👆📧✖💿📦
Whenever I find myself growing grim about the mouth; whenever it is a damp, drizzly November in my soul; whenever I find myself involuntarily pausing before coffin warehouses, and bringing up the rear of every funeral I meet; and especially whenever my hypos get such an upper hand of me, that it requires a strong moral principle to prevent me from deliberately stepping into the street, and methodically knocking people's hats off--then, I account it high time to get to sea as soon as I can.

🔈👍🔪🌐📧
This is my substitute for pistol and ball.

🖥📟🔝💼🖼🔇🥢🈁
With a philosophical flourish Cato throws himself upon his sword; I quietly take to the ship.

🔋🎋🐌🛶📇🖼📟🥢
There is nothing surprising in this.

🔘😐😕😵🥢🐈
If they but knew it, almost all men in their degree, some time or other, cherish very nearly the same feelings towards the ocean with me.

📨🖼🖼🔱📷🐚
There now is your insular city of the Manhattoes, belted round by wharves as Indian isles by coral reefs--commerce surrounds it with her surf.

🐚🕊🐌📧🥢👌
Right and left, the streets take you waterward.

👍👇🕐🈁🥢✈
Its extreme downtown is the battery, where that noble mole is washed by waves, and cooled by breezes, which a few hours previous were out of sight of land.

$%

THE EMOJI REDESIGN PROJECT

Design project
Vittorio Perotti and Giulia Zoavo

Having discovered and used Apple's proprietary emoji set for a couple of years, Milan-based illustrator Giulia Zoavo and art director Vittorio Perotti couldn't shake the feeling that they didn't fully subscribe to how the emoji looked. They decided that they would recreate each emoji in a graphically flatter, more contemporary visual style. The result, their *Emoji Redesign Project*, features 845 emoji. 'The challenge was to redesign the current emoji, maintaining their meaning and soul, but changing their appearance, giving them a contemporary style,' the pair explains. 'Fresh, flat and simple: these were the three keywords we kept in mind during our work.'

To help celebrate the completion of the full set of redesigned emoji, the duo sell various emoji-adorned products on their site, including printed T-shirts, sweatshirts and mobile phone cases.

The design duo's 'fresh, flat and simple' revamp of Apple's emoji set.

The emoji redesign project

143

145

EMOJI T-SHIRTS
Apparel
Primark

Clothing store Primark has been creating apparel sporting emoji for a few seasons, mainly T-shirts. The most recent additions to the range feature the See No Evil monkey emoji.

📖 😃

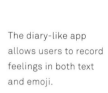

The diary-like app allows users to record feelings in both text and emoji.

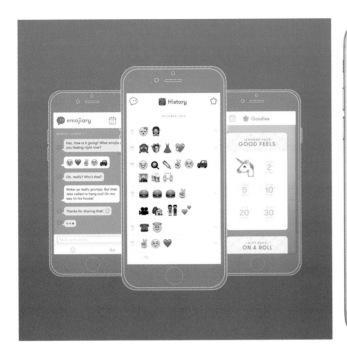

EMOJIARY
iPhone app
All Tomorrows

Created by New York-based product design studio All Tomorrows, Emojiary is an iPhone app that functions as a visual diary to record your feelings in both emoji and text form on a daily basis. The way it works is that the app chats with you, prompting you to record your feelings each day. Then, over time, you can look back on all your entries as short combinations of emoji that chart your emotional ups and downs. Emojiary also rewards

regular users with additional new characters, and it's possible to buy themed packs of emoji to make your journal more fun and express more feelings. The creators of the app hope that it will enable users to tap into their feelings and experience the reflective benefits of keeping a diary, and to better see the connections between how they feel and what they do.

'The primary need we wanted to explore was that of self-reflection and utilizing the phone as a way to promote that self-reflection and not just

as means of distraction,' explains All Tomorrows' Albert Lee. 'After prototyping a few versions, it became clear that a visual method for recording your feelings was far more effective than just text. Hence the use of emoji. Emoji are inherently emotional and expressive in nature and especially useful in a chat context, so Emojiary utilizes a chat interface as the primary mode of user interaction.'

BIG LEBOWSKEMOJI

Art project
Matthew Haughey

On 11 May 2015 Matthew Haughey, a senior content marketer at Slack Technologies, sent a series of five Big Lebowskemoji tweets that, when interpreted, represent the entire plot of the 1998 cult Coen brothers film *The Big Lebowski*. If the challenge of translating each line of emoji (a specific scene in the movie) is too much, you can find an annotated version of the project on Haughey's website, matt.haughey.com.

The project sees key scenes from cult film *The Big Lebowski* transcribed into strings of emoji characters.

SEX EMOJIS
Design project
Andrew Fox

On the face of it, UK illustrator
Andrew Fox's self-initiated *Sex Emojis*
project might seem a little indulgent;
gratuitous, even. But Fox explains
that the project was an exercise in
reduction: 'Inspired by apps such as
Tinder, I decided to come up with a
series of emoji that reduce sexual
acts into simple designs. I guess
you could call it a comment on our
generation's attitude towards
Internet-enabled casual hook-ups.
I figured that the next logical (yet
slightly depressing) step was to do
away with written conversation
entirely (or at least as much as
possible) in favour of straight-to-the-
point emoji. Like language itself, the
way we communicate online is forever
evolving. With text talk (c u l8r) and
emoji now so commonplace, it seems
as though reduction is key to the
future of digital communication.'

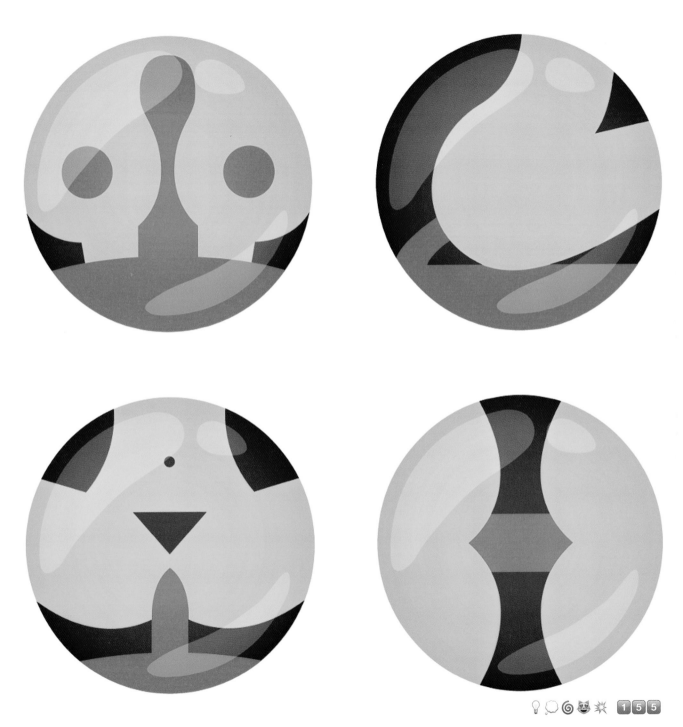

EMOJI DAYDREAM
Art project
Able Parris

Using an app called Phonto to add emoji characters to his own photographs, US-based artist and creative director Able Parris regularly creates imagery that places emoji characters in real-life scenarios and posts them on his Instagram stream. There, you might see emoji helicopters turning somersaults against a clear blue sky above a cityscape; emoji boats drifting along the East River towards Brooklyn Bridge; or an emoji monkey sitting on the lap of a man travelling on the subway. Welcome to *Emoji Daydream*!

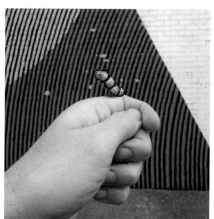

Able Parris creates his *Emoji Daydream* images using an app called Phonto to insert emoji into his own photography.

160 📖 😃

💡 💬 🌀 😼 💥 163

So, I just reached 25 million followers 🛹

DESIGNER CHARACTERS

If you could create a new emoji, what would it be? We asked a number of image-makers from around the world to design new emoji characters they wish really existed.

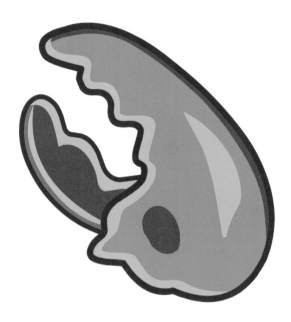

LOBSTER CLAW
Ali Graham

'My thinking behind my lobster claw
emoji was that it could be used in a
dining context, in a flirtatious way
(to give someone a cheeky pinch),
combined with the fist emoji on the
first day of the month (pinch punch)
or even combined with the Easter
Island head if you're a B52s fan!'

HIPSTER COFFEE
Hey Studio

'Hipsters have been driving the
specialist coffee market for a few
years, and nothing symbolizes the
hipster better than a waxed mous-
tache. So our emoji represents not
just any old takeaway coffee, but a
hipster coffee – usually the best
you'll find in town!'

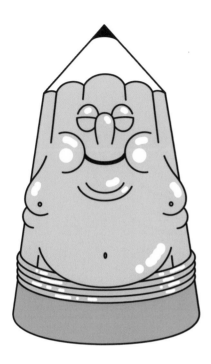

HEAVY PENCIL
Rob Flowers

'This happy and obviously heavy
pencil is for use on those occasions
when you want to put a date in the
diary for a catch up with a friend.'

MIND BLOWN
FL@33

'There are a couple of missing emoji
that I would use a lot. A "no brainer"
and also the "mind blown" emoji that
I chose to create on this occasion.
This emoji would replace my regular
use of emoticons **O_O** and **O_o** and
the alternative "OMG" and "un-be-lie-
vable" to express utter astonishment.'

GRAMOPHONE, FAN, GHETTO BLASTER & BUCKET AND SPADE
Crispin Finn

'Our four new emoji describe some of those small but important details of life: the gramophone for vinyl music lovers like ourselves; the fan to express keeping it cool under pressure or to humorously describe your fandom; the ghetto blaster for when you really need to play it loud; and the bucket and spade for those essential moments of holiday downtime.'

TYPO
Peskimo

'Our emoji features a gentleman octopus at a keyboard that's just done a typo. We use stickers and emoji regularly and haven't got one for that!'

UNDO
Matt Chase

'I personally would make great use of this – a convenient "Apple + Z" (the keyboard shortcut for "undo") for all those moments in your life when you wish you could undo the thing you've just done or uttered (or would simply like to chastise your iPhone's auto-correct function).'

**** YOU
Mr Bingo

'I often need to respond to people with this but, for some reason, angry or negative emoji seem to be really lacking from the sets I've seen.'

JUST KIDDIN
Friso Blankevoort

'When it comes to expressing yourself via emoji, it can be tricky to express negative emotions. There's nothing stronger than an angry smiley or a "thumbs down". But sometimes I do miss expressions of irony, a face-palm or maybe even a middle finger. You have to be careful with those though, because negative emotions might seem a lot more extreme in writing than in person. So, to minimize misunderstandings, I've prepared a "just kiddin" emoji. As soon as you've gone a little too far (or when you're afraid that the person you're conversing with might not get that you're joking), this one comes in handy.'

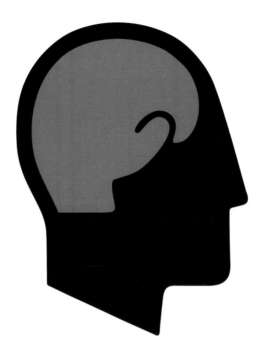

BAD HANGOVER
Noma Bar

'After exploring various options, it occurred to me that drawing a head, but with a boxing glove where the brain should be, best describes the feeling of a really bad headache. This would probably be most used as a bad hangover emoji.'

OH SHIT
Noma Bar

'Inspired by the classic poo emoji,
this particular pile of shit requires
a second look: the sides of the poo
form silhouettes of screaming
people, their eyes formed from the
flies buzzing around the poo. This is
the emoji to reach for when the shit
really hits the fan!'

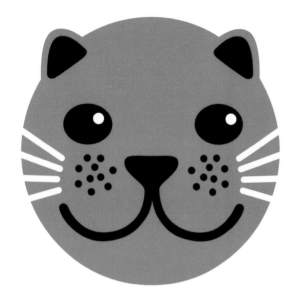

CAT, DUCK, KOALA & PANDA
Lucy Vigrass

'Having a four-year-old that enjoys delving into my phone, I wanted to create a series of emoji that would be fun for her to discover and to add to the messages we send to grandma.'

VOLUME TURNED UP TO 11
Julian Morey

'My emoji was inspired by the cult classic mockumentary *Spinal Tap*, in which all the knobs on lead guitarist Nigel Tufnel's custom-made Marshall amplifier go up to 11, rather than the standard 10. It is (quoting Tufnel) "for when you need that extra push over the cliff."'

JUGGALO
Nick Shea

'I think we can all agree that Juggalos (infamous fans of the horrorcore group Insane Clown Posse) are sorely under-represented in the emoji lexicon. Ideally this would exist as one in a series of specific subculture emoji.'

VINYL RECORD
Studio Emmi

'Music made me do it! I got into design because of music, and I get the energy to stay in design because of music. Besides, the vinyl record was missing from standard emoji sets – yet they have a minidisc? Vinyl is much more relevant to music lovers than the minidisc has ever been!'

SKATEBOARDING DINOSAUR
Matthew Bromley

'For some crazy reason there isn't a skateboard emoji in the standard set, and I wanted to right that particular wrong. So I created a skateboarding dinosaur that could be used by all of us skaters to succinctly communicate that we're busy skating!'

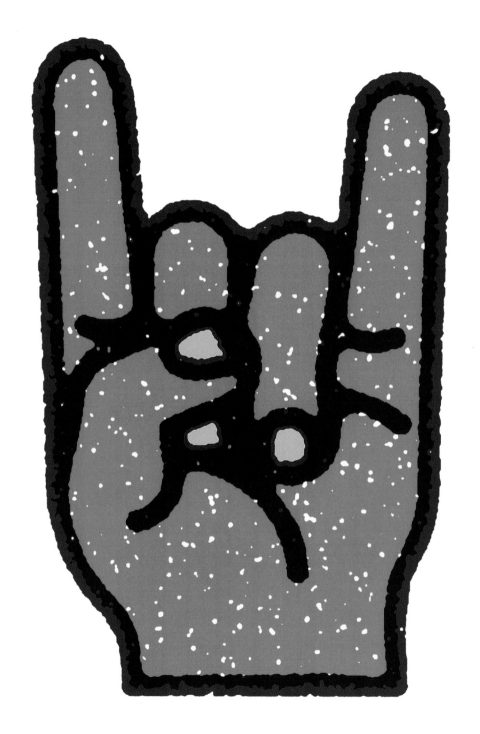

METAL SET (SATAN SYMBOL, PENTAGRAM & BEER CAN)
Tane Williams

'I've been listening to LOTS of metal lately and have found myself unable to communicate the METAL effectively with traditional emoji (except for maybe 😈), so I have created these three new emoji on that theme. These are for the metalheads!'

WORKING HARD & BEING A DICK

Jan Kallwejt

'I'm a big believer that if you work hard, you get back what you put in – so I created this happy "working hard" emoji. I'm also a believer that everyone should be themselves. Unless, of course, they're being a dick. I couldn't resist the opportunity to make this emoji for when you need to tell someone to stop being a dick.'

PAIN IN THE ARSE
Richard Hogg

'This emoji is intended to represent a sore bum – either literally, after eating spicy food, or metaphorically.'

HUMPING BUNNIES
TwoPoints

'Innuendo is all well and good, but the real power of emoji is that you can get to the point and communicate what you're thinking with just one image. So here it is, the much-needed humping bunnies emoji.'

JOHN AND YOKO
Serge Seidlitz

'Is there anything that symbolizes
peace and love more succinctly than
an image of John Lennon and Yoko
Ono naked and cuddling? I'm pretty
sure there isn't. So while this is clearly
a John and Yoko emoji, it's also a
peace and love emoji.'

BACKSTABBING
Margherita Urbani

'In general emoji are very happy and positive, playing off good or quirky vibes. Being a critical person, I wanted to create an emoji that was a little more harsh and showed one of the darker feelings that we all have sometimes.'

FINGERS CROSSED
David Henckel

'I really hope my fingers crossed emoji makes it into your emoji book!'

BACON

Liza Nelson

'Why do we need a bacon emoji? Because I've had to settle for sashimi or a kebab too many times. Because I've had to spell out the incredibly long word B-A-C-O-N on a very hungover Saturday morning too many times. Because I've had to waste precious time texting the full sentence 'If the brunch place doesn't have bacon I'm not going' too many times. Because bacon is one of my greatest passions in life and in the lives of so many people I love. Because there's already a fried egg emoji but it's just sitting there all alone. Cold. Bored. Aching for something to be near it.

We don't need every single fruit found at the grocery store (along with some that have never before been spotted in the produce section ... anywhere) when we're missing something that is one of the major food groups all on its own. Because they gave us a CD, a DVD, a minidisc AND a floppy disk – all of which are essentially extinct. And don't even get me started on the unprecedented variety of padlocks and blasting speakers they thought we needed – that would be four of each. Four. And yet only one essential, savoury breakfast food. And only one meat-related emoji I find handy at all:

the burger. When was the last time anyone suggested a Renaissance-Fair-status turkey leg for dinner and found that emoji to be a real time-saver? My point here is that the creators of emoji vastly underestimated the significance of bacon in my life and in the lives of so many other young, healthy, non-vegan Americans. And they didn't realize that it would have been one of the most truly iconic, useful, time-saving, beautifully designed, honoured and cherished characters in the history of hieroglyphics. Amen.'

FURTHER READING

Books

Christin, Anne-Marie. *A History of Writing: From Hieroglyph to Multimedia*. Flammarion, 2002.

Houston, Keith. *Shady Characters: Ampersands, Interrobangs and other Typographical Curiosities*. Penguin Books, 2013.

Sanderson, David. *Smileys*. O'Reilly Media, 1997.

Websites

Bill 'Ubi' Dwyer
ukrockfestivals.com/UBI-DWYER.html

The Canonical Smiley (and 1-Line Symbol) List by James Marshall
marshall.freeshell.org/smileys.html

Emojipedia
emojipedia.org

Harvey Ball World Smile Foundation
worldsmile.org

Martin K. Speckter's interrobang
interrobang-mks.com

SmileyWorld
smiley.com

The Unicode Consortium
unicode.org/consortium/consort.html

PICTURE CREDITS

Speaking in Pictures

© Apple Color Emoji (p. 8)

© Wingdings (top), WebSymbols (bottom) (p. 9)

© Zapf Dingbats and Wingdings (p. 10)

© Minion Ornaments, Utopia Ornaments, Linotype Decoration Pi 1, Flower Ornaments (p. 11)

© scanned and provided by Monotype Imaging (pp. 12–13)

© Linotype (left), © Rian Hughes (right) (p. 14)

© LINE (left), © Apple Color Emoji (right) (p. 15)

© Font Aid (pp. 16–17)

© Apple, Twitter, Microsoft, Samsung, LG, Mozilla, Google, EmojiOne (p. 18)

Paving the Way

© Interrobangs in Lucida Grande typeface (by Charles Bigelow & Kris Holmes) and in Wingdings 2, © Microsoft Corporation; ironieteken by Bas Jacobs of Underware; all other punctuation marks in Times New Roman, distributed by Monotype (p. 22)

© FL@33's Tomi Vollauschek (p. 24)

© British Library (p. 25)

© *Puck*, 30 March 1881, p. 65, scanned and provided by The Ohio State University Billy Ireland Cartoon Library & Museum (p. 27)

© Nick Shea, recreation of Scott Fahlman's original bulletin board post (p. 28)

© O'Reilly Media (p. 29)

© FL@33's Tomi Vollauschek (p. 30)

© grp, hjw and Sandra (p. 31)

© Jassinter Inc (pp. 32, 33 right and 35)

© World Smile Corporation (p. 33 left)

© MARK RALSTON/AFP/Getty Images (p. 34)

© Daniel Gulp (p. 36)

© Bomb the Bass (p. 37)

Emoji: Born in Japan

© Nick Shea (pp. 40, 44 left)

© Intercity (p. 41 right)

© Gavin Lucas, recreations of Shigetaka Kurita's original emoji designs (pp. 41 left, 43, 44 right, 45, 47–49, 51)

© Twitter (p. 46)

Inspired by Emoji

Emoji IRL.LOL. © Liza Nelson (emojiirllol.tumblr.com) (pp. 54–61)

Emoji.ink website © Vince McKelvie (emoji.ink) (pp. 62–63) and illustrations © Takakura Kazuki (takakurakazuki.com) (pp. 64–69)

Poo Emoji Light Wing Franklin Shoes & Button-Up Shirt © Betabrand (betabrand.com) (pp. 70–73)

Symphonieorchester © Bureau Mirko Borsche (mirkoborsche.com) (pp. 74–77)

IKEA Emoji © IKEA B.V. Nederland (ikea.com/nl/nl/campagne/emoticons. html), (Credits: Concept & App Design: Lemz, Emoticons Design: Sue Doeksen, App Developer: Elements Interactive, Film Production: 310K, Sound: Studio De Keuken, Animation: Erik Post, PR: NewsLab) (pp. 78–83)

Cindy Sherman-icon © Hyo Ju Hong (cindysherman-icon.tumblr.com) (pp. 84–85)

Politicons © +rehabstudio (rehabstudio.com/thinking/politicons) (pp. 86–91)

Who's really chatting online with your child? © Rosapark (rosapark.fr), (Credits: Creative Directors: Mark Forgan and Jamie Standen, Art Director: Mark Forgan, Copyrwriter: Jamie Standen, Illustrator/ Photographer: Baptiste Massé, 3D Production Company: Mécanique Générale) (pp. 92–95)

#EndangeredEmoji © WWF (endangeredemoji.com) (pp. 96–97)

The Emoji Art & Design Show © Forced Meme Productions & Eyebeam Art + Technology Center (emojishow.com; forcedmeme.com; eyebeam.org) (pp. 98–103)

BFF lapel pin © Valley Cruise Press (valleycruisepress.com) (p. 104)

Emoji pins © Pintrill (pintrill.com) (pp. 105–107)

Emoji Passcode © Intelligent Environments (intelligentenvironments.com) (p. 108), © Gavin Lucas (p. 109)

2015 NCAA Tournament Emoji © Julia Heffernan for *The Washington Post* (juliaheffernan.com) (pp. 110–11)

Emoji-nation © Nastya Nudnik (behance.net/fefe) (pp. 112–13)

Introji © Rebecca Evie Lynch (constructiveperseverance.tumblr.com /introji) (pp. 114–15)

Emoji Spectrum © Callum Copley (callumcopley.com/Emoji-Spectrum) (pp. 116–17)

Emojistuff.com © Richard Trautmann (emojistuff.com) (pp. 118–19)

EmotiCoke © Coca-Cola/EJE Puerto Rico (emoticoke.com) (pp. 120–23)

LINE messaging app © LINE (line.me/en; creator.line.me/en) (pp. 124–27)

Emoji set for LINE © Dan Woodger (danwoodger.com) (pp. 128–31)

Elections in Emoji © Preston City Council, film by Dave Robinson (preston.gov.uk; daverob.co.uk) (pp. 132–33)

JapaneseEmoticons.me © Peter Saydak (japaneseemoticons.me) (pp. 134–35)

Ementicons © Mentos (ementicons. mentos.com/en_GB), (Credits: Producer: Laura Graham, Creatives: Sara Watson and Laura Osbourne, Creative Directors: Shelley Smoler and Raphael Baschkin, Illustrator: Genevieve Gauckler, Client: Daan Simonis, Mentos and Perfetti Van Melle, Director of films: Matthew Pollock, Film Production Company: Indy8, App Production Company: Monterosa) (pp. 136–37)

Emoji Dick © Fred Benenson (emojidick.com) (pp. 138–41)

The Emoji Redesign Project © Vittorio Perotti and Giulia Zoavo (emojisgoflat.com) (pp. 142–45)

Primark © Allison Hekimian (p. 146), © Kylie Hong and Ida Lai (p. 147), © Peaches Beer-Jones (stylepeaches.blogspot.co.uk) (p. 148), © Primark (p. 149)

Emojiary © All Tomorrows (emojiary.com) (pp. 150–51)

Big Lebowskemoji © Matthew Haughey (matt.haughey.com) (pp. 152–53)

Sex emojis © Andrew Fox (behance.net/afox) (pp. 154–55)

Emoji Daydream © Able Parris (ableparris.com) (pp. 156–63)

Designer Characters

lobster claw © Ali Graham (grarg.com) (p. 166 left)

hipster coffee © Hey Studio (heystudio.es) (p. 166 right)

heavy pencil © Rob Flowers (robflowers.co.uk) (p. 167 left)

mind blown © FL@33's Tomi Vollauschek (flat33.com) (p. 167 right)

gramophone, fan, ghetto blaster & bucket and spade © Crispin Finn (crispinfinn.com) (pp. 168–69)

typo © Peskimo (peskimo.com) (p. 170 left)

undo © Matt Chase (chasematt.com) (p. 170 right)

**** YOU © Mr Bingo (mr-bingo.org.uk) (p. 171 left)

just kiddin © Friso Blankevoort (frisoblankevoort.nl) (p. 171 right)

bad hangover & oh shit © Noma Bar (dutchuncle.co.uk/noma-bar) (pp. 172–73)

cat, duck, koala & panda © Lucy Vigrass (lucyvigrass.co.uk) (pp. 174–75)

volume turned up to 11 © Julian Morey (abc-xyz.co.uk) (p. 176 left)

juggalo © Nick Shea (nickshea.com) (p. 176 right)

vinyl record © Studio Emmi (emmi.co.uk) (p. 177 left)

skateboarding dinosaur © Matthew Bromley (madebybromley.com) (p. 177 right)

metal set (Satan symbol, pentagram & beer can) © Tane Williams (tanewilliams.com) (pp. 178–79)

working hard & being a dick © Jan Kallwejt (kallwejt.com) (p. 180)

pain in the arse © Richard Hogg (h099.com) (p. 181 left)

humping bunnies © TwoPoints (twopoints.net) (p. 181 right)

John and Yoko © Serge Seidlitz (sergeseidlitz.com) (p. 182)

backstabbing © Margherita Urbani (margheritaurbani.com) (p. 183 left)

fingers crossed © David Henckel (davidhenckel.com) (p. 183 right)

bacon © Liza Nelson (lizanelson.com) (p. 185)

ACKNOWLEDGEMENTS

Thank you to everyone who contributed to this book, not least to Jeff Blagdon for his invaluable input and for his kind facilitating of an interview with the godfather of emoji himself, Shigetaka Kurita. Thanks also to Nagaomi Kawaharada for his assistance with said interview.

Particular thanks must go to my editor Ali Gitlow for her input, enthusiasm, guidance, support and patience – and also to Tomi and Agathe at design studio FL@33 for doing such a great job turning a bunch of words and images into this splendid book.

Sincere thanks also to Paul Barnes; Laura Graham at BBH; Alastair Coe and all at Big Active; Friso 'Freshco' Blankevoort; Andrea in the Rare Books & Music reading room, and all at the British Library; Matthew Bromley; Matt Chase; Patrick Burgoyne, Paul Pensom and all at *Creative Review*; Anna, Roger and Finn at Crispin Finn; Angela Henao and all at DDB; Rob Flowers; Kelly Reeves and all at Forced Meme Productions; Leo Walton and Patrick Marling at Golden Age; Ali Graham; Jon and Tom at Handsome Frank; Julia Heffernan; David Henckel; Hey Studio; Richard Hogg; Rian Hughes; Nathan Gale and William Hibbert at Intercity; Mr Isao Takahashi at JASS International Inc.; Martha Jay; Jan Kallwejt; Anna Kelly; Mercedes Kraus; Jenny Yoo, Dooee Kim, Kim Helen and all at LINE; Professor Peter J. Lucas; Daniel Rhatigan and all at Monotype; Julian Morey; Mum; Liza Nelson; Susan Liberator, Marilyn Scott and all at Ohio State University Libraries; Teri Finn at O'Reilly Media, Inc.; Camilla Parsons at Outline Artists; Peskimo; Andy Rementer; Emmi Salonen; Serge Seidlitz; Nick Shea; Erik Spiekermann; Martin and Lupi at TwoPoints; Margherita Urbani; Lucy Vigrass; and Tane Williams. Extra special thanks to Ravi and Amber.

A version of *'The Evolution of the Dingbat'* first appeared in the July 2012 issue of *Creative Review*.

A version of *Born in Japan* by Jeff Blagdon first appeared on The Verge on 4 March 2013: theverge.com/2013/3/4/3966140/how-emoji-conquered-the-world

© Leo Cackett (leocackett.com)

AUTHOR BIOGRAPHY

Gavin Lucas is a writer and editor with over 10 years' experience of publishing content across multiple platforms both on and offline. Formerly a senior writer at leading communication arts journal *Creative Review*, he has authored books that have been published in multiple language editions on guerrilla advertising, button badges and BMX bikes. He is an obsessive collector of art, music and books – and even more obsessive about his love of burgers which has seen him blog, exhibit, lecture and enthuse on the subject at events and for clients all over the world. Gavin is co-founder of illustration agency Outline Artists and lives in London with his wife Ravi and daughter Amber.

© Prestel Verlag, Munich · London ·
New York, 2016

© for the text by Gavin Lucas and
Jeff Blagdon, 2016

© for the images see page 187, 2016

Front cover, chapter divider
illustrations and running feet:
© FL@33's Tomi Vollauschek using
Apple Color Emoji

Back cover: Liza Nelson's 'Party' emoji
from her Emoji IRL.LOL. project

Every effort has been made to
contact the copyright holders. Any
copyright holders we have been
unable to reach or to whom in-
accurate acknowledgement has been
made please contact the publisher,
and full adjustments will be made to
all subsequent printings.

Prestel Verlag, Munich
A member of Verlagsgruppe
Random House GmbH

Prestel Verlag
Neumarkter Strasse 28
81673 Munich
Tel. +49 (0)89 4136-0
Fax +49 (0)89 4136-2335

www.prestel.de

Prestel Publishing Ltd.
14–17 Wells Street
London W1T 3PD
Tel. +44 (0)20 7323-5004
Fax +44 (0)20 7323-0271

Prestel Publishing
900 Broadway, Suite 603
New York, NY 10003
Tel. +1 (212) 995-2720
Fax +1 (212) 995-2733

www.prestel.com

Library of Congress Control Number:
2015957043

British Library Cataloguing-in-
Publication Data: a catalogue record
for this book is available from the
British Library;

Deutsche Nationalbibliothek holds
a record of this publication in the
Deutsche Nationalbibliografie;
detailed bibliographical data can be
found under: http://dnb.d-nb.de

Prestel books are available
worldwide.
Please contact your nearest book-
seller or one of the above addresses
for information concerning your
local distributor.

Editorial direction:
Ali Gitlow

Copyediting and proofreading:
Martha Jay

Design and layout:
Tomi Vollauschek and Agathe
Jacquillat, FL@33

Production:
Friederike Schirge

Origination:
Reproline Mediateam, Munich

Printing and binding:
TBB a.s., Bánska Bystrica

Printed in Slovakia

ISBN 978-3-7913-8150-3

FSC
www.fsc.org
MIX
From responsible
sources
FSC® C022120

Verlagsgruppe Random House
FSC® N001967

Printed on the FSC®-certified paper
Profimatt

THREE HUNDRED

THREE HUNDRED FIFTY YEARS

ED FIFTY YEARS

An Album of American Jewish Memory

Selected, written, and compiled by

Michael Feldberg

Karla Goldman

Scott-Martin Kosofsky

Pamela S. Nadell

Jonathan D. Sarna

Gary P. Zola

Published on the occasion of the National Dinner by

CELEBRATE 350: JEWISH LIFE IN AMERICA

in cooperation with

THE COMMISSION FOR COMMEMORATING 350 YEARS OF AMERICAN JEWISH HISTORY

The American Jewish Historical Society, The Jacob Rader Marcus Center of the American Jewish Archives, The Library of Congress, The National Archives and Records Administration

Conceived, designed, composed, edited, and produced by
Scott-Martin Kosofsky at The Philidor Company,
Lexington, Massachusetts. www.philidor.com

Project directors: Dr. Gary P. Zola and David Solomon

Printed in the United States of America
by Milllenium Graphics, Norwood, Massachusetts.
Bound by Acme Bookbinding, Charlestown, Massachusetts.
The 350th Anniversary Medal was designed by Dana Krinsky
and was rendered for the binding by Adolph Bauer Inc., Holbrook, Massachusetts.

CONTENTS

H. CON. RES. 106

Whereas in 1654, Jewish refugees from Brazil arrived on North American shores and formally established North America's first Jewish community in New Amsterdam, now New York City; (Enrolled as Agreed to or Passed by Both House and Senate)

H.Con.Res.106
Agreed to November 21, 2003

One Hundred Eighth Congress
of the
United States of America

AT THE FIRST SESSION

Begun and held at the City of Washington on Tuesday,
the seventh day of January, two thousand and three
Concurrent Resolution
Whereas in 1654, Jewish refugees from Brazil arrived on North American shores and formally established North America's first Jewish community in New Amsterdam, now New York City;
Whereas America welcomed Jews among the millions of immigrants that streamed through our Nation's history;
Whereas the waves of Jewish immigrants arriving in America helped shape our Nation;
Whereas the American Jewish community has been intimately involved in our Nation's civic, social, economic, and cultural life;
Whereas the American Jewish community has sought to actualize the broad principles of liberty and justice that are enshrined in the Constitution of the United States;
Whereas the American Jewish community is an equal participant in the religious life of our Nation;
Whereas American Jews have fought valiantly for the United States in every one of our Nation's military struggles, from the American Revolution to Operation Enduring Freedom;
Whereas not less than 16 American Jews have received the Medal of Honor;
Whereas 2004 marks the 350th anniversary of the American Jewish community;
Whereas the Library of Congress, the National Archives and Records Administration, the American Jewish Historical Society, and the Jacob Rader Marcus Center of the American Jewish Archives have formed 'The Commission for Commemorating 350 Years of American Jewish History' (referred to in this resolution as the 'Commission') to mark this historic milestone;
Whereas the Commission will use the combined resources of its participants to promote the celebration of the Jewish experience in the United States throughout 2004; and
Whereas the Commission is designating September 2004 as 'American Jewish History Month': Now, therefore, be it

> *Resolved by the House of Representatives (the Senate concurring)*, That Congress--
>> (1) honors and recognizes--
>>> (A) the 350th anniversary of the American Jewish community; and
>>> (B) 'The Commission for Commemorating 350 Years of American Jewish History' and its efforts to plan, coordinate, and execute commemorative events celebrating 350 years of American Jewish history;
>> (2) supports the designation of an 'American Jewish History Month'; and
>> (3) urges all Americans to share in this commemoration so as to have a greater appreciation of the role the American Jewish community has had in helping to defend and further the liberties and freedom of all Americans.

Attest:

Clerk of the House of Representatives.

Attest:

Secretary of the Senate.

FOREWORD

A Letter to 2054

As AMERICAN JEWRY celebrated its 350th anniversary, it was plainly no longer a community in its infancy. It had come of age. Not surprisingly, many of the themes and concerns that had marked earlier anniversaries no longer seemed pertinent. For Jews, at least, the long struggle to realize the promise of America—the promise of a nation conceived in liberty and dedicated to human equality—appeared to have met with success, at least for the time being. Those barriers to the advancement of Jews that were still standing as late as the middle of the 20th century appeared to have fallen by the century's end. American Jewry no longer wrestled with the effort to naturalize great streams of immigrants; it was at home in America. The land of the Pilgrims' pride was indeed for most the land where their fathers died. American Jewry no longer felt obliged to proclaim its patriotism or its fidelity to America's highest values. These were unquestioned except by extremist cranks. Nor did American Jewry feel the need to declaim on contributions that Jews had made to America. They were too conspicuous to require comment.

Rather, the time had come to recognize that the small, precarious settlement of 1654 had grown into the largest, freest and most secure Jewish community in all the long history of the Jewish people. The citizenship of Jews in what had become the world's foremost republic had, against all reasonable expectations, altered the course of Jewish history for ever after. And as the late Gerson Cohen, Chancellor of the Jewish Theological Seminary of America, had said some years ago, American Jewry had "achieved integration without paying the price we once feared we should have to pay—without, that is, denying our collective reality, without betraying our communal interests."

In three and a half centuries, American Jewry had absorbed millions of immigrants who had become self-sufficient and productive citizens. It had built the infrastructure of Jewish life—synagogues and cemeteries, schools and libraries, welfare agencies and community centers—and repeatedly rebuilt them as Jews moved across the continent. Although it had not yet achieved widespread Jewish literacy at a high level, it had nonetheless established institutions of higher learning and produced scholars of distinction. Although it had—to its grief—been unable to rescue European Jewry from the Holocaust, it had helped to rebuild Zion, to rescue Soviet Jewry, and to succor embattled Jewish communities in other lands. And it had done these things and more while intensely engaged in the civic and cultural life of the larger American community. Indeed, as the sociologist Marshall Sklare observed, American Jewry had been "an example of a group that does not take America for granted—a group that comprehends the greatness of America, warts and all."

At 350, then, American Jewry was coming to recognize that it was bound to take its place in the long procession of great and distinctive Jewish communities of which our collective history is comprised. The question to be pondered was what would American Jewry make of the extraordinary freedom and opportunity with which it had been blessed? In 2005, the answer to that question remained hidden in the mists of futurity, indecipherable and indeterminate. How this unprecedented experiment in the elaboration of Jewish civilization in freedom would turn out could not be foretold. But let it be said that, as we reflected on the labors of the preceding centuries, celebrated the achievements of our forebears, and assessed the challenges before us, American Jews recommitted themselves to building a future worthy of our heritage and worthy of the opportunities we enjoy as Americans.

We present this scrapbook, with its snapshots of trial and error, struggle and achievement, to those who come after. If, in 2054, our descendants gather to celebrate in joy the 400th anniversary of Jewish life in America, we will have in good measure succeeded.

—ROBERT S. RIFKIND
Chairman of the Board
Celebrate 350: Jewish Life in America

Celebrate 350
Jewish Life in America
1654 ~ 2004

LET IT BE KNOWN that in Elul 5764 (September 2004) the Jewish community of the United States began a year long commemoration marking the 350th Anniversary of Jewish settlement in this country.

WITH THE HELP OF GOD and under the protection of the Constitution of the United States, we have lived and prospered in this land. We have been an integral part of American life. We have worked with all other Americans in the never-ending effort to keep secure the democratic way of life. Our ancient prophetic ideals and the teachings of our sages serve as cornerstones of this nation's values. Our work, our hopes, and above all, our living religion have been among our proudest offerings to the American community.

IN SOME LANDS ACROSS THE SEAS the Jewish people have felt the searing flame of prejudice, persecution and death. The American Jew has had the sad yet inspiring opportunity to bring comfort to the oppressed, the joyous opportunity to participate in the reconstitution of the Jewish state on the ancient soil of Israel, and the inescapable and ennobling responsibility to mend the broken places in our world.

EVEN AS WE HAVE WORKED FOR THE WELL-BEING OF OUR PEOPLE ABROAD, the Jewish people in America have struggled to preserve our noble heritage, our historic traditions, our ancient teachings, our ethics, and our spiritual ideals in the free climate of our nation.

MINDFUL OF OUR MANIFOLD BLESSINGS and with deep gratitude in our hearts to the God of Israel, Who, in 1654, led our forebears to the shores of this great new land,

WE HAVE PROCLAIMED the period from Elul 5764 (September 2004) through Elul 5765 (September 2005) to be one of special thanksgiving, prayer, study, reflection and celebration to mark the 350TH ANNIVERSARY OF JEWISH COMMUNAL LIFE IN AMERICA.

WE CALL ON ALL AMERICAN JEWRY to participate in the observance of this anniversary; to thank God for the bountiful blessings that have been bestowed on us in this remarkable land. Let us express our collective hope that peace, security, and prosperity will reign in our nation for all. May the principles of freedom and liberty that have been the lodestar values of this great Republic continue to radiate their blessings on our nation.

CENTRAL CONFERENCE OF AMERICAN RABBIS
Rabbi Harry Danziger, President

RABBINICAL ASSEMBLY
Rabbi Perry Raphael Rank, President

RABBINICAL COUNCIL OF AMERICA
Rabbi Dale Polakoff, President

RECONSTRUCTIONIST RABBINICAL ASSOCIATION
Rabbi Brant Rosen, President

PREFACE

When the American Jewish Historical Society was founded in 1892, it became the first organization to promote an appreciation of the Jewish historical experience in North America. At both the 250th anniversary and the tercentenary of Jewish settlement in North America, in 1905 and 1954, respectively, the Society joined with other Jewish organizations to create year-long commemorations of the landing in New Amsterdam.

We are honored that, as in previous celebrations, on September 14, 2005, the President of the United States has acknowledged through personal remarks, before almost 1000 people at a dinner in Washington, D.C., the place of the Jewish people in our nation's history. We are honored by the participation and warm words of President George W. Bush. George Washington set an important precedent when, in 1790, he pledged to the Hebrew Congregation of Newport, Rhode Island, that the government of the United States would be one "which gives to bigotry no sanction, to persecution no assistance." In his remarks on September 14, President Bush quoted and reaffirmed the words of George Washington. He went on to say ". . . we're a better and stronger and freer nation because so many Jews from countries all over the world have chosen to become American citizens." The President also condemned antisemitism by saying "So to stand for religious freedom, we must expose and confront the ancient hatred of antisemitism, wherever it is found. When we find antisemitism at home, we will confront it. When we find antisemitism abroad, we will condemn it."

We believe that the present has a duty both to the past and to the future if tradition and memory are to be preserved, if values are to be transmitted, and our story can be properly told. In this way our conduct and performance as a people can be judged by the measure of history. The Celebration on September 14, 2005, and this album are part of our effort to fulfill that duty.

We are grateful for the collaboration of our friends at Celebrate 350 and the great national repositories of historical documents—the Library of Congress, the National Archives and Records Administration, the Jacob Rader Marcus Center of the American Jewish Archives—and our partners at the Center for Jewish History in New York in marking this great occasion. We are indebted to the members of the Host Committee, listed at the back of this album, whose generosity made possible our celebration on September 14 and the publication of this album.

It is my hope that at the 400th anniversary celebration, our children and grandchildren will look back with pride at the manner in which the entire United States marked the 350th anniversary, and that they will, in their own way, add another distinguished chapter to the long and proud history reflected in this album.

—KENNETH J. BIALKIN
Chairman of the Board
The American Jewish Historical Society

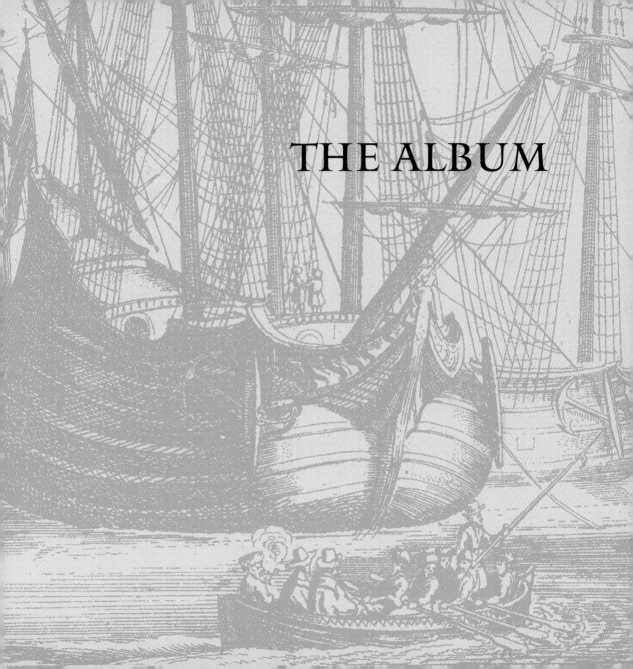

THE ALBUM

INTRODUCTION

THIS PAST YEAR, Jews across the United States have been celebrating the 350th anniversary of Jewish life in America. Books, articles, exhibits, posters, lectures, conferences, television and radio programs, films, concerts, even dance recitals have marked this momentous occasion. All four major Jewish rabbinical associations joined as one in encouraging American Jews to participate in the anniversary and "to offer thanks . . . for the bountiful blessings that have been bestowed on us in this remarkable land." The Library of Congress and the National Archives and Records Administration partnered with the American Jewish Historical Society and The Jacob Rader Marcus Center of the American Jewish Archives to establish a congressionally recognized commission that sought to "advance our understanding of the American Jewish experience as it marks this milestone anniversary" through the development of real-space and web-based exhibitions. A national umbrella organization, Celebrate 350, was created to "marshal the energy and creativity of organizations and individuals from around the country" to observe the anniversary. And both chambers of the United States Congress, recognizing Jewish participation in manifold aspects of American life, passed a concurrent resolution urging Americans generally "to share in this commemoration so as to have a greater appreciation of the role the American Jewish community has had in helping to defend and further the liberties and freedom of all Americans."

Three hundred and fifty years ago, the arrival of Jews on these shores attracted no such acclaim. In September of 1654, some twenty-three Jews, expelled from Recife, Brazil when the Portuguese recaptured it from the Dutch, arrived in New Amsterdam seeking a new home. These early Jews overcame a series of legal and political obstacles, including opposition from the colony's governor, Peter Stuyvesant. With help from the Jewish community back in Amsterdam, they won the right from the Dutch West India Company to set down roots in New Amsterdam—specifically permission to "travel," "trade," "live," and "remain," provided that "the poor among them shall not become a burden to the company or to the community, but be supported by their own nation."

The fate of Jews in New Amsterdam was tied in with that of other religious dissenters. "Giving them [Jews] liberty," Governor Stuyvesant wrote, "we cannot refuse the Lutherans and the Papists." The decision about admitting Jews to New Amsterdam was, at the deepest level, a decision about the social and religious character of New Amsterdam. Because they all did eventually receive liberty, New York became what it is today: a multi-religious, multi-ethnic, and multi-lingual community—as eventually did the nation as a whole. Small as they were in number, Jews played a conspicuous part in that early story and have remained part of the story of pluralism and tolerance in this country ever since.

This year's festivities mark the third time that the American Jewish community is celebrating its anniversary on American soil. The first time, in 1905, in the midst of massive East European Jewish immigration to the United States and as anti-Jewish violence flared in Russia, America's role as a great haven for Jews became the focal point of the commemoration. The occasion highlighted the fact that 250 years had passed since Jews had won permission "to live and reside" in New Netherlands.

Fifty years later (1954–1955), the American Jewish Tercentenary was commemorated with a nationwide series of events and observances focusing on the theme (expressed in pre-feminist language) of "Man's Opportunities and Responsibilities Under Freedom." The universalistic motif, which also echoed the language of the Cold War, expressed Jews' sense of being at home in America, and full participants in the nation's "adventure in freedom."

This time, the celebration's organizers decided against a single central theme; instead, the year's activities have been as diverse, pluralistic, and multi-focused as the American Jewish community itself. The role of women, largely ignored in previous celebrations, has been highlighted. So have Jewish cultural contributions. The overarching goal, ably expressed by The Commission for Commemorating 350 Years of American Jewish History, is "to honor the past, celebrate the present, and anticipate the future of Jewish communal life in North America."

The keepsake album before you reflects this noble goal. And it reflects the pluralistic character of both our celebration and our community. Like any album, it is filled with images—snapshots—that are evocative of that which now belongs to the ages. No one album, of course, can possibly do full justice to the wondrous breadth and depth of the American Jewish experience. There are far too many historical events, far too many significant individuals, far too many momentous contributions for us even to begin to do credit to them all. Such is the extent of the Jewish mark on America, and of America's influence on Jews.

This commemorative album is meant, instead, to serve as a mnemonic of what has been seen and read and learned over the past twelve months. Each image represents a moment, a memory, an idea larger than itself. The goal is to promote thoughtful reflection: to encourage greater self-awareness and self-understanding among Jewish Americans, and to promote greater appreciation of the American Jewish experience among all Americans.

The album also underscores the fact that Jews, whose history elsewhere has so often been shrouded in tragedy, have managed to flourish within this nation's free and pluralistic society, where church and state are separated and religion entirely voluntary. Myriad challenges continue to confront America's Jews, some of them old, some of them new. But as historian Lucy Dawidowicz recognized years ago, "the American Jewish experience—still in process, still vulnerable, still experimental—has so far shown that with the will to do so, Jews can preserve and sustain Judaism and Jewish culture while participating in the larger society."

"Not to suffer history but to make history—that is the challenge," the pioneering American Jewish historian, Jacob Rader Marcus, once wrote "Knowledge, meticulous, painfully accurate, all-embracing knowledge, brings with it the power to create, to mold, to survive." As American Jews conclude their commemoration of the 350th anniversary of American Jewish life and look ahead to the 400th, that message remains remarkably timely.

JONATHAN D. SARNA, *Chief Historian*
Celebrate 350

GARY P. ZOLA, *Chair*
The Commission for Commemorating
350 Years of American Jewish History

In 1654, twenty-three Jewish refugees from the Portuguese takeover of the Dutch colony at Recife, Brazil, sailed into New Amsterdam and petitioned Gov. Peter Stuyvesant for permission to disembark and remain there as residents. New Amsterdam was likely not their first-choice port of refuge, since it was rife with religious tensions among Protestant groups who had come there hoping to found a "New Zion," a situation different from that of Dutch enclaves elsewhere in the New World, whose culture was based largely on commerce.

At first, Stuyvesant was reluctant; in a letter to his employers, the Dutch West India Company, he expressed fear that the Jews, "who have no other God than the Mammon" would "infect and trouble" the colony, already beset by Lutherans, Catholics, and Quakers. The Company responded, saying it had among its principal shareholders "many of the Jewish nation" and ordered that the twenty-three be allowed to remain. The Company policy was most clearly expressed in 1663, after Stuyvesant banished a Quaker from the colony: "Close your eyes . . . allow everyone to have his own belief, as long as he behaves quietly and legally, gives no offense to his neighbor and does not oppose the government."

NIEUW AMSTERDAM
op t Eylant Manhattans.

"Remnant of Israel"
THE MILL STREET SYNAGOGUE, 1730
Painted ceramic by E. H. Oppenheim, 1954
Congregation Shearith Israel

In many new places of settlement, the first institution that Jews form is a burial society, to insure that burials are carried out in accordance with Jewish law. The oldest Jewish burial ground in America, on New York's St. James Street (off Chatham Square in what is now Chinatown), dates back to 1682. Many buildings may serve as a synagogue, so the creation of a new, purpose-built structure is a statement of the congregation's faith in its permanence. Shearith Israel, America's first established congregation—and New York's only congregation between 1654 and 1825—didn't have its own synagogue building until 1730, when it built one on Mill Street in New York, now known as South William Street. The structure is long gone, but an image of it survives in a map of early New York "drawn from memory" in the early 19th century. Artifacts from this synagogue building and its successors are preserved by Congregation Shearith Israel, now housed at 70th Street and Central Park West.

I am My Dear child Your Affectionate Mother"

ABIGAILL (BILHAH) LEVY FRANKS

Portrait by Gerardus Duyckinck, ca. 1735

The American Jewish Historical Society

In the 18th century, long before survey-takers recorded our beliefs, the members
of the small Jewish community struggled to lead Jewish lives. (In 1700, there were
about 300 Jews; by 1776, the number was no higher than 2500.) Among them was
the Levy-Franks family, one of the best-known Jewish families in early New York.

Abigaill (Bilhah) Levy was born in New York in 1696, a year after her parents
arrived from London. Jacob Franks, her husband, came from London, too. Much
of what we know about Jewish life in America at the time comes from Abigaill's
extensive correspondence, most of it with her son Naphtali ("Heartsey"), who lived
his adult life in London. They led prosperous and interesting lives; their friends
were the leading families of New York: the Livingstons, the Van Cortlands, the
DeLanceys. In 1734, daughter Phila (six of their children grew to adulthood) upset
her parents by eloping with Oliver DeLancey, the son of a wealthy and powerful
Huguenot family. While Jacob eventually reconciled with Phila, Abigaill, who
through all hardships maintained a Jewish home, resolved that she would not.

Westward Expansion

MICHAEL GRATZ
Portrait by Thomas Sully, 1790s
The American Jewish Historical Society

In the mid-18th century, "B. and M. Gratz" company was one of Philadelphia's most respected mercantile firms. Its senior partner, Bernard Gratz (1738–1811), immigrated to America from Upper Silesia and originally entered the shipping business. He was eager to have his younger brother join him and, in his correspondence dated 1758, Bernard urged Michael Gratz (1740–1811) to join him in Philadelphia. "If you intend to come here and live . . . you should not bring with you any merchandise whatsoever. You will be able to earn more with your money here." This proved to be sound advice. Together, the Gratz brothers made a handsome living. Soon, Michael (the more adventurous of the two) shifted the firm's focus from shipping to trading and land speculation. B. and M. Gratz played a pivotal and pioneering role in the establishment of early trade routes from the east into western Pennsylvania, Illinois, and Kentucky. Its two principals also became leading figures in Philadelphia's Jewish life, as did several of their children, the best known of whom was Michael's daughter, Rebecca Gratz.

America's Oldest Synagogue

JESHUAT ISRAEL: THE TOURO SYNAGOGUE
Architect: Peter Harrison, 1763
Interior view, photograph by John Hopf
The Jacob Rader Marcus Center of the American Jewish Archives

The oldest surviving synagogue building in North America is the noble Jeshuat Israel, built in 1763 in Newport, widely known as the Touro Synagogue, in honor of its first leader, Isaac Touro, and his family who later supported it. The building was designed by one of colonial New England's leading architects, Peter Harrison, who also built Boston's Kings Chapel and Newport's Redwood Library. It speaks fluently the New England vernacular—and of Newport's largesse—yet it does so without compromising or unnaturally adapting the halakhic requirements of synagogue architecture. It is a great American building, a great Jewish building, and a monument to religious liberty that speaks to us still.

"That it will tend to the Improvement of many of my Brethren"
THE PINTO PRAYERBOOK
Published by Isaac Pinto, 1766
The Library of The Jewish Theological Seminary

"[Hebrew] being imperfectly understood by many, by some, not at all; it has been necessary to translate our Prayers, in the Languague of the Country wherein it hath pleased the divine Providence to appoint our Lot." With these words Isaac Pinto, one of New York's most learned Jews, justfied his pioneering translation of the Sabbath and holiday Jewish prayer book into English in 1766. An anonymous translation of the high holiday services had appeared five years earlier in New York—some believe that it, too, was by Pinto—but this volume was much more substantial. Moreover, the American translation preceded by a decade the first British translation of the Jewish prayer book. Like so many subsequent English translations produced in America through the years, the volume had both a didactic and a spiritual purpose: "that it will tend to the Improvement of many of my Brethren in their Devotion."

MORNING SERVICE

OF

KIPPUR.

On the Morning of Kippur, *before* Niſhmath col Hai, *ſay this* Petition of Ribbi Yehudah Ha Levy.

Adonai negdecha col Taavati.

O LORD, thou knoweſt my whole Deſire, although I with my Lips, do not expreſs it : I humbly requeſt thy Favour a Moment, if I *then* expire : And Oh that my Requeſt were granted : I would commend my remaining Spirit into thine Hand ; then go to Reſt, and pleaſing to me, would be my Sleep.

When I depart from thee, I find Death, while I yet live ; and if unto thee I adhere, even in my Death, I have Life. But alas ! I know not what Offering I ſhall bring, and how I ſhall worſhip, or what my Duty. Teach me, O LORD, thy Ways, and deliver me from the Bondage and Captivity of my Folly. Inſtruct me while I am able to humble myſelf *before thee*, and deſpiſe not my Affliction ; before the Day *cometh*, in which I ſhall be a Burthen unto myſelf ; and when one Part of me becometh a Weight unto the other : *Even before* I be depreſſed with old Age, and my Bones become corroded, that they be weary of ſupporting me ; and that I remove to the Place where my Fathers have gone ; and retire to Repoſe, in the Place of their Reſt. I am in this World as a Sojourn-

"The Salvation of Israel"

HAIM ISAAC CARIGAL

Samuel King, Boston, ca. 1780. Based on a crayon drawing made at Newport.
Private collection, courtesy of Yale University Art Gallery

Born in Hebron of a distinguished Portuguese-Jewish family, Haham Raphael
Haim Isaac Carigal (1732–1777) was one of the most learned Jews to visit the New
World in the 18th century. A scholar and linguist, Carigal traveled across Europe
and the Middle East in his twenties, seeking funds for the Holy Land. In 1762,
he came to Curaçao, where for two years he served as the community's acting
rabbi. After several years in Europe and Palestine, he returned to the New World
in 1772, making fundraising stops in New York and Philadelphia, before arriving
in Newport. There he befriended the distinguished churchman Ezra Stiles, who
pronounced him "learned and truly modest." The two men spoke on numerous
occasions and later corresponded—in Hebrew. Carigal delivered a sermon in
Newport's synagogue on Shavuot of 1773, which Stiles attended—it is the only
published Jewish sermon from the colonial era. Carigal reciprocated by visiting
Stiles's church. Carigal moved on to Barbados, where he died at the age of forty-
five. Stiles never forgot him and, upon becoming president of Yale, sought to have
Carigal's portrait displayed as an honor to Jews and an ornament to the University.

"Sustain'd the character of being warmly attach'd to America"

LETTER FROM LEONARD GANSEVOORT

TO MAJOR GENERAL PHILIP J. SCHUYLER

New York, June 12th, 1776

The Jacob Rader Marcus Center of the American Jewish Archives

Haym Salomon (1740–1785) is an American Jewish legend. A postage stamp hails him as a "Financial Hero of the American Revolution." A monument to Salomon graces East Wacker Drive in Chicago.

Born in Poland, Salomon settled in New York City in 1772. In 1776 he received a contract to supply American troops in New York. The following year he married Rachel Franks, whose brother Isaac was on General Washington's staff. British forces twice arrested and imprisoned Salomon. The second time, sentenced to hang, he managed to escape and flee to Philadelphia.

Salomon lost a fortune during the war, though he managed to recoup it selling bills of exchange to meet federal government expenses. He personally advanced funds to members of the Continental Congress. James Madison wrote, "I have for some time . . . been a pensioner on the favor of Haym Salomon, a Jew broker."

Salomon died in 1785, leaving a wife and four children. When one of his sons petitioned for repayment of funds his father had allegedly loaned the government, Congress refused the claim. In 1936, Congress voted to erect a monument to Salomon in Washington, D.C., but never funded it.

New York June 12th 1776.

Hon.d Sir,

I am just this Moment arrived here and have not yet heard the News.

The Bearer hereof Mr Haym Solomon tells me he has laid in Stores to go Suttler to Lake George, and has been informed that the General admits none, but such as have a certificate of their being friendly to our Measures to settle there—

I can inform the General that Mr Solomon has hitherto sustain'd the Character of being warmly attach'd to America.

I am in great haste
Dr General
Your very hum: Servant
Leonard Gansevoort

"Which gives to bigotry no sanction, to persecution no assistance"
PRESIDENT WASHINGTON ADDRESSES THE JEWS OF NEWPORT
Letter from George Washington to the Hebrew Congregation
in Newport, Rhode Island, 1790
The Library of Congress

In 1789 and 1790, the newly inaugurated first president received letters of good tidings from the Jewish congregations of Savannah, Newport, and in a joint letter, the combined congregations of Philadelphia, New York, Charleston, and Richmond. While Washington's responses are uniformly gracious, the ones to the Savannah and Newport communities show Washington's desire to reassure the recipients that their contributions have been recognized and that their concerns are his concerns. Moses Seixas's letter written on behalf of the Newport congregation is redolent with biblical and liturgical language, noting past discrimination against Jews and praising the new government for "generously affording to all liberty of conscience and immunities of citizenship," and praising God "for all of the blessings of civil and religious liberty" that Jews now enjoyed under the Constitution. Especially reassuring in Washington's reply is the reiteration of Seixas's hope—a proclamation of it, in fact—that this will be a nation "which gives to bigotry no sanction, to persecution no assistance." To American Jews, who in 1790 would have been happy with mere toleration, Washington's statements took on near biblical stature.

government of the United States, which gives to bigotry no sanction, to persecution no assistance, requires only that they who live under its protec should demean themselves as good citizens, in giving it on all occasions their effectual support.

It would be inconsistent with the frankness of my character not to avow that I am pleased w your favorable opinion of my administration, an fervent wishes for my felicity.

May the children of the Stock of Abraham who dwell in this land, continue to merit and enjoy the good will of the other inhabitants, while every one shall sit in safety under his own vine and

"I am a Jew . . . I am a Republican . . . But I am poor"
GOBLET DEDICATED TO BENJAMIN NONES
Philadelphia, 1797
Photograph by Henri Silberman
Collection of Deanne and Arnold Kaplan

Benjamin Nones earned a citation for bravery in the American Revolution. After the war, as a notary public and government interpreter in Philadelphia, he barely earned enough to feed his fourteen children. Nones led the first organized Jewish charity in Philadelphia, was president of Congregation Mikveh Israel, and was active as an anti-slavery advocate.

In the 1790s, the Federalist Party represented the interests of merchants and financial speculators, while Jeffersonian Republicans courted small business owners, farmers, artisans and laborers. Many Jews in the young nation considered the Jeffersonian Republicans more favorable to religious liberty. In August 1800, Benjamin Nones became a Federalist target when he participated in a Republican convention in Philadelphia. The city's leading Federalist newspaper, the *Gazette*, published a scurrilous account of the meeting, calling all who attended "the filth of society," singling out "Citizen N---- . . . a Jew, a Republican, and poor."

The *Gazette* refused to print Nones's response, even as a paid article. The *Aurora*, the city's Jeffersonian newspaper, happily printed it. Although hot with indignation, Nones's reply conveys a dignity that speaks to us still. "I am a Jew, and if for no other reason, for that reason am I a republican," he wrote.

Humbly Presented To
the right honourable
Benjamin Nones
for his dedicated service
to the
Jewish Community
at
Philadelphia

From Cabin Boy to Commodore

URIAH PHILLIPS LEVY

Anonymous, oil on canvas, ca. 1815

The American Jewish Historical Society

In 1802, at age ten, Uriah P. Levy ran away to sea, becoming a cabin boy on a merchant vessel. According to legend, he returned home at age twelve to become bar mitzvah, after which he returned to sea, this time with his parents' blessing. By age 19, he captained his own merchant ship and, a patriot, joined the United States Navy during the War of 1812.

Fiercely proud of his Judaism, Levy was court martialed six times during his naval career for conflicts with fellow officers over antisemitic slights. Three times, his convictions were overturned. The Navy involuntarily retired Levy, but brought him back in 1857 to serve as commodore of the Mediterranean Fleet, fighting pirates off the North African coast.

Levy is best known for having rescued and restored Thomas Jefferson's beloved home, Monticello. Spurred on by the Marquis de Lafayette, Levy discovered that after Jefferson's death Monticello had fallen to ruins. A champion of religious liberty, Jefferson was Levy's idol. He purchased Jefferson's estate in 1834 and began restoring its buildings, lands and furnishings to their original condition. Uriah's nephew Jefferson Monroe Levy eventually sold the estate to a non-profit foundation in 1923.

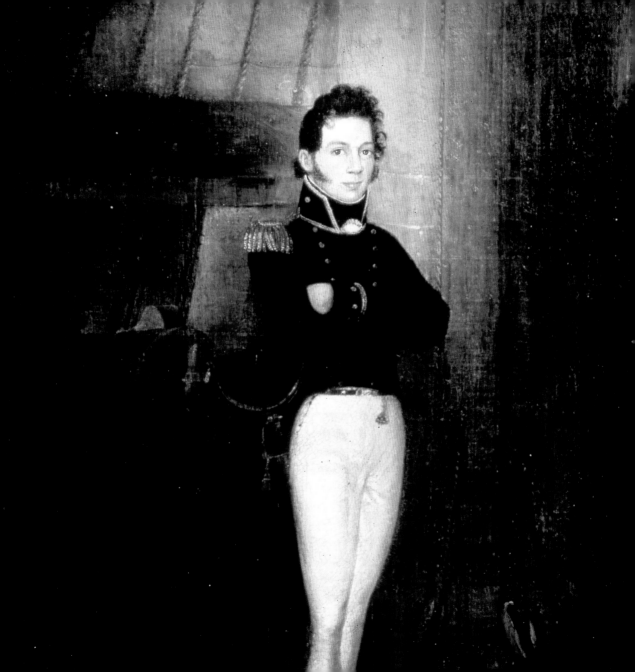

*"What the dust of antiquity may have tarnished,
an enlightened reader may restore to brightness."*

SILHOUETTE OF ISAAC HARBY

Artist unknown

The Jacob Rader Marcus Center of the American Jewish Archives

Born and raised in Charleston, South Carolina during a period of pronounced intellectual efflorescence, Isaac Harby (1788–1828) aspired to make his living by means of his pen. While he was still in his teens, Harby published *The Quiver* (1807), probably the first literary journal in this country published by a Jew. He went on to publish plays, poetry, and prose while he served as the editor of several Charleston newspapers. But it was his school for children, "Harby's Academy," that would become his chief source of income over the course of his short lifetime.

Harby ran for public office in 1822. A fellow Charlestonian wrote that Harby "not only exercises an influence with his co-religionists, but [also] in no inconsiderable degree in the state where he resides."

In 1824, Harby was one of the forty-seven Jews of Charleston who petitioned the board of Congregation Beth Elohim to institute some liturgical reforms. When this petition was rejected, Harby and a dozen or so individuals established the Reformed Society of Israelites in 1825—the first organized expression of Jewish religious reform in North America. "Our desire" Harby wrote, "is to yield everything to the feelings of the truly pious Israelite; to take away everything that might excite the disgust of the well-informed Israelite . . . . What the dust of antiquity may have tarnished, an enlightened reader may restore to brightness."

"For altho' we are free by the law, we are not so in practice"
THOMAS JEFFERSON TO MORDECAI MANUEL NOAH
Monticello, May 20, 1810
Yeshiva University Museum

In 1818, Mordecai M. Noah sent former president Thomas Jefferson a speech he delivered at the consecration of the new home of Congregation Shearith Israel in New York. In the letter shown at right, Jefferson thanked Noah for teaching him some new facts about Jewish history, and for reminding him of the long history of intolerance suffered by "your sect." Jefferson assured Noah, "Our laws have applied the only antidote to this vice, protecting our religious, as they do our civil rights, by putting all on an equal footing." However, Jefferson noted with some realism, "More remains to be done, for altho' we are free by the law, we are not so in practice."

Two years later Jefferson wrote similarly to Jacob de la Motta of Savannah that he looked forward to seeing American Jews "taking their seats on the benches of science . . . [and] at the board of government." He shared his prescription for securing religious pluralism: "The maxim of civil government being reversed in that of religion, where its true form is, divided we stand, united we fall."

Sir   Monticello. May 28. 18.

I thank you for the Discourse on the consecration of the Synagogue
in your city, with which you have been pleased to favor me. I have
read it with pleasure and instruction, having learnt from it some
valuable facts in Jewish history which I did not know before. your
sect has furnished a remarkable proof of the universal spirit of religious insole-
-rance, inherent in every sect, disclaimed by all while feeble, and
practised by all when in power. our laws have applied the only anti-
-dote to this vice, protecting our religious, as they do our civil rights
by putting all on an equal footing. but more remains to be done.
for altho' we are free by the law, we are not so in practice. public opi-
-nion erects itself into an Inquisition, and exercises it's office with
as much fanaticism as fans the flames of an Auto da fé. the prejudice
still scowling on your section of our religion, altho' the elder one, cannot
be unfelt by yourselves. it is to be hoped that individual dispositions will
at length mould themselves to the model of the law, and consider the moral
basis on which all our religions rest, as the rallying point which unites
them in a common interest; while the peculiar dogmas branching from it
are the exclusive concern of the respective sects embracing them, and no
rightful subject of notice to any other. public opinion needs reformation on
this point, which would have the further happy effect of doing away the
hypocritical maxim of "intus ut lubet, foris ut moris." nothing I think

"Desirous of rendering themselves useful to their indigent sisters of the house of Israel"

REBECCA GRATZ

Collotype from *The Jewish Cemetery, Ninth and Spruce Streets*, Philadelphia, 1906
The Library of The Jewish Theological Seminary

These words, from the constitution of Philadelphia's Female Hebrew Benevolent Society, encapsulate the lifework of its founder Rebecca Gratz. Eager to render herself useful to all indigent, to widows and orphans, Christians and Jews, Gratz established an array of nonsectarian and Jewish women's organizations. Deeply concerned for the future of American Judaism which would come in time to rest on the immigrant children pouring into the nation's seaports, she created the Hebrew Sunday School (1838) and pioneered a new role for America's Jewish women, that of religious educator. Like so many of the institutions which she led throughout her life, it flourished long beyond her death. The legend that she was the model for Rebecca of York, who in Sir Walter Scott's *Ivanhoe* refused to marry out of her faith, persists. Nevertheless, Gratz's true legacy rests upon her vision of what America's Jewish women could and must do to sustain their civic and Jewish communities.

"This synagogue is our Temple, this city our Jerusalem"
KAHAL KADOSH BETH ELOHIM, CHARLESTON, SOUTH CAROLINA
Lithograph by Solomon N. Carvalho, drawn from memory
after fire destroyed the first synagogue structure
The American Jewish Historical Society

The fourth oldest synagogue in the United States, Charleston's Kahal Kadosh Beth Elohim was formally organized in 1749. When the congregation dedicated its permanent home—a "spacious and elegant" structure—on Hasell Street, in 1794, George Washington was president. By 1810, there were nearly seven hundred Jews in Charleston, making KKBE the largest synagogue in the United States.

In 1824, forty-seven Israelites of Charleston petitioned the board of KKBE to institute some liturgical reforms. The board declined the suggestion, and the complainants organized a guild of like-minded progressives: The Reformed Society of Israelites—the first organized attempt to reform Judaism in the United States. This group published its own Reform prayer service, the first such in America.

A fire razed the synagogue in 1838. KKBE's board reconciled with the members of the RSI and a handsome new temple was erected on the very same foundation in 1841. At the dedication ceremony, KKBE's rabbi, the Reverend Gustavus Poznanski, inspired his audience of Jews and non-Jews with his now famous declaration: "This synagogue is our *temple*, this city our *Jerusalem*, this happy land our *Palestine*, and as our fathers defended with their lives *that* temple, *that* city and *that* land, so will their sons defend *this* temple, *this* city, and *this* land . . ."

"What did the wise King Solomon say?"

CATECHISM BY SOLOMON ETTING

Baltimore, 1824

The Library of The Jewish Theological Seminary

When the Jewish population spread across settled America numbered but a few thousand, one of the greatest exigencies facing Jewish families was how to educate their children in the faith. For those who did not know Hebrew well enough to teach it to their children, the problem was compounded, since there were no available English texts that covered the subject. Some families used Christian books, presumably passing over the sentences that were of concern only to Christians. Others wrote out catechisms, giving an overview of the principles of Jewish faith and practice, like this one made by Solomon Etting for his grandchildren.

"Catechesis" was the means by which a proselyte was prepared for admission to a faith. It became an important feature of Christian education, especially in Lutheran Protestantism. Though known in the Jewish world at least since the late 16th century, traditional Jewish education eschewed such works, since the entire Torah was used in basic teaching. But with the rise of the Jewish Enlightenment came secularized instruction books, some in Hebrew, but mostly in German. (An early modern example was published in Judeo-Spanish, in Amsterdam, in 1729.) Etting's catechism shown here includes a comprehensive series of questions and answers, Maimonides's "Thirteen Principles of Faith," and the Decalogue.

Q. What ought we to do, since God is so great, and so good.?

A. We should fear him, and love him and obey him.

Q. What is it to obey God.?

A. Endeavouring to do what He has commanded, and taking care not to do what he has forbidden.

Q. What is it to sin against God.?

A. To sin against God is, to do any thing that God forbids, or not to do what God commands.

Q. What did the wise King Solomon say about fearing and obeying God.?

A. "Fear God and keep his Commandmen

"An asylum for the oppressed"

MORDECAI MANUEL NOAH

Stipple engraving by Gimbrede after J. R. Smith

from *Travels in England, France, Spain, and the Barbary States*, 1819

The Library of the Jewish Theological Seminary

Mordecai Manuel Noah (1785–1851) was a writer and playwright, politician and patriot, whose father had served with the Pennsylvania militia during the Revolution. As a writer in Charleston, he was a force behind opinion supporting the War of 1812. He was the first Jew in America to lead a publicly political life, complete with its inevitable controversies. In 1819, President James Madison appointed him Consul-General in Tunis, a tenure made memorable for his involvement with the rescue of several American seamen who were held as slaves in the Barbary states.

His most extraordinary project, however, was "Ararat," a proposed American "city of refuge" for the Jews, an "asylum for the oppressed" on Grand Island in the St. Lawrence River, at the mouth of the Erie Canal near Buffalo, New York. After the plan failed, he became a vigorous supporter of Jewish settlement in Palestine.

"On the same footing as other good citizens"
PROCEEDINGS . . . ON WHAT IS COMMONLY CALLED THE JEW BILL
Baltimore, 1819
The American Jewish Historical Society

Maryland's state constitution, ratified in 1776, contained the provision that "all persons professing the Christian religion are equally entitled to protection in their religious liberty" and that any person elected or appointed to public office will declare "belief in the Christian religion." In 1797, Solomon Etting, a Jewish resident of Baltimore, petitioned the Maryland Assembly for followers of other faiths to be granted the same rights. The matter, which had become known as "The Jew Bill," lapsed in 1804, but fourteen years later, in 1818, found a champion in one Thomas Kennedy, a member of the House of Delegates, who wrote in one of his speeches:

> Lay old superstition low
> Let the oppressed people go,
> To the Bill none say no,
> Aye! unanimously.

The bill passed finally in 1825—by one vote—and became law in 1826. Later that year, Solomon Etting was elected to the Baltimore City Council; he later became its president.

SKETCH

OF

PROCEEDINGS IN THE

Legislature of Maryland,

DECEMBER SESSION, 1818,

ON WHAT IS COMMONLY CALLED

The Jew Bill;

CONTAINING

THE REPORT OF THE COMMITTEE

APPOINTED BY THE HOUSE OF DELEGATES

"To consider the justice and expediency of extending to those persons professing the Jewish Religion, the same privileges that are enjoyed by Christians:"

TOGETHER WITH

The Bill reported by the Committee,

AND

THE SPEECHES

OF

THOMAS KENNEDY, Esq. OF WASHINGTON COUNTY,

AND

H. M. BRACKENRIDGE, Esq. OF BALTIMORE CITY.

"He who granteth salvation unto kings"

THE FORM OF DAILY PRAYERS ACCORDING TO THE CUSTOM
OF THE SPANISH AND PORTUGUESE JEWS
Printed by Solomon Henry Jackson, New York, 1826
The American Jewish Historical Society

The era that saw the publication of this first complete, American-produced, Hebrew-English prayerbook was a key period in the development of American Judaism. Dispersed and often without community leaders, many of the 3,000–6,000 American Jews had fallen into laxity. They were beset by Protestant missionary organizations such as the American Society for Meliorating the Condition of the Jews and its newspaper, *Israel's Advocate*. Into this fray jumped the printer S. H. Jackson, who responded with *The Jew*, the first American Jewish periodical, which vowed to take "full advantages of the opportunities afforded a Jewish press in an open society." Jackson was a vigorous polemicist, who would go so far as to attack the very legitimacy of Christianity.

Jackson's 1826 prayerbook contains an interesting adaptation of the prayer *Ha-noten teshuah*, "He who granteth salvation unto kings," in which the offices of American government are recognized and differentiated between recess and sitting sessions. The editor of the Hebrew text was Eleazar Samuel Lazarus, a president of New York's Shearith Israel, the first American expert on Jewish liturgy, and, notably, the grandfather of Emma Lazarus.

הַנּוֹתֵן תְּשׁוּעָה לַמְּלָכִים ‏ · וּמֶמְשָׁלָה לַנְּסִיכִים · וּמַלְכוּתוֹ מַלְכוּת
כָּל־עוֹלָמִים : הַפּוֹצֶה אֶת דָּוִד עַבְדּוֹ · מֵחֶרֶב רָעָה :
הַנּוֹתֵן בַּיָּם דָּרֶךְ · וּבְמַיִם עַזִּים נְתִיבָה : הוּא יְבָרֵךְ · וְיִשְׁמֹר ·
וְיִנְצֹר · וְיַעֲזֹר · וִירוֹמֵם · וְיִגְדַּל · וְיִנַשֵּׂא לְמַעְלָה לְמָעְלָה :

During the Sitting of Congress.

The President and Vice-president of the Union, the Senate and House of Representatives of the United States of America in Congress assembled : the Governor and Lieutenant Governor and people of this state, represented in Senate and Assembly, and the Magistrates of this city.

During the Recess.

The President and Vice-president of the United States of America. The Governor and Lieutenant Governor and people of this State, represented in Senate and Assembly. The Magistrates of this city.

מֶלֶךְ מַלְכֵי הַמְּלָכִים בְּרַחֲמָיו · יִשְׁמְרֵם · וִיחַיֵּים · וּמִכָּל־
צָרָה וָנֶזֶק יַצִּילֵם : מֶלֶךְ מַלְכֵי הַמְּלָכִים
בְּרַחֲמָיו · יָרוּם וְיַגְבִּיהַּ כּוֹכַב מַעֲרַכְתָּם · וְיַאֲרִיכוּ יָמִים עַל
מֶמְשַׁלְתָּם : מֶלֶךְ מַלְכֵי הַמְּלָכִים בְּרַחֲמָיו · יִתֵּן בְּלִבָּם וּבְלֵב כָּל־

"A Western sun would gild their future day"

PENINA MOÏSE

Oil on canvas, attributed to Theodore Sidney Moïse, ca. 1840
Collection of Anita Moïse Rosefield Rosenberg
Special Collections, College of Charleston Library

Born in 1797, Penina Moïse left her mark as America's first female Jewish poet and hymnist. When Penina was twelve, her father died, leaving his Charleston, South Carolina, family impoverished. Penina's formal education ended, but legend claims that she continued reading by moonlight. Her book of Reform hymns became the first Jewish hymnal published in English on American soil. Moïse won national acclaim in 1833 for *Fancy's Sketch Book*, a collection of her poems. Her prodigious output of stories, poems, and essays appeared in national magazines and newspapers for six decades.

Moïse prefigured the writings of Emma Lazarus in "To Persecuted Foreigners," which invited Europe's oppressed Jews to "come to the homes and bosoms of the free," to "Plenty's flowering bed," where "a Western Sun would gild their future day." A proto-Zionist, Moïse hoped for a day when "Captive Judah" would be "ingathered" in Palestine, the "Land that first heard the voice of God!"

After the Civil War, suffering from near-total blindness, neuralgia, and insomnia, Moïse nonetheless opened a private school where she taught, from memory, literature she memorized while sighted. She died in 1880.

"Agitate, agitate"

ERNESTINE LOUISE ROSE

Photograph, c. 1850

Schlesinger Library, Radcliffe Institute, Harvard University

Ernestine Rose arrived in New York harbor in 1836 ready for a fight. She had already rebelled against the wishes of her Polish rabbi father that she accept a traditional arranged marriage. She had become a popular speaker among the followers of English social reformer Robert Owen. But it was in America that she would find her full voice as a creator and leader of the woman's rights movement.

She learned, soon after her arrival, that a bill proposed to the New York legis–lature would grant married women the right to control their own property and earnings. Rose drew up a petition and worked for five months to gain supporters, submitting the first petition (bearing five signatures) on the subject. Passage of New York's Married Women's Property Act was secured in 1848.

Rose traveled tirelessly, reaching twenty-three states, to speak out for women's rights, against slavery, and, eventually, for the rights of freed slaves. She addressed every woman's rights convention between 1850 and 1869. Suffrage leader Susan B. Anthony celebrated Rose's inspiration to the movement, describing her as the "most eloquent . . . speaker on our platform," keeping her portrait over her desk, and adapting her slogan, "Agitate, agitate."

The Beginnings of American Jewish Investment Banking

AUGUST BELMONT

Daguerreotype, late 1840s

The Library of Congress

The Jewish tradition in banking stemmed from necessity and opportunity in medieval Europe. The necessity came from restrictions on many forms of work; the opportunity came from restrictions on Christian involvement with usury. Jewish banking in America got off to a slow start, at first through small-scale financiers such as Haym Salomon, who were key to the success of the Revolution. The banking empire created in Europe by Mayer Amschel Rothschild began in the 1760s and it wasn't until Rothschild's agent August Belmont came to New York in 1837 that Jews became involved formally with American banking on a large scale. Belmont (né Schoenberg), who was born in Prussia in 1816, was on his way to Cuba when the 1837 Panic hit, enabling him to set up his own investment bank, A. Belmont & Co., and buy up vast properties at a great discount. His success was enormous and he became a major figure on the American scene, marrying the daughter of Commodore Perry, becoming chairman of the Democratic Party, and co-founding the Jockey Club (he is the namesake of the Belmont Stakes race). More long-lived Jewish banking houses were founded during and after the Civil War: J. & W. Seligman & Co.; Kuhn, Loeb & Co.; Lehman Brothers; Goldman, Sachs & Co.; James Speyer & Co.; and Lazard Frères.

The Damascus Blood Libel

PERSECUTION OF THE JEWS IN THE EAST

Philadelphia, 1840

The American Jewish Historical Society

The American Jewish community's involvement with the nation's foreign policy had one of its earliest—and most controversial—manifestations in 1840, the year of the infamous Damascus Blood Libel, when the Jewish community of Syria was accused of kidnapping and killing a Capuchin Friar and his young Muslim servant in order to use their blood in the making of Passover matzoh. Under torture, two witnesses told their interrogators that local Jews were responsible. Sixty-three Jewish children were seized so that the hiding place of the blood would be revealed.

The case led to international outrage, especially in England and France, but also in America. Secretary of State John Forsythe expressed President Martin Van Buren's "surprise and pain" at the charges, and urged "that justice and humanity may be extended to those persecuted people." Mobilized by Philadelphia Jewish leader Isaac Leeser, the small American Jewish community, then about 15,000, launched a public protest and petition on behalf of the Damascus Jews, adding American Jewry's voice to that of Jewish communities throughout the world.

PERSECUTION

OF

THE JEWS IN THE EAST.

CONTAINING THE

PROCEEDINGS OF A MEETING

HELD AT

THE SYNAGOGUE MIKVEH ISRAEL, PHILADELPHIA,

ON THURSDAY EVENING, THE 28th OF AB, 5600.

CORRESPONDING WITH

THE 27th OF AUGUST, 1840.

First Jewish-American Senator

DAVID LEVY YULEE

Photograph, ca. 1850

National Archives and Records Administration

David Levy was born on St. Thomas to Moses Elias Levy, a Moroccan Jew who made a fortune in Caribbean sugar planting. Moses divorced and moved with David to 50,000 acres near Jacksonville, where the elder Levy hoped—in vain—to establish a "New Jerusalem" for Jewish settlers. Despite the disappointment of his father's failed plan, David developed a taste for public administration and big projects. In 1841, David Levy served in the Florida territorial legislature and, as a delegate to Congress representing the Florida Territory, advocated for statehood. When Florida joined the Union in 1845, Florida's legislature elected Levy to the Senate, making him the first Jew to serve there.

In 1846, David Levy married into great wealth and was said to have converted to Christianity, though there is no evidence that he did more than change his name to Yulee. Antisemitism dogged his entire political career. Defeated for reelection in 1850, Yulee regained his Senate seat in 1854 and served until the Civil War.

After the war and a term in a Federal prison for disloyalty, Yulee resumed his pre-war career as a developer, marshaling state, federal, and private funds to build Florida's first railroad. It stretched across north central Florida from the Atlantic to the Gulf Coast, opening the region to settlement and commerce. Today, Yulee is remembered as the "Father of Florida Railroads."

"*Diffusion of knowledge on Jewish literature and religion*"

ISAAC LEESER AND THE OCCIDENT

Philadelphia, 1843

The American Jewish Historical Society

In April 1843, there appeared for the first time a periodical called *The Occident* that addressed the news and concerns of America's growing Jewish population. Its publisher was a young Philadelphian named Isaac Leeser and for twenty-five years, the paper created a wonderfully rich portrait of Jewish life in America and abroad. Born in Westphalia in 1806, Leeser came to Richmond, Virginia, at the age of eighteen, a young man with deep intellectual and religious leanings. After publishing a widely read article in defense of Judaism, he was invited to take the pulpit of Philadelphia's Sephardic synagogue, Mikveh Israel, in 1829. For the next forty years he played a great public role in American Jewish life. He wrote, translated, and published major and minor Jewish texts and writings for every purpose, from Hebrew readers and catechisms for children to an English translation of the Bible from Hebrew. He was also a key organizer and representative of Jewish interests to political leaders of the day.

PROSPECTUS

FOR ISSUING A SEMI-MONTHLY MAGAZINE, TO BE CALLED

THE OCCIDENT,

AND

American Jewish Advocate,

A PERIODICAL DEVOTED TO THE DIFFUSION OF KNOWLEDGE ON JEWISH LITERATURE AND RELIGION,

TO BE PUBLISHED IN PHILADELPHIA, BY AND UNDER THE EDITORIAL SUPERVISION OF

ISAAC LEESER,

AIDED BY SEVERAL CORRESPONDENTS AT HOME AND ABROAD.

THE subscriber has been frequently urged to undertake a periodical publication, calculated for the diffusion of Jewish knowledge, properly so called; but he has always felt that, besides the task being too heavy for his individual labour, the support likely to be given to the undertaking would cause it to result in a mercantile loss which his limited means will not permit him to risk. But the calls have been lately so frequent, that he has resolved, at all events, to try whether a sufficient number of subscribers, say from eight hundred to one thousand, might not be obtained, in which case immediate preparations will be made to procure the necessary literary assistance, together with all foreign periodicals and publications having any bearing upon our religion, as they issue from the press. He would merely remark that, even to his own surprise, the number of Jewish periodicals on the continent of Europe is quite large, and that, though he himself has as yet seen but few, they can still be readily procured through agents at London, Paris, and Antwerp, if the use to be made of them would warrant him to defray the considerable outlay which the purchase of them would necessarily require. In addition to the continental journals two have been commenced during the current year at London, both of which have already diffused much interesting information.

The editor's sentiments he conceives to be sufficiently well known to preclude the necessity of detailing them upon the present occasion; and he trusts that Israelites of every shade of opinion will not hesitate, from any prejudice which his oft expressed opinions may have called forth, to patronise the undertaking. And the Christian public are assured that, though he may occasionally have to examine the difference between our respective creeds, every discussion shall be conducted with fairness and candour, and that a temperate reply shall always find a ready admission into his pages.

The plan which the editor proposes to himself is, to give all current news, of whatever kind, relating to Jews; reviews of new works; extracts from old books; and original articles on scientific and religious subjects, together with poetry calculated to awaken pious feelings, and original and translated sermons by different Jewish preachers. A department will also be devoted to advertisements.

The reason which has at length induced him to venture before the public with the present plan is, that he believes much good may result from a work of the kind proposed, carefully and judiciously conducted; and as he has some experience in editorial matters of this nature, he conceives that he is not too presumptuous to offer

"Promoting their highest interests and those of humanity"

B'NAI B'RITH MANUAL, 1926

Pen and ink drawing by Ephraim Moses Lilien

Private Collection

On October 13, 1843, twelve men sat together in a cafe on New York's Lower East Side. United in their interest to organize and provide social services to their co-religionists and others, they founded what would become the world's oldest Jewish service organization: B'nai B'rith.

According to its founders, this new organization would seek to unite Jews "in the work of promoting their highest interests and those of humanity; of developing and elevating the mental and moral character of the people of our faith; of inculcating the purest principles of philanthropy, honor, and patriotism; of supporting science and art; alleviating the wants of the poor and needy; visiting and attending the sick; coming to the rescue of victims of persecution; providing for, protecting, and assisting the widow and orphan on the broadest principles of humanity."

Over the years, B'nai B'rith grew steadily into an international association of local affiliates, which today claims a membership of 180,000, who reside in more than fifty countries. American Jewry and Jews throughout the world have benefitted from B'nai B'rith hospitals, orphanages, senior housing communities, disaster relief campaigns, libraries, anti-hatred programs, and countless communal initiatives that serve the Jewish and general communities alike.

B'nai B'rith
Manual

"On to America!"

AUF NACH AMERIKA

Österreichisches Centralorgan für Glaubensfreiheit, Vienna, 1848

Private collection

"On to America!"—so proclaimed the Jewish writer Leopold Kompert as the liberal European revolutions of 1848 degenerated into anti-Jewish riots. Kompert's articles, published in a widely-read Viennese Jewish periodical, called upon Jews to take the "road to liberty" and emigrate. Thousands of central European Jews by then had already migrated to America, but in the years that followed tens of thousands more followed suit, including the editor of that Viennese periodical, Isidor Busch, and Adolf Brandeis, whose son, Louis, would become the first Jewish Supreme Court justice. "A person who is capable of becoming free, commits the greatest wrong if he does not," Kompert declared. "Whoever seizes the initiative in becoming free serves and carries the torch for thousands of Jews!"

Auf, nach Amerika.

Die Ernte ist vergangen, der Sommer ist dahin;
und uns ist keine Hilfe gekommen.
Jeremias VIII. 20.

Uns ist keine Hilfe gekommen! Die Sonne der Freiheit ist für das Vaterland aufgegangen, für uns nur als blutiges Nordlicht; die Lerchen der Erlösung schmettern in freier Luft; für uns sind es nur kreischende Möven des Sturmes. Schamröthe und bebender Zorn überwältigen uns, denken wir an das Fürchterliche, an das Haarsträubende, was uns die letzten Wochen angethan! Weil knechtische Horden und krämerische Häringsseelen den Geist der Freiheit nicht verstanden und verstehen, müssen wir es büßen. Da sei Gott dafür, daß wir unser Haupt für jeden Keulschlag bereit halten, daß unser Auge vor jedem Blitze unserer großen und kleinen Tyrannen erzittere! Dahin ist es gekommen, daß in der Stunde, wo uns die Freiheit ins Land gebracht, kein anderer Wunsch in uns ist, als: dieser — Freiheit aus dem Wege zu gehen!

Sie wollen es nicht anders und so sei es! Nicht das erste Mal ist es, daß wir ihrem Willen nachgeben. Seit Jahrhunderten ist unsere Geschichte nichts Anderes, als ein stummes Bejahen auf jede uns aufgelegte Qual, auf jede Folter und Beschränkung! Aber immer bejahen, immer den Kopf neigen? Den Nacken krumm behalten und die Hände wie zum Gebete gefaltet? Wir wollen einmal mit Erlaubniß des »souveränen Volkes« die Geduld verlieren, wir wollen einmal verneinen — und dann aus dem Wege gehen!

Nach Amerika nämlich! Erkennet, die ihr das Wesen der Geschichte nicht verstehet, darin ihren Fingerzeig, daß vor vier Jahrhunderten eben als man die Juden am heftigsten verfolgte, ein Genuese in seinem heißen Gehirne den Schöpfergedanken einer neuen Welt ausbecken mußte, daß es ihm nicht Ruhe gönnte, bis eine spanische Königin, deren Gemal die finstere Gestalt eines Torquemada und seiner mit dem Blute tausender unserer Brüder befleckten Dominikaner heraufbeschworen, bis, sagen wir, Isabella von Spanien ihrem Admiral erlaubte, Amerika zu entdecken. Nach demselben Amerika geht nun unsere Sehnsucht, dahin sollet ihr ziehen! »Auf, nach Amerika!«

Wir kennen alle eure Einwände, alle eure Erwiederungen! Aber nur der Kleingläubige und Schwachmüthige werden sie thun, der Muthige, der Gefaßte nicht! Und keinen anderen Rath könnt ihr uns geben, fragen jene, als den Wanderstab zu ergreifen und mit Weib und Kind das ferne, fremde Land aufsuchen? Die Scholle, die uns geboren, genährt, darin wir unsere Todten begraben, sollen wir verlassen? Mich dünkt, schon etwas von den Fleischtöpfen Ägyptens zu hören, von den Goldbrühen und Saftbraten den Brodem einzuathmen — aber ich sehe auch die Leute, die das Feuer schüren, und aus den Flammen des Hasses, des Vorurtheils und der Beschränktheit sein tägliches Gericht holen, bei Gott, wem darnach der Gaumen steht, der bleibe und füttere sich!«

Zwei Sätze sind es, die in dieser Zeit uns als Ausgangspuncte dienen können. Den einen sagt Moses: »Stehet fest und still;« den andern Jeremias: »Die Ernte ist vergangen und der Sommer ist dahin und für uns ist keine Hilfe gekommen.« Welchem Satze gebt ihr dem Vorzug? Stillstehen und harren, geduldig harren, bis alle uns widerstehenden Interessen versöhnt und gesühnt, bis der Geist der Humanität Sieger geworden? oder, da »uns keine Hilfe gekommen« sie uns aufsuchen — und nach Amerika ziehen?

Mich dünkt, die beiden Sätze lassen sich gar wohl vereinigen! Mögen diejenigen in unserem Vaterlande, die »fest, still stehen« wollen, diesen Standpunct in den Sand der Zukunft gründen! Wir wollen sie daran nicht hindern, wir wollen

"A temple for all the world to see"

TEMPLE EMANU-EL

San Francisco, after 1866

The Library of Congress

In September 1849, slightly more than a year after news of the California gold strike swept across the country, thirty of San Francisco's first Jews celebrated Rosh Hashanah for the first time—in a tent. A year and a half later, just in time for Passover, over one hundred "Israelites of San Francisco" gathered to form a permanent congregation and to elect officers. By the time they were done meeting, two congregations had been founded: Emanu-El for the German Jews and Sherith Israel for the Polish ones. Each set down a cornerstone two weeks apart in 1854. By 1860, San Francisco boasted four congregations and five thousand Jews. "Almost all of them are doing well," the Jewish traveler I. J. Benjamin reported with some exaggeration, "a large part of the wealth of California is in their hands." As if to prove this, Congregation Emanu-El, now firmly Reform, consecrated in 1866, "the most impressive building on the Pacific Coast"—a cathedral-like synagogue on Sutter Street, designed by the prominent British architect William Patton, with huge Stars of David, massive Tablets of the Law, and two gold-tipped spires, 165 feet high. It was "a temple for all the world to see," and it sat 1200 people. Within a decade, San Francisco would boast a Jewish community of over 15,000 Jews, second in size only to New York.

"Does Macy's tell Gimbel's? Well, Bloomingdale's does."
LEVI STRAUSS ADVERTISEMENT
San Francisco, 1870s
Collection of Deanne and Arnold Kaplan

Twenty-four-year-old Levi Strauss came to San Francisco in 1853 to open a branch of his brother's New York dry goods store. Over the next twenty years, the business flourished and Strauss took his place among the prominent citizens of the burgeoning city. One of his wholesale customers was a Reno, Nevada, tailor from Latvia, Jacob Davis, who had among his clients a man for whom he made special hard-wearing trousers, riveted at the stress points. The trousers became much in demand and Davis had a mind to produce them in quantity, but lacked the capital. For this he turned to Levi Strauss and on May 20, 1873, the two men filed a patent for the manufacture of riveted clothing made of heavy, indigo-dyed fabric. Strauss was one of many immigrant Jews involved with the manufacturing and sales of apparel, occupations that had been common among Old World Jews. But America offered limitless possibilities. Jews did not invent the department store, but they founded or developed many of the most enduring ones: Macy's, Sears Roebuck, Lazarus, Kaufman's, Gimbel's, G. Fox, Bloomingdale's, B. Altman & Co., Abraham & Straus, Bergdorf Goodman, Neiman Marcus, I. Magnin, May Co.—all of them household names for over a century.

"Minhag Amerika"

ISAAC MAYER WISE
Probably Cincinnati, late 1880s
The Jacob Rader Marcus Center of the American Jewish Archives

On the fiftieth anniversary of his rabbinic career, Isaac Mayer Wise (1819–1900) reminisced about the execrable quality of life in his native Bohemia and how he had purchased a set of journals that described the character of life in the United States of America. "That literature made of me a naturalized American in the interior of Bohemia," he said. Thus began Wise's love affair with America to which, in 1846, the young rabbi brought his family. From that time forward, he dedicated himself to the upbuilding of an American Judaism. His rabbinic career began in Albany, where Wise built his reputation as a dynamic speaker and religious reformer—not without controversy. In 1854, he became rabbi at B'nai Jeshurun in Cincinnati, which had become a principal destination for Germans and German Jews.

   With extraordinary charisma and vigor, Wise became American Judaism's institution builder par excellence. Among his many achievements, Wise founded the first national union of American synagogues (Union of American Hebrew Congregations); the nation's oldest rabbinical seminary (Hebrew Union College), and the first national rabbinical association (Central Conference of American Rabbis). This institutional pattern would ultimately be adopted by many other segments of the Jewish community, and thus Wise has been justifiably crowned the "Architect of American Judaism."

First Original Hebrew Book in America

AVNE YEHOSHUA

New York, 1860

The American Jewish Historical Society

"Oh that the munificent among our nation will purchase this book from me; multiple benefits will come to you from doing so!" The 1860 work that included this entreaty, *Avne Yehoshua* ("the Stones of Joshua"), was no ordinary volume. It was, in fact, the first original Hebrew book to be published in America, a homiletical commentary on the *Ethics of the Fathers*. Its author, Joshua Falk, earned his living as a ritual slaughterer, but he aspired to scholarship, promising a large second book (to be called "The Wall of Joshua") if his first were successful. Hebrew type had appeared before in American books—in printed Bibles, prayer books, text books, as well as in the journal *The Occident*—but *Avne Yehoshua*, unlike those books, anticipated the emergence of creative Hebrew scholarship on these shores. "I give thanks that it fell in my lot to serve as the typesetter for this learned work, the first of its kind in America," Naftali the son of Kasriel Samuel, wrote on its final page. While Falk died in Iowa in 1864, his sequel unpublished, America did in the 20th century become a center of Jewish scholarship.

ספר

אבני יהושע

על פרקי אבות

מדובר בו נכבדות הנותן אמרי ספר ללמד בני יהודה אמונות אמתיות
להבין סמוכות באמרות טהורות יגלה מהתנאים החתעלומות, להשביע
לקוראיו שובע שמחות חקירות ממתקים אמרות מנופת מתוקים
זהב מליצות התנאים מריקים, מסביר מועצות פסוקי
תורה והנביאים הרמים, ובזה החיבר אני מראה אתכם
רק נסיון ממלאכתי כאשר יבואר בהקדמה, אמנם
אם ספרי ימצא חן בעיניכם ותקנו ממני
בכסף מלא אם ירצה השם אדפיס ספר
השני אשר ידעתי נאמנה שכל אחד
יקבל נחת רוח ויראה נפלאות
אשר יש בו בכח התורה
הקדושה . חברתיו
את עשיתיו אני
הצעיר

יהושע פאלק בן כ"ה מרדכי הכהן ז"ל

מק"ק קארניק ול"ע בנואיארק:

מדפס פה ק"ק נואיארק

אצל יוסף בן יעקב ז"ל:

בשנת כתר לפ"ק

NEW YORK:

PRINTED AT "JEWISH MESSENGER" OFFICE,

15 VANDEWATER STREET.

1860.

"The Biblical View of Slavery"

ABRAHAM LINCOLN AND DIOGENES

Solomon N. Carvalho, oil on canvas, 1865
The Rose Art Museum, Brandeis University

When South Carolina seceded from the Union on December 20, 1860, following the election of Abraham Lincoln, former president James Buchanan called upon all Americans to observe a "National Fast Day" in the hope of averting the impending dissolution of the Union. It was on this occasion that Rabbi Morris J. Raphall of Congregation B'nai Jeshurun, in New York City, delivered his famous discourse on "The Bible View of Slavery." Not only did the distinguished rabbi assert that slavery is an institution that appears in the Bible, he went on to point out that— contrary to those who asserted that biblical law intended to abolish slavery— Abraham, Isaac, and Jacob were all slaveholders!

Raphall's preachment was published widely, but many Jewish voices denounced it, including the distinguished reformer Rabbi David Einhorn, who insisted that by identifying God and the Bible as proponents of slavery, Raphall had committed "blasphemy." The controversy showed that American Jews, like all Americans, were forced to choose sides in what became a bitter and bloody civil war.

In the allegorical painting at right, Lincoln is represented by the Jewish artist Solomon N. Carvalho as the embodiment of honesty, "proven" by the onlooking George Washington and the ancient Greek Cynic Diogenes, who at last has put down his lantern after finding the one, true honest man.

"The brains of the Confederacy"

JUDAH BENJAMIN
Two-dollar bill, CSA, Richmond, ca. 1862
The Library of the The Jewish Theological Seminary

Judah Philip Benjamin lies buried in Père Lachaise Cemetery, in Paris, in a grave marked "Phillipe Benjamin." Born in the West Indies in 1811 to observant Jewish parents, the brilliant young Judah attended Yale College at age fourteen and then practiced law in New Orleans. He sold his plantation and one hundred forty slaves in 1850 and, in 1852, was elected to the United States Senate. In 1853, Benjamin declined a seat on the United States Supreme Court.

When the South seceded in 1861, Benjamin served the Confederacy as Attorney General, then Secretary of War and, finally, Secretary of State. President Jefferson Davis depended heavily on Benjamin's opinion; the two men spent twelve hours a day together. Near the war's end, some Southerners found him a convenient scapegoat for the South's military setbacks, accusing him of embezzlement and calling him "Judas" rather than Judah.

After the Civil War, Northerners wrongly suspected Benjamin of plotting Lincoln's assassination. Benjamin fled to London, where he practiced law until his death in 1884, never setting foot on American soil again.

SIX MONTHS AFTER THE RATIFI
THE CONFEDERATE STAT

2

SECOND SERIES

THE CONFEDE

Will pay T

Nº

5

TWO

RECEIVABLE IN PAYMENT
OF ALL DUES

DUNCAN, COLUMBIA, S.C.

Jews and the Union

LIST OF JEWS KILLED IN THE BATTLE OF FREDERICKSBURG
The Jewish Record, New York, 1863
Private collection

The Civil War marked the first large-scale participation of American Jews in the military. Jews lived in both the North and the South and were as bitterly divided as other Americans. Though they were by numbers—about 150,000 in all—a people on the periphery, they nonetheless had a considerable influence on the mainstream in defining the civil rights of a minority people. The existing regulation governing Union chaplaincy required that chaplains be Christian, but in 1862, Philadelphia Jewish leader Isaac Leeser and others protested to President Lincoln, who had the rule amended. Rev. Jacob Frankel of Congregation Rodeph Shalom in Philadelphia became the first commisioned Jewish chaplain. But tensions between Jews and authorities grew when General Grant, suspicious of and annoyed by the activities of traders involved with smuggling and cotton speculation, issued General Order No. 11, expelling all "Jews, as a class," from the department under his command. Jews were by no means the most numerous persons involved with such activities, but they were the most identifiable by their names, accents, and manners. Jewish protests quickly reached President Lincoln who promptly rescinded Grant's order. In a follow-up meeting with Jewish leaders, Lincoln commented, "I do not like to hear a class or nationality condemned on account of a few sinners."

Army News.

The following co-religionists were either killed or wounded at the battle of Fredericksburg:

T. J. Heffernam, A, 163 N. Y., hip and arm.
Serg. F. Herrfukneckt, 7 " head.
M. Ellis, 23 N. J., hand.
Moses Steinburg, 142 Penn., legs bruised.
A. Newman, A, 72 " ankle.
Lt. H. T. Davis, 81 " arm.
J. Killenback, 4 N. J., head.
S. S. Vanuess, 15 " leg.
W. Truax, 23 " back.
J. Hirsh, 4 " "
Jacob Schmidt, 19 Penn., left arm.
Jos. Osback, 19 " wounded.
W. Jabob, 19 " left arm.
Lieut. Simpson, 19 " left leg.
Capt. Schuh, 19 " wounded.
C. M. Phillips, 16 Maine, cheek.

Hebrew Union College

HEBREW UNION COLLEGE CLASS PHOTO

Cincinnati, 1895

The Jacob Rader Marcus Center of the American Jewish Archives

Early efforts to establish schools of rabbinical learning in the United States were plagued by shortfalls in funding and enrollment, and all ended in failure. Many people believed that it would never be possible to sustain a school for higher Jewish learning in the United States. But on February 13, 1873, a Cincinnatian named Henry Adler offered Rabbi Isaac Mayer Wise a challenge grant of $10,000 to establish a "theological college"—on the condition that a union of American synagogues dedicated to its funding would be organized. In response, Wise and his supporters established, later that same year, the Union of American Hebrew Congregations, the first of its kind in America. The primary objective was achieved when the Hebrew Union College held its opening exercises on October 3, 1875. In 1883, HUC ordained its first four rabbinical graduates—the first American-educated rabbis.

At first, both liberal and traditional congregations belonged to the UAHC and supported HUC's mission. With increased immigration of traditionally trained rabbis from eastern Europe, HUC became defined as the educational center of American Reform Judaism. Nevertheless, the success of HUC established a strong precedent and became a model for many Jewish seminaries that followed.

Seligman at Saratoga

GRAND UNION IN SARATOGA

Cartoon by J. Keppler in *Puck*, June 27, 1877

The Library of Congress

As the American Jewish population approached 200,000 in the 1860s, incidents of antisemitism rose, as did occurrences of social discrimination. One such that rose to national notoriety was the barring of the German-Jewish banker Joseph Seligman from registering as a guest at the Grand Union Hotel in Saratoga Springs, New York. Seligman was not only among the wealthiest Americans but was also a friend of presidents Abraham Lincoln and Ulysses S. Grant. The event was widely reported in the newspapers and described as the first antisemitic incident in American history, which it was not.

During this time, the Jews who had arrived decades earlier and who had adapted to American ways were fearful that the new wave of immigrants, mostly Jews from eastern Europe who dressed in traditional Orthodox garb and whose practices held them separate from the general population, would create a backlash of discrimination by association. Their fears were not completely unfounded. The cumulative effect of such incidents eventually led to the founding of the American Jewish Committee (1906) and the Anti-Defamation League of B'nai B'rith (1913), although each formed in response to later antisemitic challenges.

"Who is going to Castle Garden tomorrow morning to look after those 500 Russian Jews there?"

RUSSIAN JEWS AT CASTLE GARDEN — A SCENE IN THE EARLY MORNING
Wood engraving from *Frank Leslie's Illustrated Newspaper*, August 5, 1882.
The Library of The Jewish Theological Seminary

This charge galvanized New York's Jewish philanthropists to create the short-lived Hebrew Emigrant Aid Society to relieve the suffering of the thousands of Jews who, fleeing pogroms, flooded into Castle Garden in 1881. Located at the tip of lower Manhattan in Battery Park, the former defense fort, known today as Castle Clinton, served as New York's immigration reception station from 1855 to 1890. Before Ellis Island opened its doors to immigrants on January 1, 1892, Castle Garden was the gateway to America for some eight million immigrants, among them tens of thousands of Jews escaping Old World poverty and persecution. By the 1880s, the aging immigration reception station could scarcely manage the several thousand immigrants who might in a single day crowd into its rotunda and who had to be inspected, registered, and dispatched on their way. The anarchist Emma Goldman, who passed through its walls, recalled years later the violent shock of her first moments spent on American soil within Castle Garden's overcrowded and dilapidated halls.

"*Mother of Exiles*"

THE NEW COLOSSUS

Sonnet by Emma Lazarus, holograph manuscript, 1883

The American Jewish Historical Society

This great work of public poetry—surely America's most notable sonnet—was composed in 1883 by Emma Lazarus, a fourth-generation American Jew. A seasoned professional writer, she wrote the poem expressly for a fund-raising auction held to support construction of the pedestal for Bartholdi's colossus, which was then called "Liberty Enlightening the World." While the sonnet's form is strictly classical, its content couldn't be more dismissive of classical culture, deriding the glories of the Old World as the pompous vanities of the once powerful—this in stark contrast to the new colossus, which would light the way to a golden land that welcomed the exiled, the homeless, and the tempest-tossed. Lazarus's message of refuge was her own creation, not part of an official agenda; in fact, none of the speeches given at the statue's dedication in 1886 mentioned immigrants at all. If the statue had become something of a joke to established Americans, most of whom knew it best from cartoons, there was little doubt of its meaning to the millions of immigrants coming into New York harbor—Emma Lazarus had perfectly predicted their impression. Her fourteen lines came to define not only the statue, but for many, they defined the nation itself.

Sonnets.

I.

The New Colossus.

Not like the brazen Giant of Greek fame,
  With conquering limbs astride from land to land,
Here at our sea-washed, sunset gates shall stand
A mighty woman with a torch, whose flame
Is the imprisoned lightning, and her name
Mother of Exiles. From her beacon-hand
Glows world-wide welcome; her mild eyes command
The air-bridged harbor that twin cities frame.

"Keep, ancient lands, your storied pomp!" cries she
  With silent lips. "Give me your tired, your poor,
Your huddled masses yearning to breathe free,
The wretched refuse of your teeming shore.
Send these, the homeless, tempest-tost to me,
I lift my lamp beside the golden + door!"

1883.

  (Written in aid of Bartholdi Pedestal Fund.)

"Declaration of Independence"

THE PITTSBURGH PLATFORM

Cincinnati, 1885

The Jacob Rader Marcus Center of the American Jewish Archives

The eight-point Pittsburgh Platform, promulgated by Reform rabbis called together by Kaufmann Kohler, was a set of guiding principles that sought to define "what Reform Judaism means and aims at." Stressing moral law over ritual law and universalism over particularism, it defined Jews as "no longer a nation but a religious community," forswearing a return to Zion and embracing social justice as a Jewish imperative. Described as a "declaration of independence" by Isaac Mayer Wise, the platform marked Reform's final break with Orthodoxy and the end of the once powerful dream of an American rite broad enough to encompass Jews of every stripe. It also served as a rallying cry for those opposed to Reform, who called for an Orthodox seminary and a Union of Orthodox Jewish Congregations.

for the tenth time, and I do not think that we would discover the papers in the garret."

"You are sure of it? But where can they be?" Both remained silent, engaged in deep meditation. Suddenly Freyda exclaimed:

"I know where they are, they are yonder!"

"Hersh raised up his head. His wife pointed with her finger to a large, glass covered bookcase, which was filled from top to bottom with huge tomes, in antiquated bindings.

"There?" asked Hersh with trembling voice.

"There!" said his wife. Have you not told me that these are the books of Michael Senior, and that the Ezofowicz have religiously preserved them, but that none of them have read them because Todros has forbidden the reading of such books?"

Hersh put his hand to his forehead, his wife continued:

"Michael Senior was a wise man and the future lay clear before his vision. He knew that none would read these books, and that only he who would have a desire to do so, would be that grandson, who would live at a period where a change would take place; he felt confident that he would then find his writings."

"Freyda! Freyda! You are a pearl of women."

"Hersh!" she said, "I will now go and look for our children, I hear our baby crying. I will quieten her, I will then see what the servants are doing and when I return, I will assist you in your search."

"Come back soon," replied her husband, and after she had disappeared in the next room from which the sound of children's voices was heard, he followed her with his eyes and said in a half audible whisper:

"A wise house-wife is worth more than gold and precious pearls, at her side her husband's heart is easy."

(To be continued)

AUTHENTIC REPORT

OF THE

PROCEEDINGS of the RABBINICAL CONFERENCE,

held at Pittsburg, Nov. 16, 17, 18, 1885.

III.

At the conclusion of the reading of the paper Dr. Mayer moved that the points thereof be taken as the basis for deliberation. Dr. Hirsch amended as follows: That the propositions be given into the hands of a committee which shall decide the points to be discussed, and shall classify the same. Carried. The following were appointed as the committee: Drs. Kohler, Sonneschein, Moses, Hirsch and Sale, the committee to report in the afternoon.

Dr. Mayer now reported to the Conference that a public meeting would be held at Rodef Sholem Temple in the evening, and moved that a committee be appointed to make a programme. The committee, consisting of Rabbis Moses, Mayer and Philipson, reported as follows:

Opening Prayer—Rabbi Dr. Adolph Moses; Welcome Address, by Dr. Mayer and Jos. Cohen, Esq.; Remarks on the aims of the Conference, by the President, Dr. Wise, and Drs. Kohler, Sonne-

with you. Judaism, clear and answering for all thinking Jews, will be the result of your deliberations. The blessings of our all-wise Father will be with you.   Dr. S. Hirsch.

MONDAY AFTERNOON.

The committee appointed to arrange a programme for the work of the Conference reported as follows:

1) Platform.
2) Proselyte Question.
3) Sunday Services for those who as workmen are now deprived of the privilege of religious service.
4) Agenda. Domestic Worship.
5) Reading of the Pentateuch.
6) The Sabbath School Union.
7) Other Theses.

PLATFORM.

Dr. Kohler laid the following platform before the Conference for its consideration:

"In view of the wide divergence of opinions and the conflicting ideas prevailing in Judaism to-day to such an extent as to cause alarm and feeling of uncertainty among our well-meaning co-religionists and an appaling religious indifference and lethargy among the masses, we, as representatives of Reform Judaism, here unite upon the following principles:

1) While discerning in every religion a human attempt to grasp the Infinite and Omnipotent One and in every sacred form, source and book of revelation offered by any religious system the consciousness of the in-dwelling of God in man, we recognize in Judaism the highest conception of God and of His relation to man—expressed as the innate belief of man in the One and holy God, the Maker and Ruler of the World, the King, the Father and Educator of the Human race, represented in Holy Scriptures as the faith implanted into the heart of the original man and arrived at in all the cheering brightness by the fore-fathers, the inspired prophets, singers and writers of Israel, developed and ever more deepened and spiritualized into the highest moral and intellectual power on the basis of Holy Writ by the Jewish teachers and thinkers in accordance with the philosophical and moral progress of their respective ages and under continual struggles and trials, defended and preserved by the Jewish people as the highest treasure of the human race.

2) We prize and treasure the books comprising the national library of Israel, preserved under the name of the Holy Scriptures, as the records of Divine Revelation and of the consecration of the Jewish people for this mission as priests of the one God; but we consider their composition, their arrangements and their entire contents as the work of men, betraying in their conceptions of the world the short-comings of their age.

3) While finding in the miraculous narratives of the Bible child-like conceptions of the dealing of Divine love and justice with man, we to-day, in common with many Jewish thinkers of the Spanish era, welcome the results of natural science and progressive research in all fields of life as the best help to understand the working of the Divine Love, the Bible serving us as guide to find the Divine power working from within.

4) Beholding in the Mosaic Laws a system of training the Jewish people for its mission as a

obstruct rather than enhance and encourage our moral and spiritual elevation as children of God.

6) While glorying in our great past with its matchless history of one continued wondrous struggle and martyrdom in the defence of the Unity of God, which necessitated the exclusion of the Jewish people from a world stamped with polytheism and idolatry, with all their cruelty and vice, we hail in the modern era of universal culture of heart and mind the approaching realization of Israel's great Messianic hope for the kingdom of peace, truth, justice and love among all men, expecting neither a return to Palestine, nor the restitution of any of the laws concerning a Jewish State, nor a sacrificial worship under the administration of the sons of Aaron.

7) We behold in Judaism an ever-growing, progressive and rational religion, one which gave rise to the religions which to-day rule the greater part of the civilized globe. We are convinced of the utmost necessity of preserving our identity with our great past; we gladly recognize in the spirit of broad humanity and cosmopolitan philanthropy permeating our age, in the noble and grand endeavor to widen and deepen the idea and to enlarge the dominion of man, our best ally and help in the fulfillment of our mission and the only means of achieving the end and aim of our religion.

8) We therefore hail with the utmost delight and in the spirit of sincere fellowship and friendship the efforts on the part of the representatives of the various religious denominations the world over, and particularly in our free country, towards removing the barriers separating men from men, class from class, and sect from sect, in order to cause each to grasp the hands of his fellowman and thus forming one great brotherhood of men on earth. In this growing religion of humanity, based upon the belief in one God as Father of men, and the conception of man as the image of God we find the working of the Divine plan of truth and salvation as revealed through Jewish history.

9) In view of the Messianic end and object of Jewish history we feel bound to do our utmost to make our religious truth and our sacred mission understood to all and appreciated by all, whether Jew or Gentile; to improve and reform our religious forms and habits of life so as to render them expressive of the great cosmopolitan ideas pervading Judaism and to bring about the fulfillment of the great prophetic hope and promise "that the house of God should be the house of prayer for all nations."

10) Seeing in the present crisis simply the natural consequences of a transition from a state of blind authority-belief and exclusion to a rational grasp and humanitarian conception and practice of religion, we consider it a matter of the utmost necessity to organize a Jewish mission for the purpose of enlightening the masses about the history and mission of the Jewish people and elevating their social and spiritual condition through press, pulpit and school.

On motion of Dr. Hirsch the Conference went into session as a committee of the whole with Rabbi Jos. Krauskopf as chairman, the platform as proposed by Dr. Kohler being accepted as the basis.

Dr. Sonneschein moved that in the preamble of

A Chief Rabbi Appointed and Rejected

ANNOUNCEMENT OF THE APPOINTMENT OF JACOB JOSEPH
New York City, 1888
The Library of The Jewish Theological Seminary of America

The idea of a communal rabbinic leader was a comforting one to Jews who had
come from places where such figures carried substantial religious authority.
It was hoped that a chief rabbi would expedite the settlement of disputes and
inspire a uniformity of opinion in a land that was, from an Orthodox perspective,
a religious free for all. When in 1888 the Association of American Orthodox
Hebrew Congregations hired Jacob Joseph, the communal preacher of Vilna, to
be America's chief rabbi, the dissent among New York's Jews was immediate.
From acculturated uptown Jews to the social activists and various Hasidic and
Galician elements of the Lower East Side, no one seemed to want him. Though
he had been known in Vilna as a champion of the masses, and as a man who had
been influenced by the Enlightenment, he knew nothing of American language and
culture and was dependent on others to write his speeches. The last straw came in
the form of a one penny tax that would be levied on poultry slaughtered under the
supervision of Joseph's deputies, a tax that would provide the Chief Rabbi with
his means of support. An unlikely coalition of atheist radicals, angry housewives,
competing rabbis, and butchers were infuriated, claiming it was merely an attempt
by the Association to fill its coffers. Living in obscurity, bedridden with paralysis,
Rabbi Jacob Joseph died in 1902.

ASSOCIATION OF THE

AMERICAN ORTHODOX HEBREW CONGREGATIONS
אגרת הקהלות באמעריקא.

—◆—

NEW YORK, NISSAN, 5648, April, 1888.

BRETHREN :

If there is one thought which makes the heart of the Jew leap, it is the memory of what our fathers have suffered for the sake of our religion.

Our Law has been our watchword for centuries ; it is our very life and the length of our days ; to it we owe our existence to-day, and for it there is no sacrifice too great for us to make.

But in this land, where we are at liberty to observe our religion, to study, teach, observe, perform and establish our Law, we find that our religion is neglected and our Law held in light esteem.

For many are they who stray like sheep, listening to shepherds who bid them drink from broken cisterns that hold not the true water of life. Many are they also who have been brought up in ignorance of our Holy Faith.

Their fathers or grandfathers were as orthodox as we are. Is it not our duty to prevent our children and grandchildren straying like them ?

Rouse yourselves and let not the mistake be repeated and continued by which Orthodox Judaism has lost so many who should be enlisted under its banner !

Certain congregations have united in order to create an intelligent orthodoxy, and to prove that also in America can be combined honor, enlightenment and culture, with a proper observance of religious duty.

After much care in the choice of a Chief Rabbi, we have selected the learned and pious Rabbi Jacob Joseph of Wilna. He is to be the leader in the battle which must be waged in order to keep the next generation faithful to Judaism in spite of educational, social and business influences which, in America, are so powerful to make our sons and daughters forget their duty to the religion in which their ancestors lived, and for which those ancestors died.

Assistant Rabbis will be chosen to form with him a בית דין, thus to give proper attention to religious and judicial requirements of a Jewish community, thus to correct abuses which have appeared in כשרות גטין וקדושין and which have been a reproach *for us*, and a weapon for the enemies of Judaism.

Furthermore, the object of the union is to improve the capacity and condition of our religious methods, to enlarge the resources of charitable institutions, and to secure their conformity with orthodox Jewish principles.

Join us then. Strengthen our hands. Call a meeting of your society, lodge-friends, congregation or Hebra. Place the matter before all, and we are confident that, for the sake of

"Once on shore, they were taken in hand by HIAS."

WAITING IN LINE AT HIAS OFFICE
Warsaw, 1921
Photograph by Alter Kacyzne
YIVO Institute for Jewish Research

Among the first major institutions set up by East European Jews to lend a hand to those following them to the Golden Land was the Hebrew Sheltering and Immigrant Aid Society, best known as HIAS. For more than a century, since 1889, when the Hebrew Sheltering House first opened on the Lower East Side, HIAS representatives have eased the way for immigrants and refugees. At Ellis Island its agents, clutching fistfuls of $5.00 bills and wearing strings of kosher sausages, translated for anxious immigrants and intervened whenever one failed any of the various inspections designed to keep undesirables out of the United States. HIAS reunited families, obtained affidavits of support, ran an employment bureau, and conducted religious services. After the great era of immigration came to an end, HIAS continued to settle tens of thousands of Jewish immigrants—displaced persons after World War II, Jews fleeing Cuba's Castro Revolution for Miami, and those streaming out of the Soviet Union.

"Nesher Hagadol"

JACOB P. ADLER

ca. 1910

The American Jewish Historical Society

The Yiddish theater was born in Europe, but came of age in America. Barely a decade after Avrom Goldfaden's nascent plays were staged in Jassy, Romania, the young Boris Thomashefsky, not much more than a year in America and barely the age of bar mitzvah, staged Goldfaden's *Koldunya* ("The Witch") in New York City, in 1882. Around the same time, Jacob Adler, an Odessa-born actor who had appeared in early Yiddish productions, joined the Rosenberg Troupe, a serious-minded group of traveling actors who played in Russia and Poland. Adler became a sensation when he appeared in London in the 1880s, and in 1889, already acclaimed as *Nesher Hagadol* ("The Great Eagle," a play on his last name), he settled in New York. Adler was one of the greatest tragedians in any language, becoming an international superstar when he appeared as Shylock, performing in Yiddish in a Broadway production of *The Merchant of Venice* in which all the other parts were performed in English.

Adler's third wife, Sarah, was an actress of equal brilliance. Several of their children—Stella, Celia, and Luther—became renowned actors in their own right. Stella and her husband, Harold Clurman, were founders of the Group Theatre, the most influential company of its time. She became a leading proponent of the "Method," based on the work of Constantine Stanislavsky, and devoted much of her time to teaching. Her students included Marlon Brando and Al Pacino.

"Gone to another meeting"
HANNAH GREENEBAUM SOLOMON AND
THE NATIONAL COUNCIL OF JEWISH WOMEN
ca. 1920s
National Council of Jewish Women

The 1893 Columbian Exposition held in Chicago had among it features a "Parliament of Religions," which brought together many strands of American social thought including women's suffrage and religious tolerance. It was there that Hannah Greenebaum Solomon called for the establishment of an organization to "shape the destinies" of American Jewish women's lives. In response to her call, and under her leadership, the National Council of Jewish Women was founded. The organization, which continues its important work today, has been key in providing a vast range of social services to Jewish families and women of all faiths.

"Not what has happened, but what is recorded makes history"
THE AMERICAN JEWESS
Chicago, 1895
Jewish Women's Archive

Published first in Chicago and later in New York between April 1895 and August 1899, *The American Jewess* was the first English-language publication directed to American Jewish women. Part of the emergence of new public identities for Jewish women, *The American Jewess* represented the changing aspirations of America's prosperous and acculturated Jewish women. The magazine's title reflected an emerging belief that this group constituted a new entity in Jewish life: women who did not experience the religious and national aspects of their identity as being in conflict with each other. Thoroughly American and thoroughly Jewish, the "American Jewess" felt fully at home in her overlapping worlds of American and Jewish culture. *The American Jewess* magazine set out to explore the challenges and possibilities inherent in this new identity. At its height, the magazine claimed a circulation of 31,000.

In the first issue of *The American Jewess*, its editor, Rosa Sonneschein, observed that, "Not what has happened, but what is recorded makes history." By giving voice to the aspirations, hopes, and fears of Americanizing Jewish women at the end of the 19th century, Sonneschein ensured that their experience would never be erased.

VOL. I.

No. 1.

PRICE 10 CENTS

$1.00 PER ANNUM

THE

APRIL, 1895

THE

AMERICAN JEWESS

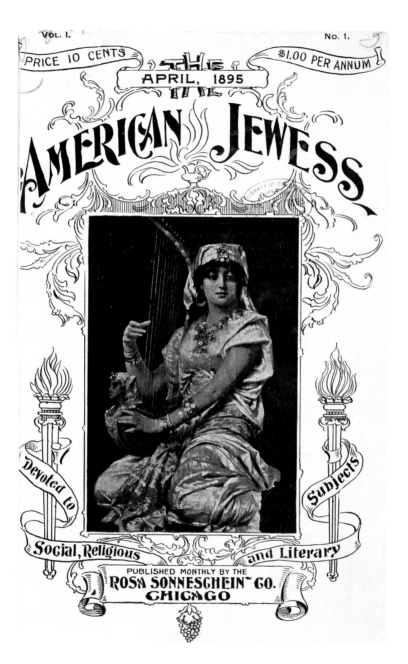

Devoted to

Subjects

Social, Religious

and Literary

PUBLISHED MONTHLY BY THE
ROSA SONNESCHEIN CO.
CHICAGO

"To unite people through their human and spiritual interests"
LILLIAN WALD AND THE HENRY STREET SETTLEMENT
Oil on cardboard portrait by William Valentine Schevill, 1919
The National Portrait Gallery, Smithsonian Institution

A visit to a sick woman in an immigrant tenement confronted medical student Lillian Wald with "all the maladjustments of our social and economic relations." Wald's response was to create New York's Henry Street Settlement (1895), pioneering the field of public health nursing, through which nurses created an organic relationship with the communities they lived in and served. Struck by the interconnectedness of illness, poverty, and despair, Wald expanded beyond public health. Soon, Henry Street offered boys' and girls' clubs; classes in arts, crafts, homemaking, and English; and vocational training.

The Henry Street work immersed Wald in ever-expanding questions of social welfare and politics. Beyond fighting for better playgrounds and housing and working conditions, she helped found the National Child Labor Committee, the Women's Trade Union League, and the National Association for the Advancement of Colored People; she spearheaded the campaign for a national Children's Bureau within the Department of Labor; campaigned for women's suffrage; and became a leader in international peace efforts.

Her Henry Street Settlement continues to serve its now Asian, African-American, and Latino neighborhood, advancing Wald's vision of a healthier world built on mutual respect and social justice.

"Zion . . . is a holy memory, but it is not our hope of the future. America is our Zion."

PROVISIONAL EXECUTIVE COMMITTEE FOR GENERAL ZIONIST AFFAIRS
New York, ca. 1918
Hadassah, the Women's Zionist Organization of America

So the Union of American Hebrew Congregations, representing Reform Jews, declared in 1898, and many an American Jew agreed. But the growth of antisemitism worldwide and the rising tide of persecuted Jews in Eastern Europe changed many minds. As America and other countries barred their doors, the idea of a Jewish homeland in the largely barren Land of Israel became increasingly inviting. The rebirth of Zion, supporters argued, would solve the "Jewish problem," revitalize Jewish culture, and extend the American dream outward. In 1909, Henrietta Szold, the most learned Jewish woman in America, traveled to Palestine and was inspired. Upon her return, she became secretary of the Federation of American Zionists, and in 1912 founded the women's Zionist organization that became Hadassah. Two years later, in response to the catastrophe facing many European Jews in World War I, the prominent Jewish lawyer Louis Brandeis, himself a recent convert to Zionism, assumed the chairmanship of the newly created Provisional Executive Committee for General Zionist Affairs and became the leader of American Zionism, bringing to it a coterie of distinguished followers. "Every American Jew who aids in advancing the Jewish settlement in Palestine," Brandeis declared, "though he feels that neither he nor his descendants will ever live there, will be a better man and a better American for doing so."

"Let the boys play baseball and become excellent at the game"
"WAITING FOR THE 'FORWARDS'"
Photograph by Lewis Hine, 1913
The Library of Congress

In New York City alone, more than one hundred fifty Yiddish newspapers and journals came into existence between 1870 and 1915, of which some twenty were dailies. For a time, around 1900, the city had six competing Yiddish newspapers that were published every day. The literary, political, and religious range of these publications was quite extraordinary: from Yiddish original novels and stories to translations of important European works from many languages; from the conservative view of the news of the day to Yiddish poetry of the labor movement; from strict orthodoxy to Marxist atheism.

Most enduring was *Der Forverts*, "The Jewish Daily Forward," founded in 1897 by the crustily independent Abraham Cahan, and continuing to this day as a weekly. At its height, the *Forward* published twelve metropolitan editions with a total circulation of around a half million (over a quarter million in New York City alone). Cahan was dedicated to the propagation of moderate socialism and the fight for social justice, but also for the Americanization of Jewish youth. "Let the boys play baseball and become excellent at the game," Cahan wrote, insisting that we "should not raise the children to grow up foreigners in their own birthplace." The *Forward* helped immigrant Jews become American, inspiring them with writing that was always engaged; in its famous column *Bintl brief* ("a bundle of letters"), it gave its readers' voices a chance to be heard.

The Galveston Plan, or, "How did you ever get there?"
JEWISH TERRITORIAL ORGANIZATION CORRESPONDENCE
Kiev, 1907
The American Jewish Historical Society

At the height of Jewish flight from Russia and Eastern Europe, a coalition of Jewish organizations funded by American Jewish financier Jacob Schiff and a German philanthropist, Baron Maurice de Hirsch, sought to direct Jewish immigrants leaving the port of Bremen away from America's crowded East Coast cities, and divert them to Galveston, Texas. There, an organization called the Jewish Immigration Information Bureau (JIIB) guided the new arrivals to small cities and farming towns in the American South and West that had Jewish populations willing to provide the immigrants with shelter, jobs, and a head start on life.

In all, between 1907 and 1914 almost ten thousand Jews spread out from Galveston to places such as Fargo, North Dakota, Palestine, Texas, and Helena, Montana. Many missed the tight-knit Orthodox communities they had left behind; others hated the prairie. Their hosts, in turn, sometimes found the newcomers demanding and ungrateful.

By 1914, with war in Europe, the JIIB office in Galveston no longer received immigrants but still helped Jewish immigrants who were here with their continuing acculturation.

E. T. O.

Центральное Эмиграціонное Бюро
ДЛЯ РОССІИ.

I. T. O.
EMIGR. CENTR. BUREAU
für Russland
Kieff.

י. ט. א.
צענטר. עמיגראצ .ביורא
פאר גאנץ רוסלאנד
אין קיעוו

Кіевъ, Оktober 16/29 дня 1907 г.

№ 4930

To the

Jewish Immigr. Infor. Bureau

Galveston

Dear Sir,

We lern from our Emigration Bureau at Odessa
that the Emigrant, Gittel Lernman, who
has been sent to Galveston with the third
party, is complaining of not yet having received
her luggage at Galveston. We have informed
her to address herself to your Bureau and
beg you to help her in getting her things
which she wants most badly.

"At the present we have no libraries, no publications and no independent scholars"

THE JEWISH ENCYCLOPEDIA

New York, 1901

The American Jewish Historical Society

Thus wrote Cyrus Adler in 1891 about Jewish scholarship in America. But even as he wrote, the situation was changing rapidly. The publication of the first volume of the *Jewish Encyclopedia* in New York, in 1902, signified that Jewish cultural authority was passing to the New World and that the language of Jewish scholarly discourse was shifting to English. Still considered an important resource, every page of the encyclopedia is available today online, as text and in facsimile. In 1971–1972, the sixteen volume *Encyclopedia Judaica* was published in Israel—also in English—and in 1997, *Jewish Women in America: An Historical Encyclopedia* was published under the auspices of the American Jewish Historical Society.

Another important contributor to the trend was the Jewish Publication Society, founded in 1888 to ensure "that Israel in America may proudly claim its literary period, as did our ancestors aforetimes." It became a publisher of both Hebrew and English-language books on both religious and secular topics of Jewish interest. Even as Hebrew was reborn as a living language and the State of Israel became an active center of publishing, English increasingly became "the international language of the Jews" in every walk of life except, perhaps, for prayer.

reign of Caligula an outbreak against the Jews occurred at Alexandria in the year 38, which Flaccus, then governor of Egypt, made no attempt to check.

Perpetual Lamp.
(From the synagogue at Strasburg.)

Philo ("In Flaccum," § 4) designates as the ringleaders (ταραξοπόλιδες) two citizens of Alexandria, Isidorus and Lampon, who for their complicity in the riot were executed under Claudius (*ib.* §§ 15, 17). The proceedings in the case before the emperor at Rome are extant in two papyrus fragments, supplementing each other, one at Berlin and the other in the museum of Gizeh.

The passage in which Lampon tries to justify himself is found in the Gizeh papyrus, which breaks off at the point where the emperor commands that Isidorus and Lampon be led away to death. That their execution really took place appears certain from a papyrus found at Oxyrhynchus, according to which a certain Appianus, in defending himself before one of the Antonine emperors, refers to the martyrdom of Isidorus and Lampon.

BIBLIOGRAPHY: T. Reinach, in *R. E. J.* xxxi. 161–178, xxxii. 160, xxxiv. 296–298, xxxvii. 219 *et seq.*; Grenfell and Hunt, *The Oxyrhynchus Papyri*, part i., No. xxxiii., London, 1898; Grätz, *Gesch.* 4th ed., iii. 331; Schürer, *Gesch.* 3d ed., i. 68, 503.

G.   S. Kr.

LAMPRONTI, ISAAC B. SAMUEL: Italian rabbi and physician; born Feb. 3, 1679, at Ferrara; died Nov. 16, 1756. His great-grandfather, Samuel Lampronti, emigrated from Constantinople to Ferrara in the sixteenth century. His father, a man of

rara, where he established himself as physician and teacher, delivering lectures for adults in his house both on week-days and on the Sabbath.

In 1709 Lampronti was appointed teacher at the Italian Talmud Torah, receiving a monthly salary of twelve scudi (= $11.64) in return for devoting the larger part of his day to teaching chiefly Hebrew grammar, arithmetic, and Italian. Lampronti gave his pupils his own homilies on the weekly sections, composed in Italian, for practise in translating into Hebrew. He also set some of his pupils to copy from the sources material which he needed for the encyclopedic work he had undertaken. The directors of the community, who thought this interfered with his duties as teacher, forbade him, in Oct.,

Activity as Teacher. 1725, to keep the material for his work in the schoolhouse. When the Spanish Talmud Torah was discontinued, in 1729, the pupils of this school also passed into the hands of Lampronti. Thus he became the teacher of most of the members of the community, and long after his death it was said in the community of Ferrara, "All the learning found among us is derived from the mouth of our father

"And the bush was not consumed"

SOLOMON SCHECHTER

New York, 1909

The American Jewish Historical Society

The Jewish Theological Seminary of America, founded in New York in 1886 and first led by a Sephardic rabbi with longtime American ties, became the center of American Jewish scholarship when the Romanian-born Cambridge scholar Solomon Schechter arrived from England in 1902 to take up the position of president. Schechter attracted some of the greatest scholars of his day and built an institution of high rigor. He also guided the development of the greatest Judaica library in the Western hemisphere. The Seminary, ever the balance point of tradition and modernity, became the home of a modified, modernized orthodoxy called "Conservative Judaism." It remains today, as it had been through much of the 20th century, a complex place that straddles the scholarly, religious, and political centers of American Jewish life.

"Bravo, bravo, bravo, Jewish women!"
THE KOSHER MEAT BOYCOTT
New York, 1902
The Library of Congress

In mid-May, 1902, the retail price of kosher meat on the Lower East Side of New York jumped from 12 to 18 cents per pound. Such dramatic price fluctuations were common as great "trusts," oligopolies controlled by industrial barons, cornered the market on commodities such as beef, steel, and oil. In response to the rise in beef prices, the retail kosher butchers of New York refused to sell meat for a week, but their boycott failed to bring wholesale prices down. So Jewish homemakers on the Lower East Side, influenced by the labor and women's suffrage movements, began to agitate for a strike. Fanny Levy, whose husband was a unionized cloakmaker, and Sarah Edelson, who owned a small restaurant, mobilized the neighborhood women by going door-to-door to persuade them not to buy kosher beef.

On May 15, the press reported that 20,000 women on the Lower East Side broke into kosher butcher shops, threw the meat into the street, soaked it with gasoline, and set it on fire. Crowds also confiscated meat from women who had purchased it from kosher butchers and destroyed that meat as well. The *Herald* reported that "an excitable and aroused crowd roamed the streets... armed with sticks, vocabularies and well-sharpened fingernails" in an effort to keep other women from purchasing kosher meat.

The *Forward* ran the headline, "Bravo, Bravo, Bravo, Jewish Women!"

CROWD GATHERED IN FRONT OF BUTCHER Shop
MEAT RIOT. N.Y.C.

"They are honorably distinguished by their industry, their obedience to law, and their devotion to the national welfare."

PRESIDENT THEODORE ROOSEVELT TO JACOB SCHIFF

Washington, November 16, 1905

The American Jewish Historical Society

In 1904, Theodore Roosevelt was President of the United States; Jacob Schiff, one of the country's foremost financiers, was "King of American Jews." That year, Schiff and a small group of American Jewish leaders decided to celebrate in grand style the 250th anniversary of Jewish settlement in North America. Schiff invited the president to address the major anniversary gathering at Carnegie Hall on the Sunday after Thanksgiving Day, 1905.

Roosevelt declined the invitation. In a private response he told Schiff that he made it a practice not to leave Washington while Congress was in session, but sent a letter that was read aloud at Carnegie Hall. Roosevelt expressed his reluctance to write to that august audience, not wishing to set a precedent for every group that wanted praise. However, his concern for the Jews of Russia, then the target of pogroms in Kishinev and elsewhere, compelled him to affirm his esteem for America's Jews who, while "loyal to their faith and their race traditions," were "indissolubly incorporated into the great army of American citizenship."

November 16, 1905.

My dear Sir:

I am forced to make a rule not to write letters on the occasion of any celebration, no matter how important, simply because I can not write one without either committing myself to write hundreds of others or else running the risk of giving offense to worthy persons. I make an exception in this case because the lamentable and terrible suffering to which so many of the Jewish people in other lands have been subjected makes me feel it my duty as the head of the American people not only to express my deep sympathy for them, as I now do, but at the same time to point out what fine qualities of citizenship have been displayed by the men of Jewish faith and race, who, having come to this country, enjoy the benefits of free institutions and equal treatment before the law. I feel very strongly that if any people are oppressed anywhere, the wrong inevitably reacts in the end on those who oppress them; for it is an

"Jews of widely different persuasions . . . all sat together"
A MEETING OF THE AMERICAN JEWISH
JOINT DISTRIBUTION COMMITTEE
New York, August 16, 1918
The Jacob Rader Marcus Center of the American Jewish Archives

In 1903 and again in 1905, American Jews were appalled to learn that riots in Kishinev, Russia, sponsored, it was alleged, by government officials, had left dozens of Jews dead and hundreds badly injured. American Jews—immigrants and natives alike—clamored for an organized and unified response. In January 1906, the distinguished lawyer and communal leader Louis Marshall proposed the establishment of a national organization to provide leadership for the community. It would be "an absolute impossibility," he wrote, "to unite as a religious body. We can, however, all unite for the purpose of aiding all Jews who are persecuted." Marshall's efforts would lead to the creation, on November 11, 1906, of the nation's oldest Jewish defense and relief agency: the American Jewish Committee.

Eight years later, the outbreak of the Great War spurred American Jews of every stripe to try to assist the 1.5 million European Jews whose lives were upended by the struggle. At first, three different organizations competed for funds, but they soon set aside their differences and joined hands to pool their resources, creating what became the American Jewish Joint Distribution Committee. "Capitalists and socialists, Reform rabbis and Orthodox ones, Jews of widely different backgrounds and persuasions, including three women, all sat together at the Joint's meetings, reaching most decisions by consensus and others by majority vote."

"The Free Synagogue"

STEPHEN S. WISE ADDRESSES 250,000 AT NAZI PROTEST RALLY
New York, May 10, 1933
© Bettmann/CORBIS

Stephen S. Wise, born in Budapest in 1874 and raised in New York, was an early Zionist activist. He attended the Second Zionist Congress in 1898 and in 1914, when Louis Brandeis became head of the American Zionist movement, Wise became his key lieutenant. In 1905, he was offered the pulpit of New York's Temple Emanu-El, considered a great plum, remarkable for a man so young, but he rejected it because the contract stated that control of the pulpit was in the hands of the board of directors. Within months, he developed a vision of "a synagogue of life and light," a union of the ideals of Judaism and American liberal democracy that included obligations to education, social justice, and community service. In 1907, having enlisted the support of many influential New Yorkers including Henry Morgenthau, Sr., The Free Synagogue was established. Morgenthau declared, "The Free Synagogue is to be free and democratic in its organization; it is to be pewless and duesless." Wise continued in the forefront of many causes; in the 1930s, he fought the antisemitic radio broadcaster Father Charles Coughlin, and he was often at the center of anti-Nazi protests.

"As free farmers on their own soil, they can make themselves useful."
EXHIBITION BY JEWISH FARMERS
Probably New Jersey, ca. 1910
The Library of Congress

A Jewish agricultural colony was founded in the United States as early as 1837, in Ulster County, New York, but it wasn't until the 1880s that Jewish agricultural efforts here reached a large scale. Most involved Jewish immigrants from Russia, many of whom were inspired by the idealism of the Russian socialist Am Olam movement. In the 1880s and 1890s, colonies were founded in Louisiana, South and North Dakota, Oregon, Colorado, Kansas, Michigan, and Connecticut. However, the largest and most durable settlements were located in New Jersey: Alliance, Carmel, Rosenhayn, Brotmanville, Norma, and perhaps the best known of all, Woodbine, which combined industry with agriculture and became the first Jewish borough to become incorporated in the United States.

Support for these efforts came mostly from grants from the Alliance Israélite Universelle, the Hebrew Emigrant Aid Society, the Montefiore Agricultural Aid Society, and most of all, from the Baron de Hirsch Fund. The German-Jewish Maurice de Hirsch (1831–1896), dedicated a fortune of $100 million to the improvement of Jews, mainly through their resettlement in lands without a long history of antisemitism. He believed Zionism to be a fantasy and turned down a request for funds from Theodor Herzl.

By the 1950s there were over 100,000 Jewish farmers in America.

EXHIBITION OF JEWISH FARMERS

ביענען זמכם

"All Israel is responsible for one another"

LA VARA, A LEVANTINE SEPHARDIC NEWSPAPER
New York, 1947
American Sephardi Federation with Sephardic House

America's first Jews were mainly Sephardim with associations to Holland, who had come through Brazil and the Caribbean. They had maintained western European connections at a time when many of their fellows had moved to North Africa and the Ottoman empire. By 1800, the early American Sephardim, though considered an elite, were outnumbered by their Ashkenazic coreligionists, who would by century's end dominate American Jewish culture. Between 1880 and 1920, as the greatest influx of Russian Jews came to these shores, some 75,000 Sephardic Jews from the Muslim Levant—from the Balkans, Greece, and Turkey—came too. They settled primarily in New York, but also established centers in Seattle, Los Angeles, Atlanta, and Cincinnati.

Many Ashkenazim—and, indeed, many old-line Sephardim—were unaware that distinct Oriental Sephardic cultures existed, and, finding themselves with little in common other than immigrant status, they frequently ignored them, both individually and organizationally. What the Oriental Sephardim had in common with each other was the Spanish-based language they spoke, which they called variously Ladino or Judezmo or Spanyolit. It was in this language that they organized a press, publishing a number of newspapers from 1910 to 1948.

יקסיסור אל פריזידינטי

LA VARA

אחד · מונדו · לה באראה

VOL. XXV, No. 45	7 RIVINGTON STREET NEW YORK 2, N. Y. Tel. GRamercy 5-7458	❋
ב"לום 25, נומירו 45		

לה סיסייון די לה קומיסייון איקונומי־
קה די לאס נאסייונינס אונידאס פור
איב"רופה. לה אקזואסייון איס איג"ה
אין סיגיינדה די איל ראפורטו דאדו אין
פ"ראנסייה אי אינגלטיירה סוב"רי
לה קונפ"ירינסייה אין פאריס די לאס
טרים גראנדים נאסייונינס קי סי אקא־
ב"ו קון אונה קריב"רה (קאליידה).

איל סוז"ימטו די איל סיקריטארייו
מארשאל פ"ואי אינקלודידו אין לה א־
יינדה די לה קומיסייון איקונומיקה
אין ג'יניב"ה אל אולטימו מינוטו.
איסטו אטירו לה ראב"ייה די איל
אימבאסאדור רוסו אין פראגה, ב"א־

סיר. רוסקין אימפוסו סו לאב"ורו 20
אנייוס אנטים אין לה אוניב"ירסידאד
די מוסקו. ס: מוז"יר דיב"ינו סו קולא־
בוראדירה דיזדי איל 1930.
אין איל 1891, און דוקטור אמירי־
קאנו ב"י. ב. קול, קונדואזייו אלגו־
נום איקספירימינטוס קי קונב"ינסי־
רון אה רוסקין קי איל סטריפטוקוקסי
(אים אונה אינפ"יקסייון קאב"זאדה
פור איל מיקרוב "יאמאדו סטריפטוקו־
קום) דיטייני איל קריסימיינטו די
קארנים קון איב"ידינסייאס ריקוז"י־
דאס, איל (רוסקין) סי טופו אונה
ג'יסטיף "יקאסייון אה סו קונב"יק־

רומפ"ידו, דיזי קליב"ה, איל
קריסי די נואיב"ו.

קומו ייה סי אב"לו די מוג"א
נירה די קורא'ם פ"ארה קאנסי־
גונה אאוטורידאד קיירין מודה
אקטיפטואר איסטי ראפורטו קי
די רוסייאה. נון איי דוב"דה אה
בילידאד די לום דום, רוסקין אי
ב"ה, סולו קי איי אין דוב"דו
מאנידרה די אינטורפירטאר סוכ
זולטאדום, אספטה קי איסטה
ב"יירטה "קי-אר" ב"ה ב"יני
פור סיר אפרוב"אדה, לום דוק
די אקי נון דישעראן די פ"ראק

"I know from experience it is up to the working people to save themselves"

PROCESSION OF MOURNERS AFTER
THE TRIANGLE SHIRTWAIST FACTORY FIRE
New York, 1911
Kheel Center, Cornell University School of Industrial and Labor Relations

On March 25, 1911, a fire broke out on the eighth floor of the Asch building on the corner of Greene Street and Washington Place in Manhattan. One hundred forty-six people—mainly young Jewish women—perished in the blaze. The victims had been trapped by blocked exit doors and faulty fire escapes.

The aftermath of the catastrophe brought grief and recriminations. Protest rallies and memorial meetings were held throughout the city. During one meeting at the Metropolitan Opera House, tension broke out between the Jews from the Lower East Side, who filled the galleries and saw class solidarity as the solution to the problems of industrial safety, and the middle- and upper-class women in the boxes, who sought institutional reforms, such as the establishment of a bureau of fire prevention. The meeting would have broken up in disorder if not for a stirring speech by Rose Schneiderman, a Polish-born former hat worker, who had once led a strike at the Triangle factory. Although she barely spoke above a whisper, Schneiderman held the audience spellbound.

"American Daughters of Zion"

NURSES AT HADASSAH WELFARE STATION, JERUSALEM

Jerusalem, 1913

Hadassah, the Women's Zionist Organization of America

Henrietta Szold enlisted generations of American Jewish women in the practical work of Zionism. As essayist, translator, and editor, she had played a foundational role in creating a meaningful American Jewish culture. Still, Szold was constrained by the limited opportunities that the Jewish world of the late 19th and early 20th centuries offered a woman of her brilliance, organizational abilities, and vision.

On February 24, 1912, thirty-eight women under Szold's leadership created what they intended to be "a large organization of women Zionists" devoted to "the promotion of Jewish institutions and enterprises in Palestine, and the fostering of Jewish ideals." Avoiding religious and political controversy, Hadassah recruited women from all streams of Judaism and reached out to non-Zionists as well as Zionists. In 1913, Hadassah sent two nurses to create a visiting nurse service in Palestine. Hadassah programs ultimately created much of the medical infrastructure, serving both Jews and Arabs, of the future state of Israel. The organization's ability to raise funds and members transformed American Zionism and thus did much to create the State of Israel.

Grasping the challenge raised and modeled by Henrietta Szold, Hadassah members showed that Jewish women could indeed change the world.

בנות ציון אמריקאניות
מכון שומרות חולים
הדסה

AMERICAN DAUGHTERS OF ZION
NURSES SETTLEMENT
HADASSAH

"The bent and heart-sore immigrant forgets exile and homesickness and ridicule and loss and estrangement, when he beholds his sons and daughters moving as Americans among Americans."

MARY ANTIN WITH CHILDREN

Probably Boston, 1916

PictureHistory.com

At the beginning of the 20th century, two Jewish immigrants, the writer Mary Antin and the editor of the *Forverts*, Abraham Cahan, presaged the vitality of American Jewish literature in what became classic accounts of the immigrants' journey into America. In her autobiography, *The Promised Land* (1912), Mary Antin celebrated Boston's public schools as her ticket to American civilization. Abraham Cahan's novel *The Rise of David Levinsky* (1917) tells of losses incurred en route to American success. That both books remain in print in this anniversary year attest to their writers' great gifts and to the power of the immigrant tales they had to tell.

Greetings
from
Mary Antin
1916.

"It is Democracy that Zionism represents"

LOUIS DEMBITZ BRANDEIS

Boston, ca. 1900

Brandeis University

In early 20th-century America, before the Holocaust, Zionism was a divisive idea in the Jewish community, especially among successful, well-established Jews. To many, America was the New Zion. But to Louis Brandeis, raised as a universalist in a German-Jewish family in Louisville, Zionism became an ideal most compatible with being a good American. "It is Democracy that Zionism represents, It is Social Justice which Zionism represents, and every bit of that is the American ideal of the 20th century," he wrote in 1914. His support of the Zionist ideal marked a turning point for many American Jews' support of a Jewish state. For others, the idea remained a theoretical entity, as physically remote as the Land of Oz. That changed for some, when they visited or heard reports about the Palestine Pavilion at the 1933 World's Fair in Chicago; it changed for nearly all in the aftermath of the Holocaust.

"A bridge over which the Torah could be brought from Europe to America"

BERNARD REVEL

United States Postal Service, 1986

Private collection

Born in Kovno and arriving in America at age twenty-one, Bernard Revel (1885–1940) had been identified at age six as a prodigy of Torah. In the new land, Revel became a peripatetic student, studying for a time at the Orthodox Rabbi Isaac Elchanan Theological Seminary in New York (the first precursor to Yeshiva University) and then at various colleges and universities, eventually completing a Ph.D. By 1915, his old seminary had merged with a similar institution, the Yeshiva Etz Chaim, and Revel was hired to direct the fortunes of what had become a rather wayward alliance. His goal was to help students harmoniously combine the best of modern culture with the learning and spirit of the Torah and the ideals of traditional Judaism. From this "Rabbinical College," as it was known for a while, grew Yeshiva College and later, after World War II, Yeshiva University. This center of "Modern Orthodoxy" has tried to remain true to its religious roots, despite the success of its thoroughly secular professional schools: Albert Einstein Medical College and the Benjamin Cardozo School of Law. It is a place in which both the clashes and successes of melding traditional Judaism with modern concerns may be seen in microcosm.

Bernard Revel

USA $1

"Hang the Jew!"

THE LYNCHING OF LEO FRANK

Marietta, Georgia, August 17, 1915

The Library of Congress

In April 1913, the murdered and presumably abused body of a thirteen-year-old girl, Mary Phagan, was discovered in the basement of an Atlanta pencil factory. The factory's manager, a northern Jew named Leo Frank, was accused of the murder. After a sensational and flawed trial that helped stoke a firestorm of hysteria and prejudice against Frank, he was sentenced to death. Georgia's governor did not believe that Frank received a fair trial and commuted his sentence to life imprisonment. In response, an outraged mob, led by some of Marietta's leading citizens, kidnapped Frank from jail and lynched him. The photo at right reprints a postcard of the scene. Lynchings were routine at this time in Southern history, and the scene conveys the relaxed attitude of the lynchers.

Many years later, an eyewitness testified that Mary Phagan was murdered by the janitor of the pencil factory, the "star witness" against Frank. Recently, the Georgia legislature voted to overturn Frank's conviction, posthumously.

"Keep the Home Fires Burning Till the Boys Come Home"
JACOB RADER MARCUS IN WORLD WAR I ARMY UNIFORM
Cincinnati, 1917
The Jacob Rader Marcus Center of the American Jewish Archives

The American Expeditionary Force (AEF) was the largest American military force deployed overseas up to that time. While the exact number of American Jews who served in the AEF is not known—estimates range from 80,000 to 250,000—World War I witnessed the mass participation of Jews to an unprecedented degree. Jacob Rader Marcus (1896–1995), the future historian of American Jewish life, then a rabbinical student at Hebrew Union College in Cincinnati, was one of approximately 700,000 American men to join voluntarily the U.S. armed services after war was declared in April 1917.

Unlike previous wars, in which Jews also served, the American Jewish soldier benefited from a new organization, the Jewish Welfare Board (JWB) established in 1917. The JWB worked with the U.S. War Department to meet the spiritual, physical, and intellectual needs of Jewish soldiers by, among other things, sponsoring rabbis to serve as Military Chaplains and setting up rest and recreation centers. In 1941, in a response to a mandate from President Franklin D. Roosevelt, the JWB joined with five other private organizations to form the USO, which undertook to address the morale and recreational needs of men and women in arms.

"The World's Problem"

THE DEARBORN INDEPENDENT AND THE INTERNATIONAL JEW
Dearborn, Michigan, May 22, 1923
The Library of Congress

Between 1920 and 1927, the legendary auto magnate Henry Ford published a series of four paperbound books entitled *The International Jew*. These were bound anthologies of antisemitic articles from his privately owned newspaper, *The Dearborn Independent*. The paper and the antisemitic anthologies were obediently hawked by Ford dealers. *The International Jew* was translated into sixteen languages and millions of copies were circulated. Its premise is based largely on the notorious fraud *The Protocols of the Learned Elders of Zion*. In 1927, following a libel lawsuit filed against him by Aaron Sapiro, a Jewish organizer of farmers' cooperatives, Ford's representatives met with attorney Louis Marshall, president of the American Jewish Committee. Ford claimed to be "deeply mortified," saying that his underlings had done this without his knowledge. He later signed a letter composed by Marshall, in which he promised to destroy all the copies. It was a fatuous promise at best—original copies circulate and are reprinted to this day. Many copies found their way to the office of Adolf Hitler who kept a portrait of Ford in his office and awarded him a special medal in 1938—which Ford accepted.

132

The Ford International Weekly
THE DEARBORN INDEPENDENT

By the Year One Dollar

Dearborn, Michigan, May 22, 1920

Single Copy Five Cents

The International Jew: The World's Problem

"Among the distinguishing mental and moral traits of the Jews may be mentioned: distaste for hard or violent physical labor; a strong family sense and philoprogenitiveness; a marked religious instinct; the courage of the prophet and martyr rather than of the pioneer and soldier; remarkable power to survive in adverse environments, combined with great ability to retain racial solidarity; capacity for exploitation, both individual and social; shrewdness and astuteness in speculation and money matters generally; an Oriental love of display and a full appreciation of the power and pleasure of social position; a very high average of intellectual ability."

—*The New International Encyclopedia.*

THE Jew is again being singled out for critical attention throughout the world. His emergence in the financial, political and social spheres has been so complete and spectacular since the war; that his place, power and purpose in the world are being given a new scrutiny, much of it unfriendly. Persecution is not a new experience to the Jew, but intensive scrutiny of his nature and super-nationality is. He has suffered for more than 2,000 years from what may be called the instinctive anti-semitism of the other races, but this antagonism has never been intelligent nor has it been able to make itself intelligible. Nowadays, however, the Jew is being placed, as it were, under the microscope of economic observation that the reasons for his power, the reasons for his separateness, the reasons for his suffering may be defined and understood.

In Russia he is charged with being the source of Bolshevism, an accusation which is serious or not according to the circle in which it is made; we in America, hearing the fervid eloquence and perceiving the prophetic ardor of young Jewish apostles of social and industrial re-

ancient prophecies to the effect that the Jew will return to his own land and from that center rule the world, though not until he has undergone an assault by the united nations of mankind.

The single description which will include a larger percentage of Jews than members of any other race is this: he is in business. It may be only gathering rags and selling them, but he is in business. From the sale of old clothes to the control of international trade and finance, the Jew is supremely gifted for business. More than any other race he exhibits a decided aversion to industrial employment, which he balances by an equally decided adaptability to trade. The Gentile boy works his way up, taking employment in the productive or technical departments; but the Jewish boy prefers to begin as messenger, salesman or clerk—anything—so long as it is connected with the commercial side of the business. An early Prussian census illustrates this characteristic: of a total population of 269,400, the Jews comprised six per cent or 16,164. Of these, 12,000 were traders and 4,164 were workmen. Of the Gentile population, the other 94 per cent,

"Kings of Tin Pan Alley"

GEORGE AND IRA GERSHWIN WITH FRED ASTAIRE
Hollywood, 1936
The Library of Congress

The 20th-century sound of America was defined in large part by Jewish composers and lyricists. In many parts of Europe, the opportunities for Jewish composers were extremely limited and America became the beneficiary of a river of talent that flowed as if had been dammed up for centuries. Nowhere was this more apparent than in the world of "Tin-Pan Alley," as the publishing machinery of the American songbook was known. The list of names is stunning even at a small sampling: Irving Berlin, George and Ira Gershwin, Jerome Kern, Richard Rodgers, Harold Arlen, Oscar Hammerstein, Sammy Cahn, Dorothy Fields, Lorenz Hart, Yip Harburg, Adolph Green—and it goes on through the next two generations that include the likes of John Kander, Jerry Bock, Burt Bacharach, Jules Styne, Stephen Sondheim, Bob Dylan, and Paul Simon. Leonard Bernstein, taking up the mantles of both George Gershwin and Aaron Copland, blurred the lines between the concert and operatic stages and the cabaret.

Not to be forgotten are the songwriters whose names are best known through their work for the Yiddish stage: Joseph Rumshinsky, Abraham Ellstein, Alexander Olshanetsky, and Sholom Secunda (of "Bei Mir Bist Du Schoen" fame)—whose works are finding new audiences today.

"You ain't heard nothin' yet!"

THE JAZZ SINGER
Movie poster, 1927
The Library of Congress

Based on Samson Raphaelson's story, "The Day of Atonement," *The Jazz Singer* became a transforming event for American Jews as well as for Hollywood. It was the first full-length talking picture (it wasn't really, but it has been said so often that it has become "fact") as well as the first major picture to depict Jewish life and its tensions in a new land. For some, not all, movie executives, who often went to great—and sometimes laughable—lengths to hide their Jewishness, the release of the picture marked a "coming out." The story, which concerns the son of a pious cantor who defies his father to pursue his dream of being a pop singer, is the American *urgeschichte* of assimilation versus tradition, always waiting to be told again, albeit with a change of makeup. And it was in many respects the real-life story of the movie's star, Al Jolson, a cantor's son born in Lithuania who became a superstar of the American stage and screen.

"The Jew will have to save Judaism before Judaism will be in a position to save the Jew."
MORDECAI M. KAPLAN (center)
WITH LOUIS FINKELSTEIN (left) AND ALEXANDER MARX
Photograph by Gjon Mili, New York, 1951
© Time & Life Pictures/Getty Images

Mordecai M. Kaplan's magnum opus, *Judaism as a Civilization*, ranks him among the most influential figures of 20th-century American Jewish thought. For over fifty years as a professor at the Jewish Theological Seminary of America, Kaplan taught hundreds of men who became Conservative rabbis. But his articulation of Judaism as a unique national civilization—comprising not just religion but also history, literature, language, folkways, and social and spiritual ideals—extended his reach across 20th-century American Jewish life. How best to reconstruct that civilization to make it amenable to moderns paved the way for Reconstructionism and earned Kaplan bitter enemies as he envisioned Judaism without supernaturalism. But his reimagining of the synagogue as a shul with a pool and his inventing the bat mitzvah for his daughter Judith, a new rite of passage which proliferated across the denominations, reveal the breadth of his influence.

"A Jewish boy from Bronxville out where Casey used to be"
HANK GREENBERG
Detroit, ca. 1934
© Underwood & Underwood/CORBIS

As if to guard their spirits against the rising Goliaths of the Great Depression and European Fascism, American Jews embraced a symbolic David in Hank Greenberg, the first great Jewish baseball star. Greenberg was more than just good, he was loyal. In 1934, when the Detroit Tigers were in a tight race for the American League pennant, the Jewish slugger faced the dilemma of whether or not to play on the High Holidays. Rabbis debated whether it was more important for him to show that Jews were dedicated to the American majority or to follow the ordinances of Judaism. Greenberg came to his own compromise: play on Rosh Hashanah and go to synagogue on Yom Kippur. His commitment to his faith was enshrined in Edgar Guest's poem, "Speaking of Greenberg," written just after the incident. Just as Louis Brandeis showed how one could be both American and Zionist, so Hank Greenberg—or, rather, the story of Hank Greenberg—defined for many the balance between Americanness and Jewishness. And, like *The Jazz Singer*, it brought before the broad American public the core issues of Jewish identity.

One hundred years ago, in 1905, a Jewish German physicist and freshly minted Ph.D. published four papers in the journal *Annalen der Physik* that forever changed human understanding of the universe. No name has ever been more associated with the word "genius" than his, despite the fact that few people are capable of fully understanding his theoretical work or its practical implications.

Einstein was as much a seeker for moral truth as he was a searcher for the essential mechanics of the universe. Though never a practicing Jew, he embraced his identity, expressing his belief in "Spinoza's God who reveals himself in the harmony of all that exists," and true to the Jewish "prime directive," he admitted to a "passionate sense of social justice and social responsibility." His celebrity gave him an influential voice that he used to champion such causes as pacifism, liberalism, and Zionism. His first visit to America was with Chaim Weizmann, to raise money for the Palestine Foundation Fund.

Einstein was quick to condemn the rise of Nazism and in 1933, just after Hitler took power, he renounced his German citizenship and settled in the United States. No single action denounced the absurdity of the Nazi enterprise quite so clearly.

PERSON OF THE CENTURY
TIME

ALBERT
EINSTEIN

"So long as the human spirit thrives on this planet, music in some living form will accompany and sustain it and give it expressive meaning."
AARON COPLAND'S *BILLY THE KID*
New York, 1938
The New York Public Library

In the art music tradition that is still referred to as "classical," a native style came slowly to America, which had looked to Europe for both guidance and guides. Aaron Copland, born in Brooklyn in 1900, the son of immigrant parents from Lithuania, studied in Paris with Nadia Boulanger, who encouraged him to go home and look for a true American art music style. The precedents were there: Gershwin's *Rhapsody in Blue* and *Porgy and Bess* had made use of everything on the urban American musical street. In 1938, Copland wrote a ballet score for Lincoln Kirstein's short-lived Ballet Caravan, based on the story of William H. Bonney, a fellow Brooklynite known as "Billy the Kid." Where Gershwin and others were resolutely urbane, Copland, who had lived in Mexico for a while, absorbed the feeling of the rural American musical idioms he found along the way. *Billy the Kid* and Copland's other enduring "American" works, such as *Appalachian Spring*, composed for Martha Graham, *Lincoln Portrait*, *Rodeo*, and *Fanfare for the Common Man*, not only created an American sound, they created the sound of America.

"We Will Never Die"

FINAL SCENE, PRAYER FOR THE DEAD
New York, March 9, 1943
The Leo Baeck Institute / The Newberry Library

In August 1942, a telegram sent by Gerhardt Riegner, an official of the World Jewish Congress in Geneva, describing plans for the Final Solution, reached England and America. Though dismissed by official U.S. government channels and given little credance by the *New York Times* and the *Washington Post*, word spread quickly through the Jewish community and beyond. On March 9, 1943, forty thousand people came to Madison Square Garden to see a pageant created by Ben Hecht, Kurt Weill, and Moss Hart. Nearly a thousand appeared on stage: rabbis, cantors, actors, musicians; the program cover was created by Arthur Szyk. Their purpose: to show solidarity and to pressure political figures to do something to stop the murder of Europe's Jews. The theatrical was called *We Will Never Die*, itself a paraphrase from Isaiah. It played in six cities to an audience of over 100,000. At the same time, the catastrophe that would become the Holocaust had been further reported by "Peter Bergson," an operative of the Irgun who had gone to Poland to smuggle Jews to Palestine. Peter Bergson was the pseudonym of Hillel Kook, the nephew of the Ashkenazic chief rabbi of Palestine. Late that year, hundreds of Orthodox rabbis marched on Washington seeking immediate rescue efforts to save the Jews of Europe, the only such march on behalf of Europe's Jews. President Roosevelt declined to meet with them.

"The day is short, the work is great"
AMERICAN CHAPLAINS PERFORM BURIAL SERVICES
FOR HOLOCAUST VICTIMS
Neunburg, Germany, April 29, 1945
Photograph by Pfc. Wendell N. Hustead
© CORBIS

Among the "Greatest Generation" who served in World War II, Jewish chaplains have rarely gotten their due. Like Christian chaplains, the three hundred and eleven rabbis who volunteered to serve as chaplains fought in battle, comforted the wounded, said prayers for the dead, and counseled spiritually bereft GI's of every faith. With dignity, the chaplains represented Judaism to the ninety-six percent of the armed forces who were Christian.

Beyond that, the chaplains in Europe tried to meet the desperate needs of liberated survivors of the Shoah even as, at first, the United States military forbade military personnel—even chaplains—to "fraternize" with civilians. Most bore up well under the stresses and responsibilities, even as they came home at war's end physically and emotionally spent. Many were ennobled by their experience, and some went on to distinguished careers.

*"Here lie officers and men, Negroes and whites,
rich men and poor men . . . together. Here are
Protestants, Catholics, and Jews . . . together."*
RABBI GITTELSOHN AT IWO JIMA
Iwo Jima, South Pacific, 1945
The American Jewish Historical Society

Brotherhood was a necessity for the valiant American soldiers in World War II,
but at the memorial service for the fallen at Iwo Jima, brotherhood found its limits
after the head Marine chaplain, a Protestant, asked Rabbi Roland Gittelsohn to
deliver the sermon at an interdenominational service. Roman Catholic chaplains
protested Gittelsohn's invitation and, in the end, three separate services were held.
Rabbi Gittelsohn did deliver a sermon at the Jewish cemetery, calling for tolerance
of men of all faiths and colors. His speech was picked up by reporter Robert
St. John and broadcast worldwide. In 1995, at the fifty-year commemoration of the
battle at its memorial in Washington, Gittelsohn was invited to read his sermon
again.

"I am become death, the destroyer of worlds"

J. ROBERT OPPENHEIMER

Ink on paper drawing by Ben Shahn, 1954

The Museum of Modern Art

Niels Bohr, the Danish atomic physicist, brought news to Albert Einstein in 1939 that the German refugee physicist Lise Meitner, working in Copenhagen, had split the uranium atom, with a slight loss of mass that had been converted to energy. Bohr speculated that, if a controlled chain-reaction splitting of uranium atoms could be accomplished, a mammoth explosion would result. Einstein was skeptical, but laboratory experiments in the United States showed the feasibility of the idea. With a European war regarded as imminent and fears that Nazi scientists might build such a bomb first, Einstein was persuaded by colleagues, notably Leo Szilard, to write a letter to President Franklin D. Roosevelt urging "watchfulness and, if necessary, quick action" on the part of the United States in atomic-bomb research. This recommendation marked the beginning of the Manhattan Project.

The project's scientific director would be J. Robert Oppenheimer, the son of a patrician New York Jewish family. Much of the staff working on the theoretical side was Jewish, the best and brightest of the world of physics including native-born Jews, such as Richard Feynman, and European-born refugees from Hitler, such as Edward Teller, Otto Frisch, and Felix Bloch.

"We appear to be treating the Jews as the Nazis treated them except that we do not exterminate them."

THE HARRISON REPORT

London, 1945

Dwight D. Eisenhower Presidential Library and Museum

In June of 1945, President Harry Truman appointed Earl G. Harrison, dean of the University of Pennsylvania Law School, to study the plight of displaced persons in Europe, especially the Jewish survivors of the Nazi death camps. The report brought forward the devastating truth that in the first months after the end of hostilities, "we appear to be treating the Jews as the Nazis treated them except that we do not exterminate them." President Truman wrote quickly to Dwight Eisenhower, the commanding general, with instructions to improve these conditions immediately. He ends with the sentence, "I am communicating directly with the British Government in an effort to have the doors of Palestine opened to such of these displaced persons as wish to go there."

London, England

The President,
    The White House,
        Washington.

My dear Mr. President:

Pursuant to your letter of June 22, 1945, I have the honor to present to you a partial report upon my recent mission to Europe to inquire into (1) the conditions under which displaced persons and particularly those who may be stateless or non-repatriable are at present living, especially in Germany and Austria, (2) the needs of such persons, (3) how those needs are being met at present by the military authorities, the governments of residence and international and private relief bodies, and (4) the views of the possibly non-repatriable persons as to their future destinations.

My instructions were to give particular attention to the problems, needs and views of the Jewish refugees among the displaced people, especially in Germany and Austria. The report, particularly this partial report, accordingly deals in the main with that group.

On numerous occasions appreciation was expressed by the victims of Nazi persecution for the interest of the United States Government in them. As my report shows they are in need of attention and help. Up to this point they have been "liberated" more in a military sense than actually. For reasons explained in the report, their particular problems, to this time, have not been given attention to any appreciable extent; consequently they feel that they, who were in so many ways the first and worst victims of Nazism, are being neglected by their liberators.

Upon my request, the Department of State authorized Dr. Joseph J. Schwartz to join me in the mission. Dr. Schwartz, European Director of the American Joint Distribution Committee, was granted a leave of absence from that organization for the purpose of accompanying me. His long and varied experience in refugee problems as well as his familiarity with the Continent and the people made Dr. Schwartz a most valuable associate; this report represents our joint views, conclusions and recommendations.

During various portions of the trip I had, also, the assistance of Mr. Patrick M. Malin, Vice Director of the Intergovernmental Committee on Refugees and Mr. Herbert Katzski of the War Refugee Board. These gentlemen, likewise, have had considerable experience in refugee matters. Their assistance and cooperation were most helpful in the course of the survey.

I

GERMANY AND AUSTRIA

Conditions

(1) Generally speaking, three months after V-E Day and even longer after the liberation of individual groups, many Jewish displaced persons and other possibly non-repatriables are living under guard behind barbed-wire fences, in camps of several descriptions, (built by the Germans for slave-laborers and Jews) including some of the most notorious of the concentration camps, amidst crowded, frequently unsanitary and generally grim conditions, in complete idleness, with no opportunity, except surreptitiously, to communicate with the outside world, waiting, hoping for some word of encouragement and action in their behalf.

"More interest in breaking idols than making them"

MARK ROTHKO IN HIS STUDIO
Photograph by Hans Namuth, 1964
© 1991 Hans Namuth Estate,
Center for Creative Photography, University of Arizona

The Jewish relationship with visual art has long been an uncomfortable one, determined largely by one's interpretation of the Second Commandment prohibition of graven images. In America, a liberal interpretation has largely prevailed. There were few Jewish artists in 19th-century America, not surprising given the small size of the population. But from the great tide of immigrants who arrived late in the century and early in the 20th, came a profusion of artistic creativity—if not from them directly, then from their children or grandchildren. Jews produced art of every kind, but emerging into the highest realms of artistic achievement were two strains: the representational that effortlessly and without compromise blurred the boundary between "art" and "illustration," such as the work of Ben Shahn, Saul Steinberg, and Leonard Baskin; and the school of Abstract Expressionism, as exemplified by Mark Rothko, Barnett Newman, and Adolph Gottlieb.

Perhaps this profusion of Jewish genius was the product of centuries of pent-up creativity that had had no outlet; or perhaps it was a coincidence of time that these American Jewish artists came of age in the Modern era, when "art had more interest in breaking idols than making them."

"The Jewish DPs will never forget the generous impulses and the unprecedented humanitarianism of the American forces."

TRACTATE KIDDUSHIN, TITLE PAGE
Munich/Heidelberg, 1948
Mendel Gottesman Library. Yeshiva University

In the aftermath of the Harrison Report, the situation of the Jewish DPs improved, with special attention given to their spiritual needs. In 1946, a touching and fascinating Haggadah was published, created by the survivors for the first Passover after their liberation, and now known as the "Survivors' Haggadah." Later, DP rabbis asked the Army to publish a Talmud. Despite severe shortages of paper, the Army requisitioned a plant in Heidelberg that had formerly printed Nazi propaganda. The five hundred sets appeared in 1948. The Talmud, for so long the target of persecution in Europe, was for the first time in history published by a government. Its preface reads:

> *This edition of the Talmud is dedicated to the United States Army. The Army played a major role in the rescue of the Jewish people from total annihilation, and their defeat of Hitler bore the major burden of sustaining the DPs of the Jewish faith. This special edition of the Talmud, published in the very land where, but a short time ago, everything Jewish and of Jewish inspiration was anathema, will remain a symbol of the indestructibility of the Torah. The Jewish DPs will never forget the generous impulses and the unprecedented humanitarianism of the American forces, to whom they owe so much.*

משעבוד לגאולה מאפלה לאור גדול

מסכת
קדושין
מן
תלמוד בבלי

עם כל המפרשים כאשר נדפס מקדם ועם
הוספות חדשות כמבואר בשער השני.

יצא לאור ע"י ועד אגודת הרבנים
באזור האמריקאי באשכנז

בסיוע שלטון הצבא דארצות הברית והדזוינט
בגרמני'

מינכן–היידעלבערג
שנת חמשת אלפים ושבע מאות ותשע לב"ע

כמעט כלוני בארץ ואני לא עזבתי פקודיך

מחנה עבודה באשכנז בימי הנאצים

"The United States recognizes . . . the new State of Israel."

PRESIDENT TRUMAN RECOGNIZES THE STATE OF ISRAEL

Memorandum, May 14, 1948

The Truman Library, Independence, Missouri

When Harry Truman became president in 1945, Chaim Weizmann attempted to persuade him of the justice of creating a homeland for Jewish Holocaust survivors. In the aftermath of the U.N. resolution calling for the division of British Palestine and the creation of a Jewish state, The Jewish Agency announced that on May 14, 1948, it would establish the new State of Israel. Arab neighbors threatened war.

While Truman favored Israel's independence, he bridled at pressure from Jewish groups to commit to recognition. Exasperated, he refused to meet with Weizmann again. Activists persuaded Eddie Jacobson, Truman's former partner in a Kansas City men's haberdashery, to persuade the President to see Weizmann. Jacobson obliged and Truman was happy to see him, but was reluctant to discuss the Zionist issue. Stymied, Jacobson pointed to a bust of Andrew Jackson in the Oval Office and compared Weizmann to "Old Hickory." Truman laughed, made an off-color remark, and told Jacobson he would meet with Weizmann.

On March 18, 1948, Truman promised Weizmann that, when the British Mandate expired, he would recognize the Jewish state. Moments after midnight on May 14, as the British withdrew, David Ben Gurion declared Israel established. Truman extended recognition eleven minutes later.

This Government has been informed that a Jewish
state has been proclaimed in Palestine, and recognition
has been requested by the *provisional* Government thereof.

The United States recognizes the provisional government as the de facto authority of the new ~~Jewish~~ *State of*
~~state~~. *Israel.*

Harry Truman

Approved.
May 14, 1948.

6.11

"Women in chemistry and physics? There's nothing strange about that."
GERTRUDE ELION

Glaxo Laboratories, Triangle Park, North Carolina, ca. 1980
GlaxoSmithKline Archives / Jewish Women's Archive

Gertrude Elion knew what she wanted to do—but nobody seemed ready to let her do it. New York's Hunter College provided her with a free education during the Depression, but when she graduated at age 17, summa cum laude and Phi Beta Kappa, not one graduate school would provide her with financial aid.

Unable to find a laboratory job, she started secretarial school. Supporting herself as a doctor's receptionist and a substitute high school science teacher, Elion eventually earned a master's degree in chemistry (she was the only woman in her classes). With more lab opportunities open to women during World War II, Elion found a job at Burroughs Wellcome, a pharmaceutical company, in 1944.

Elion's research led to the first effective treatment for childhood leukemia and to immunosuppressants that made organ transplants possible. Her anti-viral research led to treatments for many ailments including AIDS. Elion, whose doctorates were all honorary, received the Nobel Prize in Medicine, together with her partner George Hitchens and British scientist James Black, in 1988.

Elion thus joined an impressive list of American Jewish Nobel Prize winners in science that also includes American-born Rosalyn Yalow (1977), and Gerty Theresa Radnitz Cori (1947) and Rita Levi-Montalcini (1986), who were born and educated abroad.

"Risks, I like to say, always pay off"

THE SALK INSTITUTE

La Jolla, California

Architect: Louis I. Kahn, 1959–1966

© CORBIS

In the early 1950s there was no time more miserable than summer. A polio epidemic that afflicted 20,000 persons a year, mostly children, kept people away from swimming places and movie theaters. It was a disease that played no favorites, afflicting the poor and a president alike. Then suddenly, on April 12, 1955, the development of a preventive vaccine was anounced. Eight years in the making, it had been developed by an immunologist named Jonas Salk, a fellow of the University of Pittsburgh Medical School working with National Foundation for Infantile Paralysis.

Salk, the son of Russian-Jewish immigrants, became an international celebrity, a status that enabled him to raise funds to build the Salk Institute in La Jolla, California. His goal was to establish an institute that would explore questions about the basic principles of life. He wanted to make it possible for biologists and others to work together in a collaborative environment that would encourage them to consider the wider implications of their discoveries for the future of humanity.

In December 1959, Salk and architect Louis I. Kahn began a unique partnership to design such a facility. Salk summarized his aesthetic objectives by telling the architect to "create a facility worthy of a visit by Picasso." Kahn, a dedicated painter as well as an architect, responded to this challenge.

"God Bless America"

THE AMERICAN JEWISH TERCENTENARY DINNER:
IRVING BERLIN SINGS "GOD BLESS AMERICA"
Drawing by Al Hirschfeld
Harvard University Theater Collection

The American Jewish Tercentenary Dinner was held in New York City at the Astor Hotel on October 20, 1954. It was an auspicious occasion: President Dwight D. Eisenhower addressed the assembled crowd, Eddie Fisher and the Jewish Chapel Choir of the United States Military Academy performed. But the highlight of the event was a performance of "God Bless America" by its composer, Irving Berlin.

Irving Berlin (1888–1989), born Israel Baline in Russia, had become suffused with the music of his new country. In his first big hit, 1911's "Alexander's Ragtime Band," he updated ragtime syncopations with jazzier rhythms and added a sweet glance backward with a quotation from Stephen Foster's "Old Folks at Home." His 1935 "Cheek To Cheek" is still the musical embodiment of urbane suavity. And then there is "Easter Parade" and "White Christmas"—need one say more? No one ever expressed such unalloyed joy in being an American.

The Tercentenary was a time of mixed feelings. There was happiness over the new State of Israel, but it was also a time when many American Jews were just coming to grips with the devastation of the Holocaust. Some months before the September anniversary, the Army-McCarthy hearings began to unravel; a little more than a year before, the Rosenbergs were executed. Few, however, questioned the worthiness of celebrating the anniversary.

"The triple melting pot"

PROTESTANT — CATHOLIC — JEW
Dustjacket, 1955
Private collection

Two American books from the postwar era helped to elevate the self-esteem of
American Jews in the years after the Holocaust. Rabbi Joshua Loth Liebman's
Peace of Mind (1946) was an astonishing success, long at the top of the *New York
Times*'s best-seller list—and still in print. It became the prototype for dozens
of self-help books that followed, combining universal religious feeling with
psychological self-understanding. In a different vein, Will Herberg's 1955 best-seller
Protestant–Catholic–Jew, was a popular work about the sociology of American
religion. It elevated Jews to insider status in American religion, introducing the
concept of a religious "triple melting pot" and establishing the idea of a common
"Judeo-Christian" tradition.

PROTESTANT

CATHOLIC

JEW

"The broken windows of our sanctuary bear mute evidence to the contrast between the ideals of religious faiths and the practices of godless men."

THE TEMPLE BOMBING

Atlanta, 1958

The Jacob Rader Marcus Center of the American Jewish Archives

In the dark before dawn on the morning of October 12, 1958, a few short hours before Atlanta's Jewish children would wake for Sunday School, white supremacists dynamited the city's oldest synagogue. The chief target of the bombing was the Temple's rabbi, Jacob Rothschild, an outspoken integrationist, who had welcomed African-Americans onto his pulpit and into his home. But the Temple bombing was only one among a series of attacks upon synagogues, Jewish community centers, and rabbis' homes across the South that began even before the Supreme Court's 1954 ruling in favor of desegregation. So far no one has been convicted of bombing the Temple on Atlanta's famed Peachtree Street, or of the attacks that shattered Miami's Orthodox Temple Beth-El and Nashville's Jewish community center, or of planting the dynamite that failed to explode at Birmingham's Conservative Beth-El.

"I believed it was important to a little girl's self-esteem to play with a doll that has breasts."

RUTH HANDLER AND THE 40TH ANNIVERSARY BARBIE

Photograph by Jeff Christensen, New York, 1999

© Reuters

Ruth Handler invented an American icon when she launched the Barbie doll in 1959. Barbie's colossal success propelled Mattel, the company founded by Ruth and Elliot Handler with Harold "Matt" Matson, into the ranks of Fortune's 500. But Barbie and her entourage are only part of the story of how America's Jewish women pioneered a rapidly expanding consumer culture. That history includes the famous, like Helena Rubenstein in cosmetics and Jennie Grossinger in resorts. But it also includes many whose names are less well known, like Rose Blumkin of Omaha's Nebraska Furniture Mart and Sylvia Weinberger who, with a sprinkling of matzoh meal and a pinch of salt, turned chopped liver into a commercial success.

Long before the Holocaust burst hugely into American consciousness and well before Elie Wiesel became its Nobel-laureate international witness, American Jews were already grappling with its aftermath. Many faced it personally and alone as had Rebbetzin Anna Alstadt Hertzberg who, on the eve of Yom Kippur in 1946, lit thirty-six memorial candles, one for each member of her family struck down by the Nazis. But other American Jews were encountering it publicly in the faces of the survivors settling among them or when they read Anne Frank's diary, first published in America in 1952 and adapted as the 1956 Pulitzer prize-winning play, *The Diary of Anne Frank*. By decade's end, a vast body of literature—documentary, personal memory, analytical—gradually took shape. It included English translations of Primo Levi's *Survival in Auschwitz* (*If This Is a Man*) and Elie Wiesel's *Night*.

Zionism on Screen

EXODUS POSTER

Printed poster designed by Saul Bass, 1961

The Library of Congress

Modern Zionism and the movies were born around the same time and became acquainted with one another while still in their youth. Film presentations were an important feature of Zionist promotional and fundraising events. The fifty-five-minute feature *Land of Promise*, released in 1935, was no doubt the most widely seen movie about Jewish Palestine. Made for the Palestine Foundation Fund by a crew from Fox studios, it had a five-week run at New York's Astor theater at a time when three weeks was considered a major success by Hollywood standards. Later, it was seen all over the world: Jewish troops saw it during World War II; in the early years of the State of Israel it was frequently screened in transit camps for new immigrants. Even today, few documentaries dealing with the pre-state history of Israel do not use images taken from *The Land of Promise*.

In the post-state years, a number of films were made about Israel's founding, including *The Juggler* and *Cast A Giant Shadow*. The best-known of these, however, is the 1961 blockbuster *Exodus*, directed by Otto Preminger and based on Leon Uris's best-selling 1958 novel.

OTTO PREMINGER PRESENTS PAUL NEWMAN, EVA MARIE SAINT, RALPH RICHARDSON, PETER LAWFORD, LEE J. COBB, SAL MINEO, JOHN DEREK, HUGH GRIFFITH, GREGORY RATOFF, FELIX AYLMER, DAVID OPATOSHU, JILL HAWORTH IN "EXODUS." SCREENPLAY BY DALTON TRUMBO. BASED ON THE NOVEL BY LEON URIS. MUSIC BY ERNEST GOLD. PHOTOGRAPHED IN SUPER PANAVISION 70, TECHNICOLOR® BY SAM LEAVITT. TODD AO STEREOPHONIC SOUND. A UNITED ARTISTS RELEASE. PRODUCED AND DIRECTED BY OTTO PREMINGER.

New American Jewish Populations

FREE SOVIET JEWS!

Poster produced by the Greater New York Conference on Soviet Jews

Illustration by Julia Noonan

The Museum of Jewish Heritage—A Living Memorial to the Holocaust

In the years leading up to the Six Day War, many American Jews and Jewish organizations focussed their efforts on the protection of the more than two million Jews living in the Soviet Union. The cause became something akin to a Jewish Civil Rights Movement, sometimes discussed in the same breath. Two specific organizations formed in 1964: The American Jewish Conference on Soviet Jewry and Student Struggle for Soviet Jewry. But it wasn't until after the Six Day War that the major effort began. The movement was an enormous success, as over 1.5 million Jews left the Soviet Union for the United States, Israel, and elsewhere.

Other Jews suffering oppression were also aided by American Jewish organi–zations, notably the Jews of Ethiopia and Eritrea. Another important Jewish population imperiled in recent years was the Jews of Iran, who departed in large numbers from the home where they had lived since the time of the Babylonian Exile. Many of them settled in the United States, especially Los Angeles. In that city, too, as elsewhere across the United States, tens of thousands of Israelis have also made new homes.

SOLIDARITY SUNDAY
MAY 21st. CITY HALL TO BATTERY PARK
MARCH BEGINS 12 NOON, BDWY & MURRAY ST.
THE GREATER NEW YORK CONFERENCE ON SOVIET JEWRY. (212) 354-1316
SUPPORTED BY THE UNITED JEWISH APPEAL OF GREATER NEW YORK & THE FEDERATION OF JEWISH PHILANTHROPIES.

"The Writer in the Family"

PHILIP ROTH

Connecticut, 1990s

Photo by Nancy Crampton / Random House

In 1977, the critic Irving Howe, remembered by so many for his evocative *World of Our Fathers*, argued that the American Jewish writing whose vitality and energy he celebrated in the writings of Isaac Bashevis Singer, Henry Roth, and Saul Bellow had peaked. He doubted the possibility that a new generation of writers would emerge to contribute the distinctive sensibility of America's Jews to American literature. A quarter of a century later, we know Howe was wrong. Not only did some of those he included then in his pantheon, like Philip Roth and Cynthia Ozick, continue to extend the canon of American Jewish literature, but a host of new voices—Tony Kushner, Allegra Goodman, Nathan Englander, Dara Horn, Michael Chabon, Lara Vapnyar, to name but a handful—found their literary imaginations fueled by scenarios Howe scarcely envisioned.

"As though my legs were praying"

ABRAHAM JOSHUA HESCHEL AND MARTIN LUTHER KING, JR.,
AT THE MARCH FOR PEACE, ARLINGTON NATIONAL CEMETERY
Photograph © by John C. Goodwin
Arlington, Virginia, February 6, 1968

There was an immediate and deep affinity between Abraham Joshua Heschel and Martin Luther King, Jr., who first met in Chicago in 1963, at a conference on religion and race. At the deepest level, they shared a belief in the central message of Exodus, how it was inevitably intertwined with politics. As King persuaded Heschel to become more involved with the Civil Rights struggle, Heschel convinced King to take a more active stand against the war in Vietnam. The image of the two men arm-in-arm at the head of the march from Selma to Montgomery, in March 1965, and again in other protests, became an emblem of an era. King was elated by Heschel's participation, writing, "I cannot tell you how much your presence means to us." For Heschel, it was a holy event. He wrote to King, "The day we marched together out of Selma was a day of sanctification . . . [I felt] as though my legs were praying." In 1968, King was the keynote speaker at a dinner in honor of Heschel's sixtieth birthday, an event organized by the Rabbinical Assembly. Ten days later he was shot dead in Memphis. Heschel was the rabbi who spoke at King's funeral.

"Worship God through joy!"
SHLOMO CARLEBACH AT THE VILLAGE GATE
Vanguard Records, New York, 1963
Photograph by Norman C. Vershay
YIVO Institute for Jewish Research

Shlomo Carlebach (1925–1994) was born to a distinguished line of German rabbis. After Talmud study in the United States, he became attached to the court of the Lubavitcher Rebbe Joseph Schneersohn. A gifted singer and songwriter, Carlebach was encouraged by Schneersohn to make his an outreach ministry, teaching Jews of all stripes by song—in their own milieu. Carlebach's great success was in coffeehouses, at youth gatherings, in hippie communes, at music festivals, in performance, and on record. In 1966 he appeared at the Berkeley Folk Festival in California, along with Pete Seeger and Joan Baez; a year later, he opened The House of Love and Prayer in San Francisco's Haight-Ashbury district.

Carlebach's brand of counterculture Judaism eventually broadened its appeal, becoming identified with the "Jewish Renewal" movement of the post-1960s period. Within this realm were two other highly individualistic leaders: Zalman Schachter-Shalomi, whose spirituality had a fashionably Far-Eastern flair, and Rebbetzin Esther Jungreis, whose stadium presentations were reminiscent of Christian evangelists.

פתחו לי שערי צדק

SHLOMO CARLEBACH
AT THE
VILLAGE GATE

Design Jules Halfant · Photo Norman C. V.

America and the Six Day War

MOSHE DAYAN VISITS PRESIDENT NIXON
Washington, December 12, 1970
© Bettmann/CORBIS

Following three weeks of fear and trembling, war erupted early on June 5, 1967, and in six days the Arab armies were routed, leaving Israel in control of the Sinai Peninsula, the west bank of the Jordan River, the Golan Heights, and most important of all for Jews, the Old City of Jerusalem. Throughout the United States, Jews flocked to synagogues to express relief and give thanks; some talked of having witnessed a "miracle," a signal from God. More tangibly, Jews donated unprecedented sums of money: $240 million in donations and $190 million in Israel bonds. As the United States military stumbled in Vietnam, Israel's smashing victory offered a sense of reassurance: its victory was widely perceived as a victory for America itself. Israel's Defense Minister, Gen. Moshe Dayan, became as much a hero in America as in Israel. The Six Day War also marked for some "a turning point in American Jewish consciousness," changing the way American Jews thought "not only about Israel but about themselves." It has been said that 1967 became the demarcation of when the contemporary era for American Jews began. But in the context of what America as a whole was undergoing—Vietnam, Black militancy, the assassinations of Martin Luther King, Jr., and Robert Kennedy, the election of Richard Nixon—and Israel's later struggles, the perception of the event has changed.

Tradition and Innovation

HAVURAT SHALOM

Somerville, Massachusetts, 1994

Photograph by Carl Mastandrea

The Combined Jewish Philanthropies of Greater Boston

Judaism in America is often described in terms of its four major denominations, but not without a nod to one of the 1960s counterculture's lasting edifices. In Somerville, Massachusetts, in the environs of Harvard, Brandeis, and Tufts universities, Havurat Shalom was founded in 1968 as a spiritual community where members would take control of their own Jewish lives. This *havurah* (community of friends) was established as a place for study, worship, and social action, inspiring the founding of similar groups around America and the world.

Members of Havurat Shalom extended their brand of non-hierarchical Judaism with the publication of *The Jewish Catalog: A Do-It-Yourself Kit* in 1973, offering others the tools to "do Jewish" for themselves.

The community remains a progressive pioneer in Jewish life. Since the 1980s, Havurat Shalom has led the way in its commitment to feminist and egalitarian liturgy and principles. A perpetual advocate for inclusion within Jewish life, Havurat Shalom continues to combine tradition with innovation.

"How can all this concretely be applied to our daily lives?"

In 1940, Rabbi Joseph I. Schneersohn, the sixth Hasidic rebbe in the dynasty of Lubavitch, arrived in a wheelchair in the United States. Saved by a presidential visa from the clutches of the Nazis, he settled in the Crown Heights section of Brooklyn and set to work establishing in America a "new center for Torah and Judaism." Under the energetic leadership of his son-in-law, Rabbi Menahem Mendel Schneerson, who became the seventh Lubavitcher Rebbe in 1951, the Lubavitch movement spread. His *shluchim* (emissaries) set up Jewish institutions wherever Jews lived or visited, seeking to strengthen Jewish religious consciousness and hasten the coming of the messiah. The Rebbe's death, in 1994, disappointed those who had come to believe that he himself was the messiah, but the movement soldiered on, carrying the Rebbe's legacy forward.

SCENE FROM *THE PRODUCERS*

Film written and directed by Mel Brooks, 1968

The New York Public Library

Set up as a liturgical year-end antidote to painful collective memories, the holiday of Purim is the Jewish Feast of Fools, the day on which the Talmud teaches that one should become so drunk as to forget the difference between the hymns "Blessed Be Mordecai" and "Cursed Be Haman." One of the most beloved customs of the day is the performance of a *purimshpil*, a play in which the world is turned upside down. There have been *purimshpiln* to suit all times, needs, and bad memories; Haman, the villain of the biblical Purim story, has been envisioned as various cruel popes and sundry tsars, a cavalcade of crusaders, grand (and not-so-grand) inquisitors. In America, in the late 1920s, there were *purimshpiln* in which the notoriously antisemitic Henry Ford was the day's Haman. And the tradition lives on, nowhere more famously (infamously, to some tastes) than in *The Producers*, the 1968 film by Mel Brooks (and its 2001 incarnation as a Broadway musical), in which all are invited to dance on Hitler's grave—in jackboots, no less.

"This Woman's Place"

BELLA ABZUG RUNS FOR CONGRESS
Campaign poster, New York, 1970
The Library of Congress

Bold, brazen, and true to her heart, Bella Abzug fought in the frontlines for all the great causes of her lifetime: women's rights, civil rights, social justice, workers' rights, the environment, and against the abuses of government. Her legacy endures in the important pieces of legislation she authored or coauthored: the Freedom of Information Act, the Government in the Sunshine Act, and the Right to Privacy Act. She wrote the first law banning discrimination against women in obtaining credit cards, loans, and mortgages, and introduced pioneering bills on comprehensive child care, Social Security for homemakers, and family planning. "Battling Bella" was always the people's warrior.

"Jewish Women Call for Change"

RABBI SALLY PRIESAND ON THE 25TH ANIVERSARY
OF HER ORDINATION

Hebrew Union College, Cincinnati, March 1997

Private Collection

In March 1972, a small group of young, highly educated women calling themselves Ezrat Nashim (the name for the women's section of a synagogue, also translated as "help of women") pushed the Conservative rabbinate to institute gender equity. Its manifesto, "Jewish Women Call for Change," demanded women's full participation and leadership in Conservative Judaism. Ezrat Nashim applied its emerging American feminist consciousness to Judaism just as Sally Preisand was completing her studies. Priesand became the first American woman rabbi when she was ordained at Hebrew Union College–Jewish Institute of Religion in June 1972. Sandy Sasso became the first Reconstructionist woman rabbi in 1974; Amy Eilberg was ordained by the Conservative Movement in 1985.

Changing expectations created by female rabbis have profoundly reconfigured American Jewish ritual and life. Orthodox communities are encouraging unprecedented female engagement in advanced textual study. In the liberal movements, Sally Priesand's ordination and more than seven hundred subsequent female ordinations have led to a deepening emphasis on spirituality, a turn to the healing possibilities of Jewish tradition, challenges to continued exclusions within Jewish tradition and life, such as those against gays and lesbians, and a general democratization of access to ritual participation, education, and leadership.

"The New Jewish Literacy"

ME'AH CLASSROOM AT HEBREW COLLEGE
Newton Centre, Massachusetts, 2004
Photograph © by Paula Lerner

Lifelong learning among Jews is rooted in the Book of Deuteronomy and flourished for millennia wherever Jews lived. In America, publications designed to educate Jewish adults about their history and faith began to emerge as early as the 1840s. Thereafter, programs of adult Jewish education developed in waves, often in response to eras of change. The late nineteenth century witnessed a dramatic spurt in Jewish educational opportunities for women as well as for men, including the establishment of the first Jewish teachers' colleges, the creation of major Jewish library collections, and, in 1893, the founding of the Jewish Chautauqua Society. Another spurt took place beginning in the late 1930s, in response to Nazism, domestic antisemitism and the waning of the Great Depression. By the late 1950s, adult Jewish education had grown into "an effort of major proportions and national impact," though many programs subsequently stagnated. More recently, an era of great change in Jewish life spawned a renewed hungering for adult Jewish learning. Three nationwide programs of adult Jewish education took off: the Wexner Heritage Program (1985), the Florence Melton Adult Mini-Schools (1986), and the Me'ah ("one hundred [hours]") Program (1994). Each attracted thousands of committed Jewish adults, women in particular, interested in learning more about Jewish history, texts, ideas, and practices.

The Difference Between a Bookkeeper and a Supreme Court Justice
RUTH BADER GINSBURG IS SWORN IN TO THE SUPREME COURT
Washington, August 10, 1993
Collection of the Supreme Court of the United States

The story of Associate Justice of the Supreme Court Ruth Bader Ginsburg
illustrates the opportunities of the American education system, and how
through diligence, brilliance, and luck, an ambitious woman could overcome
the many barriers set before her. It shows how an inspired litigator could
push courts to honor and expand the American tradition of justice. It gives
us an eminent American judge who points proudly to the strength she draws
from Judaism's eternal pursuit of justice. Finally, Justice Ginsburg's life
demonstrates what she sees as America's preeminent challenge of celebrating
difference while unifying for the common good.

In joining in numerous 350th anniversary commemorations of Jewish life in
America, Justice Ginsburg has offered a telling question as an illustration
of what it is that has made the United States a unique home for so many Jews
and other Americans. What is the difference, she has asked, between a Lower
East Side garment district bookkeeper and a Supreme Court Justice. Her
answer, pointing to her mother's experience and her own: "one generation."

"The quality of human life depends greatly on what we remember, how we remember, and why we remember"

THE UNITED STATES HOLOCAUST MEMORIAL MUSEUM
Architect: James Ingo Freed
Opened Washington, D.C., 1994
© PictureNet/CORBIS

The first steps toward memorials to the victims of the Holocaust were tentative and slow in coming. It was some years before the collective psyches of the surviving victims and the public were able to comprehend the events. The capture and trial of Adolf Eichmann, 1960–1962, made clear the narrative of the perpetrators for the first time; the heartbreaking memoirs of the survivors and books of historical analysis attempted to fill out the story. Justice would be pursued in the courts, but the quest for public recognition reached its apogee more than thirty years later, in 1994, when the United States Holocaust Memorial Museum opened in Washington, D.C., and Steven Spielberg's film *Schindler's List* was released throughout the world.

The Washington museum, which became one of the top attractions in a city of museums and memorials, was built during a time when many local memorials to the victims of the Holocaust were appearing around the country. The memorials, which take a great variety of forms, are most often connected to educational programs, whether locally originated or coordinated through international organizations such as the Brookline, Massachusetts-based Facing History and Ourselves.

"Only in America"

JEWISH CAMPAIGN BUTTONS 2000, 2004
Skirball Cultural Center and Museum, Los Angeles

In the year 2000, Senator Joseph Lieberman was nominated for the vice-presidency of the United States on the Democratic ticket, the first Jew ever to be selected by a major political party for such high office. "Only in America," he exclaimed. His nomination was widely viewed as a sign that antisemitism had declined to historically low levels in the United States. Being Jewish was no longer an obstacle to political success. Just forty years earlier, another Jewish senator from Connecticut, Abraham Ribicoff, declined John F. Kennedy's invitation to serve as his Attorney General for fear that the country was not ready for a Jew to appear in such a visible position of power. The Lieberman nomination, by contrast, met with wall-to-wall approbation, even from Republican opponents. This result demonstrated that a Jewish candidate no longer had to worry about being "too Jewish" in order to succeed. An American could observe the Sabbath, keep kosher, and aspire to high office as well. Indeed, in 2004, Lieberman cast his hat into the ring as a candidate for the presidency. Three other Democratic contenders touted Jewish family connections that year: one was the son of a Jew, one the grandson, and one was married to a Jewish woman.

EDITORIAL COMMITTEE & CAPTION AUTHORS

We wish to thank LYN SLOME *and* KEVIN PROFFITT *for their invaluable advice and assistance in image research and permissions. We also thank* ALICE HERMAN, DAVID SOLOMON, *and* RACHAEL DORR *for their tireless support throughout the project.*

Manfred Anson, Statue of Liberty Hanukkah menorah (cast brass), New Jersey, 1985/2004. The Library of Congress. Gift of Dr. Aaron J. Feingold (in memory of Saul Feingold) and Peachy and Mark Levy.

NATIONAL DINNER
SEPTEMBER 14, 2005

NATIONAL DINNER SPONSORS

CELEBRATE 350: JEWISH LIFE IN AMERICA

Robert S. Rifkind, Chair

Alice Herman, Executive Director

in collaboration with

THE COMMISSION FOR COMMEMORATING 350 YEARS OF AMERICAN JEWISH HISTORY

comprising

THE LIBRARY OF CONGRESS

Dr. James H. Billington, Librarian of Congress

THE NATIONAL ARCHIVES AND RECORDS ADMINISTRATION

Dr. Allen Weinstein, Archivist of the United States

THE AMERICAN JEWISH HISTORICAL SOCIETY

Kenneth J. Bialkin, Chair

Sidney Lapidus, President

David Solomon, Executive Director

THE JACOB RADER MARCUS CENTER of the AMERICAN JEWISH ARCHIVES

Dr. Gary P. Zola, Executive Director

NATIONAL DINNER COMMITTEES

HOST COMMITTEE

CHAIRS

Len Blavatnik

Lester Crown

Marilyn and Sam Fox

Diane and Guilford

Ilene and Stanley Gold

Ruth and David Gottesman

Susan and Roger Hertog

Linda and Michael Jesselson

Deanne and Arnold Kaplan

Ruth and Sidney Lapidus

Ronald S. Lauder

Barbara and Ira A. Lipman

Ms. Sharon Handler
   and Amb. John L. Loeb, Jr.

Ingeborg and Ira Rennert

Susan and Jack Rudin

Mrs. Edmond J. Safra

Jeanie and Jay Schottenstein

Lynn Schusterman

Katherine Farley
   and Jerry Speyer

Merryl H. and James S. Tisch

Joan and Sandy Weill

Fred S. Zeidman

The Zell Family

Roy J. Zuckerberg

Mort Zuckerman

VICE CHAIRS

Brenda and Burton Lehman

Phyllis and William Mack

Leonard P. Shaykin

Alan B. Slifka

Jessica M. Bibilowicz

Wendy and Mark Biderman

Dr. Ronald Dozoretz

Mel Fisher

Emanuel and Patricia Gantz

Nancy Goldstein-Levine

Eugene and Emily Grant
   Family Foundation

Cheryl Halpern

Frances A. Hess

Robert S. Kaplan

Mr. and Mrs. Peter L. Malkin

Leo Nevas

Bruce Ramer

Richard Ravitch

Leonard A. Wilf

HONORARY COMMITTEE

His Eminence Theodore
   Cardinal McCarrick

The Rt. Rev. John Bryson Chane

Sheldon S. Cohen

Rabbi Dan Ehrenkrantz

Amb. Stuart Eizenstat

Rabbi David H. Ellenson

Beverly Sills Greenough

Amb. Martin S. Indyk

Richard M. Joel

Dr. Henry A. Kissinger

Dr. Norman Lamm

Robert M. Morgenthau

Amb. Alfred H. Moses

Dr. Jehuda Reinharz

Amb. Dennis Ross

Dr. Ismar Schorsch

Elie Wiesel

SUPPORTERS

Dr. Ira A. Abrahamson

M. Bernard Aidinoff

Robert Arnow

The David Berg Foundation

Mandell L. Berman

Bethesda Oak Hospital

Anne E. and Kenneth J. Bialkin
  /Bialkin Family Foundation

Jacob and Hilda Blaustein Foundation

Mr. and Mrs. Frank Bloom

George S. Blumenthal

Susan Brenner and Steve Mombach

Otto M. Budig, Jr.

Carnegie Corp. of New York

Lucille and Charles Carruthers

Maureen and Marshall Cogan

Mr. and Mrs. Philip S. Cohen

Lester Crown

Mr. and Mrs. Bernard Dave

Deloitte and Touche

Helen DeMario Foundation

Dinsmore & Shohl

Dorot Foundation

Duro Bag

Amb. Stuart E. Eizenstat

Amb. Edward E. Elson

Henry and Edith Everett

Federated Department Stores

Fifth Third Bank

Norman and Rebecca Frankel
  and Susan Marcus

Dr. and Mrs. Richard Freiberg

Mr. and Mrs. William Friedlander

Shelly and Michael Gerson

Barbara and Charles Glueck

Stanley Gold

William Goldberg

Jerome R. Goldstein

E. Robert Goodkind

The Gottesman Fund

The Greater Cincinnati Foundation

Greenbaum, Doll & McDonald, PLLC

Alan C. Greenberg

Gary Greenberg

Stephen & Myrna Greenberg (JCF)

Anne and Burton G. Greenblatt

Leonard A. Wilf

Toni and Stewart Young

Harry and Jeanette Weinberg

The Norman and Rosita Winston
Foundation

David and Nancy Wolf

Genevieve and Justin Wyner

Dr. and Mrs. Jeffrey Zipkin

Roy Zuckerberg

PARTICIPATING ORGANIZATIONS

Information was provided by the individual organizations.

AMERICAN JEWISH JOINT
DISTRIBUTION COMMITTEE, INC.
711 Third Avenue, 10 Floor
New York, NY 10017-4014
www.jdc.org

JDC is the overseas arm of the American Jewish community. We sponsor programs of relief, rescue and renewal and help Israel address its most urgent social challenges. We are committed to the idea that all Jews are responsible for one another.

Judge Ellen M. Heller, President
Eugene J. Ribakoff, Chairman
Steven Schwager, Executive Vice-President

AMERICANS FOR PEACE NOW
1101 14 Street, NW, Suite 6
Washington, DC 20005
www.peacenow.org

Americans for Peace Now is a Jewish, Zionist organization dedicated to enhancing Israel's security through peace and supporting the Israeli Peace Now movement. We are proud to be the preeminent voice for pro-Israel, pro-peace members of the American Jewish community.

Luis Lainer, Chairman
Martin Bresler, Secretary
Elaine Hoffman, Treasurer
Debra DeLee, President & CEO
Mark Rosenblum, Founder

AMERICAN JEWISH CONGRESS
825 Third Avenue
New York, NY 10022
www.ajcongress.org

Defense of the Jewish People in the US, Israel and overseas.

Paul S. Miller, President
Jack Rosen, Chair
Harley Lippman, Chair, Governing Council
Neil B. Goldstein, Executive Director

AIPAC
440 1st St., NW
Washington, DC 20001
www.aipac.org

Domestic lobby organization for a strong US-Israel relationship

Bernice Manocherian, President
Howard Kohr, Executive Director

AMERICAN-ISRAEL FRIENDSHIP
LEAGUE
134 E. 39 Street
New York, NY 10016
www.aifl.org

The America-Israel Friendship League is a non-sectarian, grass roots organization dedicated to supporting US-Israel friendship by stressing our mutual commitment to democratic principles, respect for human rights and dignity, and highlighting Israel's efforts to implement that freedom and democracy in the Middle East.

Kenneth J. Bialkin, Chairman and President
Mortimer B. Zuckerman,
     Honorary President
Dr. Charlotte K. Frank,
     Chair, Executive Committee

William H. Behrer, III,
     Chief Operating Officer

AMERICAN CONFERENCE OF CANTORS
213 N. Morgan Street, Suite 1A
Chicago, Illinois 60607
www.accantors.org

The ACC, affiliated with the Union for Reform Judaism, supports its members in their sacred calling as emissaries for Judaism and Jewish music. We provide our communities with compelling experiences of music, text, learning, interpersonal relationship and connectedness to God.

Cantor Richard Cohn, President
Cantor Susan Caro, Vice President
Cantor Jessica Epstein, Vice President
Cantor Marshall Portnoy, Vice President
Cantor Judith K. Rowland,
     Immediate Past President

AMIT
817 Broadway
New York, NY 10003
www.amitchildren.org

AMIT enables Israel's youth to realize their potential and strengthens Israeli society by educating and nurturing children from diverse backgrounds within a framework of academic excellence, religious values and Zionist ideals.

Jan Schechter, National President
Marvin Leff, Executive Director
Deanne Shapiro, First Senior Vice President
Audrey Lookstein, Chair, National Board
Debbie Moed, Chair, Board of Directors

THE AMERICAN JEWISH COMMITTEE
The Jacob Blaustein Building
165 E. 56 Street
New York, NY 10022
www.AJC.org

AJC protects the rights of Jews the world over; combats bigotry and anti-Semitism and promotes human rights for all; works for the security of Israel; and advocates public policy positions rooted in democratic values and perspectives of the Jewish heritage.

 E. Robert Goodkind, President
Richard J. Sideman,
    Chair, Board of Governors
Julie Baskes, Chair, National Council
David A. Harris, Executive Director
Shula Bahat, Associate Executive Director

AMERICAN ORT
817 Broadway
New York, NY 10003
www.aort.org

Founded in 1922, American ORT supports a global network of schools, colleges and training programs that boasts more than 3 million graduates and provides a cutting edge education to more than 300,000 students in 60 countries annually.

Joe Cohen, President
Robert L. Sill,
    Chairman of National Board of Directors
Jeffrey M. Reiff,
    Chairman, Executive Committee
Paul B. Firstenberg, Executive Director
Irma Friedman,
    National Campaign Director

AMERICAN JEWISH PRESS ASSOCIATION
1255 New Hampshire Ave., NW #702
Washington, DC 20036
www.ajpa.org

The AJPA mission has remained constant over the years: to enhance the status of American Jewish Journalism and to provide a forum for the exchange of ideas and cooperative activities among the American Jewish Press.

Toby Dershowitz, Executive Director
Rich Waloff, President
Rob Certner, 1st Vice President

AMERICAN SEPHARDI FEDERATION
with SEPHARDIC HOUSE
15 West 16 Street
New York, NY 10011
www.americansephardifederation.org

The American Sephardi Federation, founded in 1973 to support, revitalize and strengthen American Sephardic communities, recently joined forces with Sephardic House to create one united Sephardic organization whose mission is to promote and preserve the spiritual, historical, cultural and social traditions of all Sephardic communities and assure their place as an integral part of Jewish heritage.

Leon Levy, Honorary Lifetime President
David E. R. Dangoor, President
Mike M. Nassimi, Chairman of the Board
Esme E. Berg, Director

ANTI-DEFAMATION LEAGUE
823 United Nations Plaza
New York, NY 10017
www.adl.org

Since 1913, the Anti-Defamation League has been the world's leading organization fighting anti-Semitism, racism and all forms of bigotry, prejudice and discrimination through investigation, education, protection, legislation, litigation, communication and persuasion.

Abraham H. Foxman, National Director
Barbara B. Balser, National Chair
Glen A. Tobias, Hon. Nat'l Chair
Howard P. Berkowitz, Hon. Nat'l Chair
David H. Strassler, Hon. Nat'l Chair

ASSOCIATION OF JEWISH LIBRARIES
c/o NFJC
330 Seventh Avenue – 21 Floor
New York, NY 10001
www.jewishlibraries.org

The Association of Jewish Libraries promotes Jewish literacy through enhancement of libraries and library resources and through leadership for the profession and practitioners of Judaica librarianship. The Association fosters access to information, learning, teaching and research relating to Jews, Judaism, the Jewish experience and Israel.

Rhonda Rose, President

Laurel Wolfson,
   Vice President/President Elect
Pearl Berger, Past President
Peggy Pearlstein, President—The Research
   & Special Libraries Division
Linda R. Silver, President —The Synagogue,
   School, & Center Division

ASSOCIATION FOR JEWISH STUDIES
15 W. 16 Street
NY, NY 10011
www.brandeis.edu/ajs

*Founded in 1969, the Association for
Jewish Studies is a learned society and
professional organization that seeks to
promote, maintain, and improve teaching,
research, and related endeavors in Jewish Studies in colleges, universities, and
other institutions of higher learning.*

Judith R. Baskin, President
Sara R. Horowitz, Vice President
Arnold Dashefsky, Vice President
Ephraim Kanarfogel, Vice President
Steven J. Zipperstein, Vice President
Rona Sheramy, Executive Director

ASSOCIATION OF MODERN ORTHODOX
DAY SCHOOLS AND YESHIVA HIGH
SCHOOLS

500 West 185 Street
Suite FH413
New York, NY 10033
www.AMODS.org

*The Association of Modern Orthodox
Day Schools and Yeshiva High Schools
(AMODS) networks and services those who
pass on our knowledge, values, and vision
to our children. AMODS seeks to create an
energized educational system dedicated to
excellence, a community for educators and
concerned lay leaders, and a portal through
which all of these constituencies can draw
upon the expertise of the schools, programs,
and initiatives of Yeshiva University.*

Rabbi David A. Israel, Director
Nathan Kruman, Assistant Director
Toby Goldfisher Kaplowitz, Coordinator
Rabbi Robert S. Hirt, Co-Chair
Matthew J. Maryles, Co-Chair

BALTIMORE HEBREW UNIVERSITY
5800 Park Heights Ave.
Baltimore, MD 21215
www.bhu.edu

*The mission of Baltimore Hebrew University
is to preserve, generate, transmit and apply
knowledge of Judaism, its culture and its*

civilization within the context of world civilizations and thereby strengthen and deepen Jewish identity and communal continuity.

Herschel Langenthal,
  Immediate Past Chair of Board
Judith Langenthal
Dr. Frank Schuster
Susan Schuster, Vice Chair of Board
Dr. Barbara Zirkin, Dean

B'NAI B'RITH INTERNATIONAL
2020 K Street, NW, 7th Floor
Washington, DC 20006
www.bnaibrith.org

B'nai B'rith is an international organization committed to the security and continuity of the Jewish people and the State of Israel; defending human rights; combating anti-Semitism, bigotry and ignorance; and providing service to the community on the broadest principles of humanity. Its mission is to unite persons of the Jewish faith and to enhance Jewish identity through strengthening Jewish family life and the education and training of youth; broad-based services for the benefit of senior citizens; and advocacy and action on behalf of Jews throughout the world.

Joel S. Kaplan, President

Moishe Smith, Chairman of the Executive
Daniel S. Mariaschin,
  Executive Vice President
Harold Shulman, Treasurer
Dennis W. Glick, Chair, Center for Human
  Rights & Public Policy

BRANDEIS UNIVERSITY
415 South Street
Waltham, MA 02453
www.brandeis.edu

Founded in 1948 by members of the American Jewish community, Brandeis University is non-sectarian yet committed to serving the Jewish community. It combines the academic rigor of top research universities with personal interaction of the finest liberal arts colleges.

Mr. Stephen B. Kay, Chairman of the Board
Mr. Gershon Kekst, Vice Chair of the Board
Mr. Malcolm L. Sherman,
  Vice Chair of the Board
Dr. Jehuda Reinharz, President
Dr. Marty Wyngaarden Krauss, Provost

CENTER FOR CHRISTIAN-JEWISH
UNDERSTANDING OF SACRED HEART
UNIVERSITY
5151 Park Avenue

Fairfield, CT 06825
www.ccju.org/

CCJU encourages interreligious dialogue through understanding and promotes harmony between religions through many programs, lectures, etc., locally and internationally.

Rabbi Joseph Ehrenkranz,
    Executive Director
Dr. David Coppola,
    Assistant Executive Director

CENTER FOR JEWISH HISTORY
15 W. 16 Street
New York, NY 10011
www.cjh.org

The Center for Jewish History is a central repository for the cultural and historical legacy of the Jewish people. The Center embodies the unique partnership of five major institutions of Jewish scholarship, history and art.

Bruce Slovin, Chairman
Joseph D. Becker, Vice Chairman
Kenneth J. Bialkin, Vice Chairman
Erica Jesselson, Vice Chairman
Ira Berkowitz, CFO
Michael Glickman,
    Director of Public Affairs

CLAL
440 Park Ave. South, 4th floor
New York, NY 10016
www.clal.org

Founded in 1974, CLAL—The National Jewish Center for Learning and Leadership is a leadership-training institute, think tank, and resource. A leader in pluralism, CLAL's innovative programs connect Jewish wisdom to contemporary experience, creating spiritually rich and engaged Jewish lives.

Fern K. Hurst, Chairman
Rabbi Irwin Kula, President
Donna M. Rosenthal,
    Executive Vice Chairman
Rabbi Brad Hirschfield, Vice President
Rabbi Jennifer Krause,
    Associate Vice President

COMBINED JEWISH PHILANTHROPIES
126 High Street
Boston, MA 02110
www.cjp.org

Central fundraising and community building organization of the Boston Jewish Community, committed to principles of Torah, Tzedek, and Chesed.

Robert L. Beal, Chair
Barry Shrage, President

CONFERENCE OF PRESIDENTS OF MAJOR
AMERICAN JEWISH ORGANIZATIONS
633 Third Avenue, 21 Floor
New York, NY 10017
www.conferenceofpresidents.org

*The central umbrella body for 52 national
Jewish organizations, the Conference of Presidents of Major American Jewish Organizations is the address for policy formulation and
collective action to strengthen all aspects of
the U.S.-Israel relationship, to protect and
enhance the security and dignity of Jews
at home and abroad and to address foreign
policy issues that impact our community.*

Harold Tanner, Chairman
Malcolm Hoenlein,
    Executive Vice Chairman
James S. Tisch, Immediate Past President
    and Chairman of the Conference of
    Presidents Fund

CONGREGATION MICKVE ISRAEL
Monterey Square, P.O. Box 816
Savannah, GA 31402-0816
www.mickveisrael.org

*Founded 1733, third oldest Jewish synagogue
in America. In a unique Gothic structure,
circa 1876, its museum collection includes
the two oldest Torahs in America, and a
collection of Presidential letters including
George Washington, Thomas Jefferson, James
Madison and 20th century presidents.*

Arnold Mark Belzer, Rabbi
Anne B. Maner, Executive Director
Daniel B. Nagelberg, Parnas/President
Marjorie Levy, Vice-President
Steve Gordon, Treasurer

CONGREGATION SHEARITH ISRAEL
8 West 70 St.
New York, NY 10023
www.shearith-israel.org

*In September 1654, twenty-three Jews fleeing
the inquisition in Recife, Brazil landed
in New Amsterdam where they founded
the Spanish and Portuguese Synagogue,
"Shearith Israel." Although the tradition of
the Congregation is Sephardic and follows
the Spanish and Portuguese customs and
traditions, membership is open to all Jews.
No other congregation holds such diversity
among congregants, making a true gathering
of Jews from the four corners of the earth.*

Rabbi Dr. Marc D. Angel, Senior Rabbi
Rabbi Hayyim Angel, Associate Rabbi
Rev. Ira Rohde, Hazan
Peter Neustadter, Parnas
David J. Nathan, Michael Katz, Seganim
Dr. Alan M. Singer, Executive Director

CONGREGATION MIKVEH ISRAEL
44 North Fourth Street
Philadelphia, PA 19106
www.mikvehisrael.org

Mikveh Israel, "The Hope of Israel," founded in 1740 is an unparalleled American Jewish Institution. It is a synthesis of the Spanish-Portuguese Jewish ritual and the ongoing development of the American Jewish community. Among the most revered members were Haym Salomon, financier of the Revolutionary War, Nathan Levy, whose ship brought the Liberty Bell to this country, and Rebecca Gratz, a Jewish woman of great stature in the community in the 19th Century.

Mikveh Israel has a membership of approximately 350 families. The Sephardic service has remained unchanged since 1740.

Albert E. Gabbai, Rabbi
Leon L. Levy, Parnas/President
Robert L. Franklin, Esq.,

Segan/Vice President
Maurice Sady, CPA, Treasurer
Mrs. Dorothy Kligerman,
   Recording Secretary

COUNCIL OF AMERICAN
JEWISH MUSEUMS
Center for Judaic Studies,
University of Denver
2000 East Asbury Ave., Suite 157
Denver, CO 80208
www.jewishculture.org/cajm

The Council of American Jewish Museums is committed to strengthening the Jewish museum field in North America through training of museum staff and volunteers, information exchange, and advocacy on behalf of Jewish museums.

Macy B. Hart, Chair
Gabriel Goldstein, Vice-Chair
Judith C. Siegel, Secretary
Marcia Zerivitz, Treasurer
Joanne Marks Kauvar, Executive Director

GOLDRING/WOLDENBERG INSTITUTE
OF SOUTHERN JEWISH LIFE (ISJL)
P.O. Box 16528
Jackson, Mississippi 39236

www.isjl.org

The mission of the Goldring/Woldenberg Institute of Southern Jewish Life is to preserve and document the practice, culture and legacy of Judaism in the South.

B.J. (Jay) Tanenbaum III,
    Chairman, Board of Directors
Rayman L. Solomon,
    Vice Chairman, Board of Directors
Alan Franco,
    Vice Chairman, Board of Directors
Macy B. Hart, President
Dr. Stuart Rockoff, Director,
    History Department

GREATER MIAMI JEWISH FEDERATION
4200 Biscayne Blvd.
Miami, FL 33137
www.jewishmiami.org

The Greater Miami Jewish Federation exists to ensure that we act collectively & responsibly to meet the needs of and safeguard the freedom of all Jewish people.

Michael Adler, President
Jacob Solomon, Executive Vice President

HADASSAH, THE WOMEN'S ZIONIST ORGANIZATION OF AMERICA, INC.
50 West 58 St.
New York, NY 10019
www.hadassah.org

Founded in 1912, Hadassah, the Women's Zionist Organization of America, is a volunteer women's organization, whose members are motivated and inspired to strengthen their partnership with Israel, ensure Jewish continuity, and realize their potential as a dynamic force in American society.

In Israel, Hadassah initiates and supports pacesetting health care, education, youth institutions, and land developments. In the United States, Hadassah enhances the quality of American and Jewish life through its education and Zionist youth programs.

June Walker, National President
Morlie Levin, National Executive Director
Ruth B. Hurwitz, National Treasurer

HEBREW COLLEGE
160 Herrick Rd.
Newton Centre, MA 02459
www.hebrewcollege.edu

Through the study of Jewish religion, culture, civilization and Hebrew language,

Hebrew College is committed to educating students of all ages and backgrounds to become knowledgeable, creative participants, educators and leaders in the Jewish community and larger world.

Dr. David M. Gordis, President
Leslie Bornstein Stacks,
   Chair, Board of Trustees
Amb. Alfred Moses, Chair, National Board

HEBREW UNION COLLEGE–
JEWISH INSTITUTE OF RELIGION
One West 4th Street
New York, NY 10012
www.huc.edu

Hebrew Union College-Jewish Institute of Religion, the academic and professional leadership development center of Reform Judaism, educates men and women for service to American and world Jewry as rabbis, cantors, educators, and communal service professionals, and offers graduate programs to scholars of all faiths. With campuses in Cincinnati, Jerusalem, Los Angeles, and New York, HUC-JIR offers renowned libraries, archives, museums, research institutes and centers, biblical archaeology excavations, and academic publications.

Rabbi David Ellenson, Ph.D., President
Dr. Alfred Gottschalk, Chancellor Emeritus
Dr. Norman J. Cohen, Provost
Burton Lehman, Chair, Board of Governors
Stanley P. Gold,
   Chair Emeritus, Board of Governors

HIAS, INC. (Hebrew Immigrant Aid Society)
333 Seventh Avenue, 16th Floor
New York, NY 10001
www.hias.org

HIAS embodies the American Jewish community's commitment to welcome the stranger. Dedicated to assisting persecuted and oppressed people worldwide and delivering them to countries of safe haven, HIAS has, since 1881, rescued more than 4.5 million people.

Jerome S. Teller, Chair of the Board
Neil Greenbaum, President and CEO
Sanford Mozes, Vice Chair
Jacqueline Levine, former Vice Chair
Carl Glick, Chair Emeritus

HILLEL: THE FOUNDATION FOR
JEWISH CAMPUS LIFE
800 Eighth Street, NW
Washington, DC 20001
www.hillel.org

Hillel is an international community devoted to learning, personal growth, pluralism, Israel, Jewish celebration and the perpetuation of the Jewish people. Student by student, community by community, country by country, Hillel is forging a strong Jewish future.

Avraham Infeld, President of Hillel
Randall Kaplan, Chairman, Hillel
    International Bd. Of Directors
Edgar M. Bronfman, Chairman, Hillel
    International Bd. Of Governors
Lynn Schusterman, Co-Chair, Hillel
    International Bd. Of Governors
Michael Steinhardt, Co-Chair, Hillel
    International Bd. Of Governors

JESNA (Jewish Education Service
of North America)
111 Eighth Avenue, 11th Floor
New York, NY 10011
www.jesna.org

JESNA seeks to make engaging, inspiring, high quality Jewish learning available to every Jew in North America by building an educational system of consistent excellence.

Diane Troderman, Chair
Mandell L. Berman, Honorary Chair

Jonathan S. Woocher, Ph.D.,
    Chief Executive Officer
Donald A. Sylvan, Ph.D., President & COO

JEWISH COMMUNITY RELATIONS
COUNCIL OF NEW YORK, INC.
70 West 36 Street, Suite 700
New York, NY 10018
www.jcrcny.org

The Jewish Community Relations Council of New York is the central coordinating and resource body for more than 60 civic, communal, educational and religious organizations. Central to the JCRC's mission is the protection and strengthening of the rights and interests of the Jewish community in New York.

Matthew J. Maryles, President
Michael S. Miller,
    Executive Vice President and CEO

JEWISH FEDERATION OF CINCINNATI
4050 Executive Park Dr., #300
Cincinnati, OH 45241
www.jewishcincinnati.org

The Jewish Federation of Cincinnati is committed to providing resources and planning to all members of the Jewish community

*seeking to participate in the enhancement
and perpetuation of Jewish faith, values
and life in all of its diversity at home,
in Israel, and throughout the world.*

Shep Englander, CEO
Sharon Stern, COO
Danielle Minson, FRD Director
Dick Friedman, President
Marc Fisher, President-elect

JEWISH FEDERATION OF
GREATER HOUSTON
5603 S. Braeswood Blvd.
Houston, TX 77096
www.houstonjewish.org

*The mission of the Jewish Federation of
Greater Houston is to preserve & enrich
Jewish communal life through innovative &
visionary leadership that is responsive and
responsible to Jewish communities locally,
nationally, in Israel, and around the world.*

Lee Wunsch, CEO
Joe Williams, President
Suzanne Jacobson,
    Assoc. Exec. VP/Campaign Dir.
Mary Ward-Hecksel, Assoc. Exec. VP/CEO

JEWISH FEDERATION OF
GREATER LOS ANGELES
6505 Wilshire Blvd.
Los Angeles, CA 90048
www.jewishla.org

*The Jewish Federation Council mobi-
lizes and integrates human, financial and
organizational resources to foster a sense
of common Jewish purpose and to enhance
Jewish identity to meet critical human
needs in a Jewish context, and to inten-
sify our bonds with the people of Israel.*

Harriet Hochman, Chair of Board
Michael Koss, Chair Designate
Laurie Konheim, Campaign Chair
Gary Brennglass, Chair Valley Alliance
John Fishel, President

JEWISH FUNDERS NETWORK
330 7th Ave.
New York, NY 10001
www.jfunders.org

*JFN is an international network of indi-
viduals, families, foundations, and professionals committed to advancing the quality
and growth of Jewish philanthropy, in both
Jewish and secular endeavors. We engage*

*all individuals and institutions interested
in past and contemporary Jewish life.*

David Smith, Esq.,
   President of the Board of Trustees
Allan R. Frank, Chairman
David Lerman, First Vice President
Dr. Ellen Frankel, CEO and Editor-in-Chief
Carol Hupping, COO and
   Publishing Director

JEWISH FEDERATION OF ST. LOUIS
12 Millstone Campus
St. Louis, Missouri 63146-5776
www.jewishinstlouis.org

*Founded in 1901, Federation is the central
fundraising, planning and community-build-
ing organization of the 60,000 member
Jewish community. Federation mobilizes
the human and financial resources needed
to preserve and enhance Jewish life in St.
Louis, Israel and around the world.*

Heschel. J. Raskas, Ph.D., President
Barry Rosenberg, Executive Vice President

JEWISH NATIONAL FUND
42 East 69 Street
New York, NY 10021
www.jnf.org

*Jewish National Fund is the caretaker of
the land of Israel, on behalf of its owners—Jewish people everywhere.*

Ronald S. Lauder, President
Russell Robinson, CEO
Leonard Kleinman, First Vice President
Bud Levin, Vice President, Campaign
Art Silber, Treasurer

JOFA
The Jewish Orthodox Feminist Alliance
15 East 26 Street, Suite 915
New York, NY 10010
www.jofa.org

*JOFA seeks to expand the spiritual, ritual,
intellectual, and political opportunities for
women, and advocates for their meaningful participation to the full extent possible
within the framework of halakha. Our
commitment is rooted in the belief that
fulfilling this mission will enrich and uplift
individual and communal life for all Jews.*

Carol Kaufman Newman, President
Belda Lindenbaum, VP Development
Robin Bodner, Executive Director
Blu Greenberg, Founding President
Audrey Trachtman, Treasurer

JEWISH RECONSTRUCTIONIST
FEDERATION
7804 Montgomery Ave. #9
Elkins Park, PA 19027
www.jrf.org

Founded in 1955, and celebrating its 50th birthday year, the Jewish Reconstructionist Federation is the rapidly growing synagogue organization of the Reconstructionist movement. Serving more than 100 congregations and havurot (fellowships) across North America—and with an increasing number of international Associate members—the JRF provides a wide array of services to its affiliates in all areas of congregational life.

Daniel G. Cedarbaum, President
Robert Barkin, Vice President
Myrna Sigman, Vice President
Leah Kamionkowski, Vice President
Carl A. Sheingold, Executive Vice President

JEWISH THEOLOGICAL SEMINARY
3080 Broadway
New York, NY 10027
www.jtsa.edu

Preeminent center for academic study of Judaica outside of Israel, one of preeminent centers worldwide . . . training center for scholars to advance that study; educates Jewish professionals/lay leadership in the spirit of Conservative Judaism for the total community through formal/informal academic and religious programs.

Dr. Ismar Schorsch, Chancellor
Mr. Gershon Kekst, Chairman of the Board
Dr. Michael B. Greenbaum,
    Vice Chancellor &COO
Rabbi William Lebeau, Vice Chancellor &
    Dean of Rabbinical School
Rabbi Carol Davidson, Vice Chancellor,
    Institutional Advancement

JEWISH UNITED FUND/JEWISH FEDERATION OF METROPOLITAN CHICAGO
Ben Gurion Way—One S. Franklin St.
Chicago, IL 60606
www.juf.org

JUF Federation serves as the central address of Chicago's Jewish community, providing the critical resources that bring food, refuge, health care, education and emergency assistance to 300,000 Chicagoans of all faiths and 2 million Jews worldwide.

Midge Perlman Safton,
    Chairman of the Board

Robert M. Schrayer, Vice Chair & 2005
  JUF General Campaign Chairman
Max R. Schrayer, Vice Chair & 2006 JUF
  General Campaign Chairman
Dr. Betsy R. Gidwitz, Chair of Overall
  Planning & Allocations
Dr. Steven B. Nasatir, President

JEWISH WAR VETERANS OF THE USA
1811 R Street, NW
Washington, DC 20009
www.jwv.org

*Our mission: To support veterans of
all faiths, to fight bigotry in any form,
to maintain the National Museum of
American Jewish Military History*

David L. Magidson, National Commander
Robert M. Zweiman, Chairman
Jack Berman, Museum President
Arlene Kaplan, President, Ladies Auxiliary
Herb Rosenbleeth,
  National Executive Director

JEWISH WOMEN'S ARCHIVE
138 Harvard Street
Brookline, MA 02446
www.jwa.org

*The mission of the Jewish Women's Ar-
chive is to uncover, chronicle and transmit
the rich legacy of Jewish women and their
contributions to our families and our communities, to our people and our world.*

Dr. Gail Twersky Reimer, Executive Director
Nicki Newman Tanner, Chair
Barbara B. Dobkin, Founding Chair

JEWISH WOMEN INTERNATIONAL
2000 M St., NW, Suite 720
Washington, DC 20036
www.jwi.org

*Jewish Women International is dedicated to
ensuring that every woman and girl is safe,
in her home and in her relationships. JWI
is recognized as the leading Jewish organization committed to ending the cycle of
family violence and to promoting safe homes,
strong women and healthy relationships.*

Loribeth Weinstein, Executive Director
Sandy Unger, International President

JUDAH L. MAGNES MUSEUM
2911 Russell St.
Berkeley, CA 94705
www.magnes.org

The Magnes is a museum of art and history focused on the Jewish experience. Through its world-class collections, original exhibitions and programs, the museum demonstrates a balanced commitment to tradition and experimentation that contributes generously to international scholarship and culture.

Irving Rabin, President, Board of Trustees
Terry Pink Alexander, Executive Director

LEO BAECK INSTITUTE
15 West 16 Street
New York, NY 10021
www.lbi.org

The Leo Baeck Institute is a research library and archive dedicated to documenting the history and culture of German-speaking Jewry. The books, memoirs, photos and artwork in the LBI collections are the foremost resource for scholarship on a rich and varied heritage that the Nazis could not destroy. "Modernity" in the 20th century could hardly be imagined without the contributions of German Jewry, from science and medicine to literature, journalism and a host of other fields.

Dr. Ismar Schorsch, President
Carol Kahn Strauss, Executive Director

MUSEUM OF JEWISH HERITAGE—
A LIVING MEMORIAL TO THE
HOLOCAUST
36 Battery Place
New York, NY 10280
www.mjhnyc.org

The Museum's mission is to educate people of all ages and backgrounds about modern Jewish history and the Holocaust.

David G. Marwell, Ph.D., Director
Hon. Robert M. Morgenthau, Chairman
George Klein, Vice-Chair
Senator Manfred Owenstein, Vice-Chair
Howard J. Rubenstein, Vice-Chair

NATIONAL COUNCIL OF
JEWISH WOMEN
53 West 23 Street
New York, NY 10010
www.ncjw.org

The National Council of Jewish Women is a volunteer organization that has been at the forefront of social change for over a century. Inspired by Jewish values, NCJW courageously takes a progressive stance on issues such as child welfare, women's rights, and reproductive freedom.

Stacy H. Kass, Acting Executive Director
Phyllis Snyder, President

NATIONAL FOUNDATION FOR
JEWISH CULTURE
330 7th Ave., 21 Floor
New York, NY 10001
www.jewishculture.org

*The National Foundation for Jewish
Culture supports Jewish artistic creativity, scholarship and cultural preservation
in America. The NFJC's grants, awards,
conferences and programs serve to enhance
Jewish identity and bring the best of the
Jewish experience to the American public.*

Richard A. Siegel, Executive Director
Larry Pitterman, COO
Carol Spinner, President
Charlotte Newberger, Chair of Board

NATIONAL MUSEUM OF
AMERICAN JEWISH HISTORY
Independence Mall East
55 N. 5th Street
Philadelphia, PA 19106
www.nmajh.org

*Our mission is to present educational pro-
grams and experiences that preserve, explore
and celebrate the history of Jews in America.*

Gwen Goodman, Executive Director/CEO
Dr. D. Walter Cohen,
    Chairman, Board of Trustees
George M. Ross,
    Member, Board of Trustees
Lyn M. Ross, Member, Board of Trustees

NCSJ: ADVOCATES ON BEHALF OF
JEWS IN RUSSIA, UKRAINE,
THE BALTIC STATES & EURASIA
2020 K St., NW, Suite 7800
Washington, DC 20006
www.ncsj.org

*NCSJ, the mandated central coordinat-
ing agency of organized American Jewry
for policy and activities on behalf of the
estimated 1.5 million Jews in Russia and
Eurasia, protects and empowers Jews through
advocacy, monitoring, information dis-
semination and public policy analysis.*

Robert J. Meth, M.D., Chairman
Joel M. Schindler, Ph.D., President
Mark B. Levin, Executive Director

NAAJHS
North American Association of
Jewish High Schools

c/o Akiba Hebrew Academy
223 N. HighlandAve.
Merion, PA 19066
www.naajhs.org

To provide a network for the exchange of information and ideas relating to Jewish high school education, develop and share curriculum, train educators and lay leaders, bring students together from member schools and serve as an advocate for the advancement of Jewish day high schools in North America.

Rabbi Philip D. Field, President
Jonathan Cannon, VP —Israel Programs
Simcha Pearl, VP—Youth Programs
Paul Shaviv, VP—Curricular Projects
Rennie Wrubel, Ph.D., VP—Lay
    & Professional Development

RABBINICAL ASSEMBLY
3080 Broadway
New York, NY 10027
www.rabbinicalassembly.org

The Rabbinical Assembly is the international association of Conservative/Masorti rabbis. Since its founding in 1901, the Assembly has provided leadership for the Conservative/Masorti movement and its rabbis have served the Jewish people through-out the world. The Assembly provides for the professional and personal needs of its membership, publishes learned texts, and administers the movement's Placement Commission and Committee on Jewish Law.

Rabbi Perry Raphael Rank, President
Rabbi Alvin Berkun, Vice President
Rabbi Jeffrey Wohlberg, Treasurer
Rabbi Gulah Dror, Financial Secretary
Rabbi Joel H. Meyers,
    Executive Vice President

RABBINICAL COUNCIL OF AMERICA
305 Seventh Avenue, 12 Floor
New York, NY 10001
www.rabbis.org

The Rabbinical Council of America, established in 1935, advances the cause and the voice of Torah and the rabbinic tradition by promoting the welfare and professionalism of Orthodox rabbis around the world, and by being in the forefront of issues at the nexus of the interaction of Torah in the world around us.

Rabbi Dale Polakoff, President
Rabbi Basil Herring,
    Executive Vice President

Rabbi Shlomo Hochberg,
First Vice President
Rabbi Kenneth Auman,
Honorary President

RECONSTRUCTIONIST RABBINICAL
ASSOCIATION
1299 Church Rd.
Wyncote, PA 19095
www.therra.org

The RRA is the professional association of Reconstructionist rabbis and represents our members collectively in the Jewish and general communities. Our mission is to advance Judaism as a religious civilization, balancing the claims of Jewish tradition with the needs of the contemporary Jewish community.

Rabbi Brant Rosen, President
Rabbi Richard Hirsh, Executive Director
Rabbi Toba Spitzer, 1st VP
Rabbi Ira J. Schiffer, 2nd VP
Rabbi Amy Small, Immediate Past President

RECONSTRUCTIONIST RABBINICAL
COLLEGE
1299 Church Rd.
Wyncote, PA 19095
www.rrc.edu

The College's primary mission is to train rabbis, as well as other Jewish leaders, to teach Torah and provide Jewish leadership in congregations and in other roles throughout the Jewish community.

Rabbi Dan Ehrenkrantz, President
Donald L. Shapiro, Board Chair
Aaron Ziegelman, General Chair
David Roberts, Vice Chair
Susan Beckerman, Vice Chair

RELIGIOUS ZIONISTS OF AMERICA
7 Penn Plaza – Suite 205
New York, NY 10001
www.RZA.org

The Religious Zionists of America (RZA) is an ideological and educational organization that seeks to reach all segments of the American Jewish population through adult education, pro-Israel advocacy, promoting aliyah, strengthening and developing a creative curriculum on religious Zionism for Jewish day schools and encouraging the knowledge and use of Hebrew.

Alan A. Mond, Executive Vice President
Rabbi Yosef Blau, President
Martin Oliner, Chairman of the Board

REPUBLICAN JEWISH COALITION
50 F Street, NW, Suite 100
Washington, DC 20001
www.rjchq.org

We seek to foster ties between the American Jewish community and Republican decision-makers. We work to sensitize Republican leadership to the concerns of the Jewish community, while advocating Republican ideas and policies within the Jewish community.

Sam Fox, National Chairman
Matthew Brooks, Executive Director

ROCKY MOUNTAIN JEWISH HISTORICAL SOCIETY & BECK ARCHIVES
University of Denver
2000 E. Asbury, Suite 157
Denver, CO 80208
www.du.edu/cjs/rmjhs

The Rocky Mountain Jewish Historical Society and Beck Archives work in tandem to publicize and preserve the vibrant Jewish history of the Rocky Mountain Region, with an emphasis on Colorado.

Dr. Jeanne Abrams, Director
Mark Boscoe, President

SKIRBALL CULTURAL CENTER
2701 N. Sepulveda Blvd.
Los Angeles, CA 90049
www.skirball.org

The Skirball Cultural Center is dedicated to exploring the connections between 4,000 years of Jewish heritage and the vitality of American democratic ideals.

Uri D. Herscher,
　Founding President and CEO
Howard I. Friedman,
　Chairman, Board of Trustees
Kathryn Girard, Chief of Staff
Lori Starr, Senior Vice President
　and Museum Director

SSDSA
Solomon Schechter Day School Association
USCJ
155 Fifth Ave., Fifth Floor
New York, NY 10010
www.ssdsa.org

The SSDSA, supported by the United Synagogue of Conservative Judaism, provides services, resources, professional development, leadership training and expertise to its affiliated schools and their professional and lay leaders throughout North America. We promote collaboration among member schools and excellence in Jewish and general education.

Rabbi Robert Abramson, Director,
    Dept. of Education, United Synagogue
Dr. Elaine R.S. Cohen,
    Assoc. Director, Dept. of Education
Andy Cohen, President,
    SSDSA Board of Directors
Dr. Karen Ceppos, Immediate Past
    President, SSDSA Board of Directors
Rabbi Jim Rogozen, President,
    Solomon Schechter Principals Council

SOUTHERN JEWISH HISTORICAL SOCIETY
1718 Peachtree Street NW
South Tower, Suite 990
Atlanta, Georgia 30309-2409
www.jewishsouth.org

The purposes of this society shall be the collection, preservation, exhibition, publication, and popularization of materials referring to the history and life of Jews in the South and the promotion of research in and the study of the Jewish history and life of this region.

Sumner I. Levine, President
Mark K. Bauman, Vice President
Bernard Wax, Treasurer
Scott M. Langston, Secretary
Minette Cooper, Immediate Past President

SPERTUS INSTITUTE OF JEWISH STUDIES
618 South Michigan Avenue
Chicago, IL 60605
www.spertus.edu

Spertus invites people of all ages and backgrounds to explore the multi-faceted Jewish experience. Through its innovative public programming, exhibitions, collections, research facilities and degree programs, Spertus inspires learning, serves diverse communities and fosters understanding for Jews and people of all faiths, locally, regionally and around the world.

Marc Wilkow, Chairman of the Board
Howard A. Sulkin, Ph.D., President & CEO
Dean P. Bell, Ph.D.,
    Dean/Chief Academic Officer
Rhoda Rosen, Director-Spertus Museum
Hal Lewis, D.J.S.,
    Dean-Public Programming

TOURO SYNAGOGUE
85 Touro Street
Newport, RI 02840
www.tourosynagogue.org

*Our mission is to strengthen the presence
of Touro Synagogue as a symbol of religious
freedom and diversity, and of Jewish survival;
to engage children and adults (members
& visitors) in meaningful and enjoyable
dialogue and prayer through participa-
tory religious services and programs.*

Rabbi Mordechai Eskovitz, Rabbi, Touro's
    Congregation Jeshuat Israel
Laura Freedman Pedrick, President, Touro's
    Congregation Jeshuat Israel
Michael Balaban, CEO,
    Touro Synagogue Foundation
M. Bernard Aidinoff, Chair,
    Touro Synagogue Foundation

UJA-FEDERATION OF NY
130 E. 59 Street
New York, NY 10022
www.ujafedny.org

*UJA-Federation cares for those in need,
rescues those in harm's way, and renews
and strengthens the Jewish people in New
York, in Israel and around the world.*

John S. Ruskay,
    Executive Vice President & CEO
Morris W. Offit, President
Susan K. Stern, Chair of the Board

UJA FEDERATION OF NORTHERN
NEW JERSEY
111 Kinderkamack Rd.
River Edge, NJ 07661
www.ujannj.org

*The UJA Federation of Northern New Jersey
strives to help rescue the imperiled, care for
the vulnerable, revitalize Jewish life and build
community in Israel and around the world.*

Daniel Silna, President
Howard E. Charish,
    Executive Vice President
David Gad-Harf, Associate EVP & COO
Dana Egert, 2006 Campaign Chair

UNION OF ORTHODOX JEWISH
CONGREGATIONS OF AMERICA
11 Broadway
New York, NY 10004
www.OU.ORG

*The "Orthodox Union," is in its second
century of service to the Jewish community,*

providing community and synagogue services, adult education, youth work and political advocacy. Its kosher supervision label, the O-U, is the world's most recognized kosher symbol.

Stephen Sanitsky, President
Rabbi Tzvi Hersh Weinreb,
    Executive Vice President
Harvey Blitz, Board of Directors Chair
Mark Bane,
    Sr. Vice President for Public Policy
Nathan Diament, Director of Public Policy

UNION FOR REFORM JUDAISM
633 Third Ave., 7th floor
New York, NY 10017
www.URJ.ORG

As the congregational arm of the Reform Movement, the Union for Reform Judaism strives to create and sustain vibrant Jewish communities wherever Reform Jews live by providing leadership, vision and materials on spiritual, ethical and political issues.

Rabbi Eric Yoffie, President
Robert Heller, Chair, Board of Trustees
Rabbi Lennard Thal, Sr. V.P.
Rabbi Daniel Freelander, V.P.
Russell Silverman, Immediate Past Chair

UNITED JEWISH FEDERATION OF PITTSBURGH
234 McKee Place
Pittsburgh, PA 15217
www.ujfpittsburgh.org

UJF is the central fundraising and planning organization for the Pittsburgh Jewish community.

Richard E. Kann, Chair of the Board
Jeffrey H. Finkelstein, President and CEO

UNITED SYNAGOGUE OF CONSERVATIVE JUDAISM
155 Fifth Avenue
New York, NY 10010
www.uscj.org

The United Synagogue of Conservative Judaism promotes the role of the synagogue in Jewish life in order to motivate Conservative Jews to perform mitzvoth encompassing ethical behavior, spirituality, Jewish learning, and ritual observance. The mission of the United Synagogue of Conservative Judaism is to strengthen and serve our congregations and their members.

Judy Yudof, International President
Rabbi Jerome M. Epstein,
    Executive Vice President

Arnold Most, Secretary
Gary Rosenthal, Financial Secretary
Jay Wiston, Treasurer

U. S. HOLOCAUST MEMORIAL MUSEUM
100 Raoul Wallenberg Place, SW
Washington, DC 20024-2126
www.ushmm.org

*The U. S. Holocaust Memorial Museum
is a living reminder of the moral obligations of individuals and societies, ensuring
that millions of people from all over the
world will learn its timely lessons about
anti-Semitism, hatred and indifference.*

Fred S. Zeidman, Chair
Ruth B. Mandel, Vice Chair
Sara J. Bloomfield, Director

WOMEN'S AMERICAN ORT
250 Park Avenue South
Suite 600
New York, NY 10003
www.waort.org

*Women's American ORT is a national Jewish
organization that strengthens the worldwide Jewish community by empowering
people to achieve economic self-sufficiency
through technological and vocational education. WAO provides financial support and
leadership within the global ORT network
of schools and programs in 60 countries,
including Israel, CIS and Baltic States and
South America. In U.S., a two year college,
technical institutes and resource centers
provide training and services to Jewish
students, teachers and community groups.*

Judy Menikoff, National President
Shelley Fagel, National First Vice President
Hope Kessler, National Executive Director
Terry Azose, Vice President,
    Leadership Development/Outreach
Kay Freeman, Vice President; Field
    Development & Field Operations
Linda Kirschbaum, Vice President,
    Fundraising
Sara Trub, Vice President,
    Strategic Development

YESHIVA UNIVERSITY
500 West 185 Street
New York, NY 10033
www.yu.edu

*Founded in 1886, Yeshiva University is
ranked among the nation's leading academic
research institutions. About 7,000 students
study at its four New York City campuses.*

You don't have
to be Jewish

to love Levy's
real Jewish Rye

ALBUM PARTNERS

CELEBRATE 350, INC.

BOARD OF DIRECTORS

Robert S. Rifkind, Chairman

Lester Crown

Dr. David Ellenson

Stanley Gold

Gershon Kekst

Lynn Korda Kroll

Dr. Norman Lamm

Dr. Jehuda Reinharz

Dr. Ismar Schorsch

Roselyne Swig

Roy J. Zuckerberg

Alice Herman, Executive Director

STEERING COMMITTEE

Rabbi Marc Angel
   Shearith Israel Congregation

James August

Dr. Steven Bayme
   American Jewish Committee

Alice Herman

Prof. Sara Lee
   Hebrew Union College

Michael M. Lorge

Rabbi Janet Marder
   Congregation Beth Am

Dr. Gail Twersky Reimer
   Jewish Women's Archive

Martin Raffel
   Jewish Council for Public Affairs

Robert S. Rifkind

Prof. Jonathan Sarna (chief historian)
   Brandeis University

Richard Siegel
   National Foundation for Jewish Culture

David P. Solomon
   American Jewish Historical Society

Dr. Gary P. Zola
   The Jacob Rader Marcus Center of
   the American Jewish Archives

Rabbi Sheldon Zimmerman
   United Jewish Communities

THE JACOB RADER MARCUS CENTER
of the AMERICAN JEWISH ARCHIVES

AT HEBREW UNION COLLEGE–JEWISH INSTITUTE OF RELIGION

STAFF & ADMINISTRATION
Dr. Gary P. Zola, Executive Director
Lisa B. Frankel, Director of
    Programs and Administration
Kevin Proffitt, Senior Archivist
    for Research and Collections
Frederic Krome, Academic Associate,
    Managing Editor, *The American
    Jewish Archives Journal*
Dorothy Smith, Coordinator of

Archival Operations and
    Information Technology Specialist
Eleanor Lawhorn, Administrative
    Assistant to the Executive Director
Christine Schmid, Associate Archivist
Devhra BennettJones, Coordinator of
    Historical Research and Special Projects
Phillip Reekers,
    Design and Digitization

EZRA CONSORTIUM
Michael M. Lorge, Chair
Winifred Barrows
Robert Block
Nancy and Joseph Brant
Roberta and Maxwell Burstein
Barton Cohen
    and Mary Davidson Cohen
Beth and Rand Curtiss
Jerome Dave

Bernard Dave
Susan and Marvin Dickman
Lori Fenner
Scott Golinkin

Arnold and Dee Kaplan
Clementine Kaufman
Jerry and Nancy Klein
Morton and Ruth Klein
Leo Krupp

244

Alan M. Edelstein

Ruth B. Fein

George M. Garfunkel

David Gordis

Robert D. Gries

David Hershberg

Michael G. Jesselson

Arnold H. Kaplan

Daniel Kaplan

Samuel R. Karetsky

Harvey M. Krueger

Sidney Lapidus

Philip Lax

Ira A. Lipman

Norman Liss

Kenneth D. Malamed

Deborah Dash Moore

Edgar J. Nathan III

Arthur S. Obermayer

Jeffrey S. Oppenheim

Steven D. Oppenheim

Nancy T. Polevoy

Leslie M. Pollack

Arnold J. Rabinor

Harold S. Rosenbluth

Louise P. Rosenfeld

Zita Rosenthal

Bruce Slovin

David Solomon

Joseph S. Steinberg

Morton M. Steinberg

Ronald S. Tauber

Saul Viener

Sue R. Warburg

Efrem Weinreb

Norbert Weissberg

Justin L. Wyner

Roberta Yagerman

Laurence Zuckerman